WILEY/IRM SERIES ON MULTINATIONALS

Appropriate or Underdeveloped Technology?
Arghiri Emmanuel

The Threat of Japanese Multinationals: Can the West Respond?
Lawrence G. Franko

The New Multinationals: The Spread of Third World Enterprises
Sanjaya Lall

International Disclosure and the Multinational Corporation
S. J. Gray, J. C. Shaw, L. B. McSweeney

Multinational Enterprises, Economic Structure and International
Competitiveness
Edited by John Dunning

Britain and the Multinationals
John Stopford and Louis Turner

State-owned Multinationals
J. P. Anastassopoulos, G. Blanc, P. Dussauge

State-owned Multinationals

Jean-Pierre Anastassopoulos,
Georges Blanc and Pierre Dussauge
*Hautes Etudes Commerciales and
Institut Supérieur des Affaires Jouy-en Josas, France*

Preface by Eneko Landaburu

Translated by Valerie Katzaros

JOHN WILEY & SONS
Chichester · New York · Brisbane · Toronto · Singapore

Library of Congress Cataloging-in-Publication Data:

Anastassopoulos, J. P.
  State-owned multinationals.

  (Wiley/IRM series on multinationals)
  Translation of: Les multinationales publiques.
  Bibliography: p.
  Includes index.
  1. International business enterprises. 2. Government
business enterprises. I. Blanc, Georges.
II. Dussauge, Pierre. III. Title. IV. Series.
  HD2755.5.A613 1987   338.8′8   87–2033
  ISBN 0 471 91502 5

British Library Cataloguing in Publication Data:

Anastassopoulos, Jean-Pierre
  State-owned multinations.—(Wiley/IRM
  series on multinationals).
  1. International business enterprises
  2. Government business enterprises
  I. Title   II. Blanc, Georges
  III. Dussauge, Pierre   IV. Les multinationales
  publiques. *English*
  338.8′8   HD2755.5
  ISBN 0 471 91502 5

Phototypeset by Input Typesetting Ltd, London SW19 8DR
Printed in Great Britain by St. Edmundsbury Press, Bury St. Edmunds

Contents

Foreword

The present book is the fruit of a research project conducted by the authors with the collaboration of Dominique Gueudet and Pascal Hawat, research assistants. It has greatly benefited from the contribution of all our colleagues in the Department of Strategy and Business Policy at the Centre HEC–ISA. We are also indebted to Danièle Alix and Jacqueline Podechard for their efficiency and kindness while typing the manuscript.

The project itself, financed primarily by the IRM, was initiated by Michel Ghertman and supported by Eneko Landaburu, who encouraged us all along. We are grateful to both of them as well as to Miss Gerta Unger for her efficiency in managing all the practical aspects of this project.

We are also grateful to all those who contributed the data on which the book is based: managers and high-ranking civil servants — more than 200 in over 20 countries — whom we interviewed in the course of our research. Unfortunately, they are too numerous to be cited here by name, but they have provided invaluabe information.

Lastly, we are grateful to the Paris Chamber of Commerce and Industry for the facilities and working conditions offered to us on the Jouy-en-Josas campus. We hope this project will serve as an example for others to come.

Preface

It is commonly admitted by observers of the international scene that the interdependence of nations today constitutes one of the fundamental aspects of any national economic and social policy. The internationalization of economy has become a reality. The necessary links between western economies as well as the notion of a large market on which major companies operate are now widely accepted.

The Institute for Research and Information on Multinationals (IRM), which promotes research on the role and impact of multinational firms within an international economy, has chosen to study the new forms of multinationalization of enterprises as part of its principal lines of research. Thus, in 1984, we published a book dealing with the emergence of multinationals originating from third world countries.[1] We are now presenting this study on state-owned multinationals.

The project of the present book sprang from a threefold assessment. First, we found that the multinationalization of state-owned enterprises was not limited to a few cases of somewhat special firms: more and more state-owned enterprises have begun to set up beyond their frontiers. Secondly, the analysis of certain statistics showed that state-owned multinationals represented a group of enterprises whose impact on the international economic scene was not insignificant. Lastly, we realised that no in-depth and serious study had so far been carried out.

Thus, we decided to undertake this research of which the book of J. P. Anastassopoulos, G. Blanc and P. Dussauge is the fruit. The authors begin their study by focusing on a paradoxical situation, or at least a striking contradiction. Indeed, how can the terms 'multinational' and 'state-owned' go together, when each of them has been associated with epithets which, juxtaposed, are antinomical? The image of the multinational is still that of an enterprise whose values are efficiency and profitability. On the other hand, the image of the state-owned firm is often that of an enterprise which respects the social environment and serves the national interest.

To go beyond the scope of perception and image, which often cover only a partial view of reality, more profound theoretical reasons can

---

[1] Sanjaya Lall, *The New Multinationals: The Spread of Third World Enterprises*, John Wiley & Sons/IRM, Chichester, 1983.

be found in the present analysis, allowing a better definition of this antagonism. It is admitted that multinationality stresses the interests of the enterprise and places these above the national interests of all the countries where it operates. On the other hand, nationalization or state ownership puts the primary emphasis on the interests of the State, relegating those of the enterprise to a secondary position. Thus nationalization can prove to be a serious obstacle to the multinationalization of a firm.

The contradiction between multinational and state-owned is even greater when one analyses the specific constraints imposed by the owner-state on the enterprises under its control. These constraints, devised by the government and aimed at safeguarding the interests of the nation, are usually incompatible with the direct interests of the enterprise.

In the first place, the government seeks a national orientation for its industrial and technological policy (contracts for the purchase of domestic products and technologies, etc.), thus checking any international strategy which is possibly more profitable for the enterprise. Secondly, the financial policy imposed on the enterprise can be constricting and problematic for its expansion abroad. Thirdly, the state-owned enterprise is compelled to observe a social policy laid down by the government which proves to be a handicap as far as its foreign investments are concerned. The government's social policy aims not only at creating new jobs but also at ensuring a more even geographical distribution of employment in the country. The obstacles in the way of the multinationalization of state-owned enterprises are legion, since governments utilize them as instruments of their foreign policy while host countries often regard them as representatives of a foreign state.

At this stage of the analysis it can be asserted that though being state-owned does not necessarily exclude multinationalization (as shown by the extensive list of enterprises in Chapter One), the nature of state ownership, as we have seen, is more of a hindrance than a help. However, the authors have gone further in their study and examined the distinctive characteristics which can, on the contrary, facilitate the multinationalization of state-owned enterprises compared to that of private firms. In a purely free market system, state-owned enterprises can be unfair competitors and thus extend their expansion abroad, since they are not subjected to the same rules as private companies.

These accusations of unfair competition are based on three main arguments. First, state-owned enterprises are accused of benefiting systematically from government contracts and receiving massive aid for research and development, thereby being able to sell their best products abroad at prices which do not take the real costs into consideration.

Secondly, since profitability is not the sole criterion for evaluation of performance, subsidies accorded by the State to cover operating losses enable the enterprises to sell their products on foreign markets at a loss. Lastly, the State can also help through economic and diplomatic pressures or bilateral agreements with other countries. In such cases, the state-owned enterprise will enjoy a protection which is usually inaccessible to private companies.

If the argument of the constraints imposed by the State shows that the state-owned enterprise is hindered in its multinationalization process and the counterargument emphasizes the advantages which favour this foreign expansion, the synthesis presented by the authors through a detailed and illustrative analysis of the complexity of strategies and practices of firms proves that state-owned enterprises are no better nor worse than their private counterparts. Does this imply that state-owned multinationals are identical to other multinationals? It can only be pointed out that there exists a wide range of state-owned multinationals, from those that are almost indistinguishable from private companies, enjoying a large measure of autonomy and having a resolutely international strategy, to enterprises which are above all public services and whose multinationalization process is hampered by the interventionist State. It appears therefore that the distinctive characteristics of a state-owned multinational do not depend exclusively on its sector of activity, or the nature of the state which controls it, or even totally on the level of economic development of its country of origin. Its ability to manage the paradoxical situation of belonging to one state while setting up in another is also a crucial factor. Consequently, as has been convincingly demonstrated by the authors, success or failure is less dependent on the policy of the controlling authority than on the capacity of the management to formulate complex strategies in which state ownership, far from being a handicap, is an additional asset in the multinationalization process. The key to success lies in the ability to reconcile two opposing logics, that of the State and that of the enterprise.

Is this effort to harmonize two conflicting logics illusory? The authors seem to think so, as borne out by the title of the concluding chapter: 'Nationalization and Multinationalization: The Breaking Point in Perspective'. In their opinion, either the state-owned enterprises will extend their multinationalization, the State being obliged to slacken its hold, or the intervention of the owner-state will inevitably hamper their efforts at internationalization. The first case will lead to multinationals which are identical to others, whereas the second will result in standard state-owned enterprises with no international outlook.

In view of recent developments, this conclusion is likely to be controversial. This is to be welcomed, since one of the aims of the IRM is to stimulate debates and encourage reflection on an important economic phenomenon. Whatever the results of this debate, the present study proves that all industrial systems give rise to organizational structures which transcend national boundaries. The characteristics of the international division of labour and the imperatives of worldwide competition go beyond ideologies. There are countless examples showing that 'leftist' governments adopt free market strategies, and conversely, rightwing governments resort to interventionist measures in their policy regarding state-owned multinationals.

Most governments, at least in Europe, whatever their political leanings, recognize that the worldwide market for the large enterprise, whether private or state-owned, is at once an essential and a privilege. The company's importance, indeed its survival, depend on its ability to operate on an international scale.

This book of J. P. Anastassopoulos, G. Blanc and P. Dussauge is remarkable for its perceptive analysis of a complex reality. Their original contribution will help in upsetting fixed ideas and further our knowledge of a subject which, being extremely political, is controversial. We are grateful to them.

E. LANDABURU
Director of the Institute for
Research and Information on
Multinationals (IRM)

Chapter One

A Paradox

INTRODUCTION

Multinational and state-owned: the juxtaposition of the two terms to characterize one and the same enterprise is paradoxical, even disturbing, suggesting as it does some more or less monstrous hybrid. State-owned multinationals do nevertheless exist. They are much more numerous than is generally thought and are set up just about everywhere in the world; indeed several of them are household names. Some come across simply as multinational companies and people both outside and inside them tend to forget that their major shareholder is the State. On the other hand, others are regarded, and function, as state-owned enterprises, or even public utilities, and very few people suspect that they are at the same time real multinational companies. Lastly, others tend to emphasize their state-owned character here (generally in their country of origin) and their multinational one there (in the host countries); some even claim to be neither state-owned nor multinational. In any case, very few of the state-owned multinationals are happy to accept their double status or mention it explicitly, nor do the strategies they implement reflect all the consequences of this twofold situation.

The two terms, multinational and state-owned, applied to a company, seem to conjure up two quite contradictory images.

When multinationals are mentioned, one immediately thinks of ITT, IBM or Coca Cola. For the general public, the predominant image, though it has improved slightly over the last few years, remains very negative.[1] People think of them as powerful organizations that put

---

[1] Cf J. Attali, M. Holthus, D. Kebschull, G. Peninou and P. Uri, *L'opinion Européenne Face aux Multinationales*, Edition d'Organisation–CEEIM, 1975; J. M. Cotteret, C. Ayache and J. Dux, *L'Image des Multinationales*, IRM–PUF, 1984.

their own interests before any other consideration and dictate their conditions to the governments of the countries in which they are set up. One thinks of ITT in Chile and the part it played in overthrowing the Allende régime, or of United Fruit, making and breaking the governments of the Central American Banana Republics, and also of IBM, whose dominating position in the computer field is thought to be likely to threaten the independence of certain countries, even developed ones. Many books and films as well as statements from politicians, have helped reinforce this image in the minds of the public. At the same time and more positively, multinationals are perceived as extremely efficient enterprises, very well run and very profitable.

In contrast, state-owned companies are generally seen as badly run, as pouring money down the drain, employing a staff that is overpaid, over-protected and overabundant, as operating in a very bureaucratic way, caught up in a network of contradictory constraints imposed by the State, and as being frequently paralysed by strikes. At the same time, these state-owned companies are seen to serve the general interest, to provide vital services at preferential rates and to be concerned with the social environment, job creation, etc. . . .

It would seem that these two virtually opposed views of multi-nationals on the one hand and of state-owned companies on the other make the very idea of state-owned multinationals hard to accept. More-over, enterprises which happen to be at the same time multinational and state-owned seek to define their position in terms of either one or the other and have problems reconciling the two notions — when they do not actually reject them outright.

DID YOU KNOW?

The following multinationals are state-owned enterprises

Many people in France know that Renault, the country's major car manufacturer, is a nationalized company, but how many people in the United States who buy the 'Alliance' (Renault 9) or the 'Encore' (Renault 11) are aware of this? How many employees of American Motors, Renault's subsidiary in the United States which makes the 'Alliance' and the 'Encore' over there, know that Renault and also, to a certain extent, American Motors are controlled by the French State? In the same way, which of AHC's (American Helicopter Corporation) customers, suppliers or employees in the United States know that AHC, whose share of the helicopter market in the United States is as high as 25%, is a subsidiary of Aerospatiale (Société Nationale Industrielle Aérospatiale), which owns 100% of the shares — and as such is subject to direct supervision by the French Ministry of Defence? Very few people indeed; except of course those competing directly with AHC who, as we shall see, seek to take advantage of this rather peculiar, not to say suspicious, characteristic, especially in the eyes of Americans, fervent advocates of private enterprise and free competition as they are.

Keppel Shipyard is one of the major industrial groups of Singapore. The activities of this group, centring on shipbuilding and maritime equipment, have been widely diversified and developed abroad in the last few years, with industrial subsidiaries being installed in different countries of the ASEAN,[2] particularly shipyards which employ more than 400 people in the Philippines. To hear Mr Loh Wing Siew, general manager of the group, talk about the profits that his company has made or will make in the future, the growth he hopes to bring about and the essential task of increasing investment in other countries, it is difficult to imagine that Keppel Shipyard is a state-owned group, 70% of whose equity is held by the State of Singapore. Moreover, less than five years ago Keppel Shipyard was no more than a department of the Singapore port administration.

The Italian Company SGS advertises a job which, while promising, as Churchill promised the English people, blood, sweat and tears, nevertheless offers exciting experience in a job with a future. Would any young Italian electronics engineer attracted by such an ad realize that SGS is a state-owned company, actually a subsidiary of IRI, a huge holding company set up by Mussolini which controls thousands of Italian industrial firms in a large number of sectors? Indeed, it is a surprising statement for a state-owned company to make, especially one belonging to IRI, whose role is rather to 'bail out' Italian industry and help firms in difficulty. It is true, however, that SGS is a somewhat particular case, one of Italy's, indeed Europe's, leading electronic components firms. It is among the companies in the semiconductor sector that have grown most over the last few years, and it became the world's twentieth largest producer in 1983. SGS is also truly multinational. It has several industrial subsidiaries in countries as varied as the United States, Malaysia, Malta, France and Singapore, and modifies the production capacities of its factories in the different countries according to the needs of the market, the labour and the manufacturing

[2] Association of South East Asian Nations.

costs, as any private multinational would do. The recent laying off of scores of employees of its factory in Catania, Sicily, while a second production unit was being built in Singapore is revealing in this respect. For a state-owned company to obtain consent from the controlling authority to carry out such an operation successfully without causing social unrest is most unusual. The personality of Pasquale Pistorio, chairman and managing director of SGS, probably has a part in this, since before heading SGS he was international director of the American group Motorola and therefore had considerable experience in managing a private multinational enterprise. The few examples described above of multinationals which also happen to be state-owned companies are far from being isolated cases. Among many others, we could also mention Embraer, the main Brazilian aircraft manufacturer which has set up in Europe and in the United States, makes 50% of its turnover abroad and is controlled by the Brazilian Air Ministry; and ENASA (Empresa Nacional de Autocamiones SA), the Spanish commercial and heavy goods vehicles manufacturer (using the Pegaso trademark) which has industrial subsidiaries in several Latin American countries and has recently bought up Seddon Atkinson, a lorry manufacturer in the United Kingdom. Like CASA (Construcciones Aeronauticas SA), the Spanish aircraft manufacturer set up in Indonesia, ENASA is a subsidiary of INI (Instituto Nacional de Industria), a holding company established by General Franco in 1946 which supervises the whole of the participation of the Spanish State in industry.

If there are indeed a great number of enterprises known to be multi-nationals which turn out to be state-owned, there are also well-known state-owned enterprises which are found to be multinational.

The following state-owned enterprises are multinationals

If it seems quite natural that, given the nature of their activity and the absence of oil resources in the subsoil of their respective countries, major state-owned groups such as Elf-Aquitaine in France, ENI (Ente Nazionale Idrocarburi) in Italy or Petrobras in Brazil have become truly multinational, it is perhaps more surprising to note that enterprises which would not normally be expected to operate abroad, such as the RATP (Régie Autonome des Transports Parisiens), Indian Railways or DSM (Dutch State Mines), are also multinational companies.

The RATP, which is responsible for public transport (mainly tube and bus services) in the Paris area, had few reasons for developing its activities in other countries. This did not prevent it from creating a subsidiary, Sofretu (Société Française d'Etude et de Réalisation de Systèmes de Transports Urbains), designed to export its technology and expertise, which has so far been very successful. The RATP was responsible for designing and building dozens of underground systems all over the world in cities as different as Montreal, Cairo, Mexico City, Rio de Janeiro, Santiago de Chile, Caracas, etc., . . . and most recently in Orlando (Florida). Today, through the intermediary of Sofretu, the RATP has installed more urban transport systems throughout the world than any other enterprise. Equally, Indian Railways, which barely manages to operate one of the biggest rail networks in the world, exports its knowhow to a number of African countries via its subsidiary, RITES (Rail India Technical and Economic Services). Its success in exporting in the face of competition from countries far more developed and technologically more advanced than India is surprising.

DSM, a state-owned enterprise whose original role was to exploit the natural resources of the Netherlands, particularly coal, is today a multinational chemical company with industrial subsidiaries in the United States, Mexico and most Western European countries, though its initial purpose was not a natural starting point for this development. Nevertheless, DSM has developed activities in the field of fertilizers, plastics, resins, organic chemistry, etc., and has set up in a great number of countries. DSM's activities in the United States are particularly important as it owns two industrial subsidiaries: Columbia Nitrogen Corporation, which produces fertilizers, and Nipro Incorporated, which is one of the main American producers of caprolactam, a raw material essential in the manufacture of nylon. It might be pointed out that, as with Renault or Aerospatiale, very few people in the United States suspect that Nipro or Columbia Nitrogen are 100% subsidiaries of a Dutch group. Still less do they suspect that the Dutch State has a 100% stake in this group.

Kuwait Petroleum Corporation (KPC), the state-owned firm responsible for exploiting the oil resources of the emirate, has set up a subsidiary, Kuwait Petroleum International (KPI), to conduct its operations in Europe. KPC acquired two refineries in Europe (in Rotterdam and Copenhagen) from Gulf Oil as well as service stations from Elf-Aquitaine in Belgium thus controlling over 3000 retail outlets in Europe which give it a share of between 4 and 12% of the market in the countries where it has operations also bought up Gulf's distribution network in Belgium, Denmark, Italy, Luxembourg, the Netherlands and Sweden. In late 1986, Kuwait Petroleum further expanded its service station network in Europe by taking over about 800 outlets, previously owned by Hays Petroleum Services, in the UK and acquiring 30 additional service stations also in the UK. At the time, according to company officials, Kuwait Petroleum sold roughly three-quarters of its total production in the form of refined products, a significant part of which (about 250 000 barrels per day) were marketed directly by the firm through its own retail network and under its recently created 'Q 8' brand name. KPC also acquired Santa Fe International Corporation, a US oil services company, for 2.5 billion dollars in 1981 and is trying to buy a distribution network in the United States. Finally, KPC owns significant shares of three well known German firms, Daimler-Benz (14%), Hoechst (24.9%) and Metallgesellschaft (20%) but has remained a passive investor for the time being.[3]

In addition to these examples, there are many state-owned enterprises which turn out to be multinationals. We might also mention one other case, that of the Indian group IBP–BL (Indo Burma Petroleum–Balmer-Lawrie), consisting of a number of companies established by English businessmen in the nineteenth and at the beginning of the twentieth century, which have been progressively nationalized since Indian independence. This group, with its very varied, not to say radically different activities (oil distribution, chemicals, import–export business, electrical equipment, industrial equipment, travel agencies, warehouses, etc.), whose image does not at first sight correspond in the slightest to standard notions of multinationals, nevertheless set up a subsidiary in Dubai a few years ago, which produces metal containers and barrels. It is currently setting up another industrial subsidiary in Saudi Arabia. The reason why one is so often unaware of the multinational character of many state-owned enterprises or the state-owned character of a number of multinationals is that these enterprises are very discreet and even reject one or the other, or both, of these labels.

ON THE DEFENSIVE

Multinationals that deny being state-owned

Many state-owned multinationals' managers whom we approached in the course of our research were surprised at our going to see them. They felt unable to tell us anything about the matter inasmuch as theirs

[3] See J. Arbose, 'The mighty oil midget that's storming out of the Gulf', *International Management*, March 1986; also see *Le Monde*, 30 October 1986, 'La Compagnie Nationale du Koweit achète 830 stations-service en Grande Bretagne'.

was not a state-owned company or, alternatively, was neither state-owned nor multinational. Thus, for instance, the managers of Matra, one of the French industrial groups which have experienced the highest growth rate in the course of the last few years, as well as those of Norsk-Hydro, the major Norwegian oil, chemicals and metals group, rejected outright the idea that their company was state-owned since, in both cases, the State holds 'only' 51% of the authorized capital.

One might be astonished to learn that the threshold of 51% is regarded as having no particular significance as to the state-owned character of the enterprises concerned. Does this mean that a majority shareholding does not give any controlling influence? Moreover, the same enterprises consolidate the accounts of subsidiaries of which they hold over 50% of the shares, considering that they are part of the same group. What is still more significant is the fact that the State is particularly careful, when there are increases in capital, to make up its participation so as to maintain it above the crucial 50% threshold. If some state-owned companies thus obstinately refuse to own up to the 'state-owned' label, could it be because this label is somewhat pejorative?

There are indeed a great number of examples of groups that refuse to be labelled 'state-owned' or that at the very least are reserved about it. Thus, the important Swedish paper manufacturing group Assi, which has industrial subsidiaries in many Northern and Western European countries and of which the State holds 100% of its equity, makes no mention at all of this in its presentation brochures and includes only a very discreet reference to the point in its annual reports, despite the fact that it can hardly be considered as having no importance. The chairman and managing director of SGS, all of whose capital is held, through IRI, by the Italian State, himself defines his enterprise as 'an electronics multinational, certainly not a state-owned firm'. Here again, the brochures of the company are very secretive about its links with IRI and even more so about the relation between the latter and the State. How can this attitude of state-owned multinationals, recurring as we have seen time and again, be explained? Could their bad reputation as far as efficiency is concerned make them appear at first sight as doubtful economic partners? The mistrust concerning state-owned enterprises is indeed rather widespread, particularly in traditionally 'capitalist' countries. When a private company is in a position to choose, all other things being equal, it will generally prefer to deal with another private company, especially if this involves going into partnership. The American chemical group Occidental Petroleum, associated for several months in a joint venture with ENI, very rapidly withdrew from the association, asserting that the Italian government constantly forced ENOXI, the common subsidiary, to buy up small Italian chemical ailing

firms so as to preserve employment while thereby signing away the
profitability and the future development of the operation. Faced with
the apprehension of their industrial and commercial foreign partners,
the five big industrial multinational groups, Thomson (electronics),
Rhône-Poulenc (chemicals), Péchiney (aluminium), Saint-Gobain (glass
and building materials) and CGE (electric and electronic equipment),
fully nationalized in 1982 by the French government, made strenuous
efforts to persuade their partners that nationalization was not going to
bring any change. It is said, however, that contracts were lost and some
operations cancelled because of the mistrust felt by foreign customers
or partners after nationalization.

But such anxiety about the state-owned character of enterprises is
very ambiguous as it is fuelled by contradictory arguments. Thus, in
the United States, where mistrust concerning state-owned and, what is
more, foreign companies is more widespread, it is based on their
supposed inefficiency but also on accusations of their being able to
engage in unfair competition. All enterprises the property of the State
are automatically suspected of receiving subsidies from it and therefore
of being unfair competitors, enjoying illicit advantages in the interplay
of free competition.

The importance of this current of opinion in the United States is
borne out by the great number of recent publications on this theme.
Besides the regular publication of articles on the subject,[4] it is particularly significant that an interval of only four years separates the publication of two books entitled, respectively, *Foreign State Enterprises*[5]
(1979) and *Nationalized Companies*[6] (1983), which both have the same
quite explicit subtitle: *A threat to American business*. The following
passages taken from the introduction of each of the two books illustrate
most eloquently the feeling aroused in the United States by the mere
mention of state-owned multinationals.

> Capitalism in Western Europe is changing rapidly. In some countries
> state-owned companies amount to nearly half of the industrial sector,
> including control of key industries. European governments now have
> a direct ownership stake in over half of Europe's fifty largest
> companies. Few Americans are aware that many familiar companies

    [4] See among others:
H. D. Menzies, 'U.S. companies in unequal combat', *Fortune*, April 9, 1979.
R. Mazzolini, 'Are state-owned enterprises unfair competitors?' *California Management
Review*, Winter 1980.
K. D. Walters and R. J. Monsen, 'State-owned business abroad: new competitive threat',
Harvard Business Review, March-April 1979.
    [5] Douglas F. Lamont, *Foreign State Enterprises*, Basic Books, New York, 1979.
    [6] R. Joseph Monsen and Kenneth D. Walters, *Nationalized Companies*, McGraw Hill,
New York, 1983.

are government-owned. Renault, Alfa Romeo, British Petroleum, Airbus, British Leyland, Volkswagen, Swedish Steel, and Rolls Royce — to name only a few — are companies in which governments are the sole or largest shareholder. Government companies in Western Europe make aluminium pans, airplane engines, tractors, computer software, cakes, office equipment, advanced electronic equipment, computers and cars and trucks — and run hotel chains. Although the private sector is for the moment larger than the state-owned sector, the state-owned segment is beginning to dominate in more and more industries, and it expands to new products and markets each year.

The spread of European state-owned companies has also affected the United States in a variety of ways:

— The direct purchase of United States companies by foreign state-owned enterprises (such as Sohio, Ashland Coal, Copperweld, Mack Trucks, Texas Gulf)

— The temptation to American politicians to have government take over, (directly or indirectly), large companies in trouble

— The competitive threat that nationalized companies, because of their special advantages, represent to private companies.

(*Nationalized Companies: A threat to American business* by R. J. Monsen and K. D. Walters: Excerpt from introduction)

The controversial thesis of this book is that the time has come for our government to insist that enterprises in the U.S. receive only those rights that they are willing to grant U.S. firms overseas, and no more. Indeed, because the competition of foreign state multinationals is based largely upon special privileges — ranging from low cost loans and subsidies to outright capital grants — the author urges that the U.S. Government also embark on a policy of state capitalism . . . For, whether we like it or not, state capitalism is a fact of international economic life. If we do not want foreign governments to gain control of our economy at home, our government will have to play a more direct role in supporting U.S. business abroad.

(*Foreign State Enterprises: A threat to American business* by D. F. Lamont: Excerpt from foreword)

In more concrete terms, the accusation of unfair competition also directly affects state-owned multinationals in their activities in the United States.

Boeing regularly accuses Airbus Industrie, the European consortium which makes airliners, of receiving subsidies and therefore of being able to survive only with the support of the governments participating in the project. According to this company, the Airbus aircraft can compete with those of Boeing only because they are sold at a price considerably lower than their real cost. Boeing asserts that its main competitor on the civil aircraft market is not Airbus Industrie as such, but an actual coalition of European governments. This being the case, the David and Goliath image frequently used to describe Airbus's struggle against the giant Boeing is immediately turned on its head.

Those accused of unfair competition are sometimes brought before the courts. Thus, in 1984, a private American satellite-launching firm brought an action against Arianespace, another European consortium responsible for marketing the launching of satellites using the European rocket Ariane, accusing it of selling its launching services at a price considerably lower than their real cost owing to the subsidies it received from the various European States involved in the consortium.

Though legal action over unfair competition is not very frequent, foreign state-owned enterprises in the United States are nevertheless sufficiently impressed to want to avoid this kind of trouble.

State-owned enterprises that deny being multinational

If many state-owned multinationals try to make their foreign partners ignore, or at least forget, their links with the State, others are as discreet as possible in their home country about their investment abroad, and even more so about the jobs they are thus creating while perhaps at the same time cutting jobs at home.

The fact that in France Renault prefers to present itself in its brochures and advertisements as 'the first French exporter' rather than as an actual automobile multinational like Ford, General Motors, Volkswagen and others is revealing. When an enterprise is state-owned, it generally seems preferable that it should appear as an exporting company rather than as a real multinational.

In the same way, Petroleos Mexicanos (Pemex) as well as Petroleos de Venezuela (PDVSA), the two firms responsible for exploiting the oil resources of Mexico and Venezuela respectively and which each have a large participation in refining firms in Europe, try to minimize the scale of these investments by presenting them as exceptional operations which will not recur. However, the strategic role of such investments is not negligible, since they make it easier for Pemex and PDVSA to export oil to Europe. Nevertheless, these industrial investments abroad are clearly hard to justify and to take responsibility for. Does this mean that the term 'multinational' is somewhat pejorative for a state-owned enterprise? Do the companies which invest abroad appear as 'betraying' the national interest?

In any case, the state-owned enterprises seem to have valid reasons for being discreet about their investment abroad. SGS clearly states that since success in the semiconductor field depends on whether a company is really multinational or not, it is obliged to pursue a conscious strategy of multinationalization. Yet even SGS is reluctant to talk about the production units it sets up abroad; so much so that one of the managers of IRI, the government holding which owns the capital of the firm, told us — it later turned out that he was wrong — that SGS had not installed new production units abroad since becoming a state-owned company as it preferred to allocate its resources to the development of production capacity in Italy. The fact is that SGS is now expanding its plants in France and building new factories in Singapore and in the United States. However, even some of the top managers of IRI, its major shareholder, are unaware of this.

A WORLDWIDE AND SPREADING PHENOMENON

Are state-owned multinationals an economic aberration? Perhaps . . . but certainly not a marginal phenomenon involving a few isolated and untypical cases. By this stage, we hope that the reader's response to the title of this book will have changed, after reading these few pages of introduction, from one of incredulity into one of curiosity, even interest. Be that as it may, before ending this first chapter we would like to convince the reader about the importance of state-owned multinationals in the world economy today and show that this importance is bound to increase over the next few years.

First of all, the place occupied by state-owned enterprises among the world's top companies is often not widely appreciated. For instance, how many people know that on the 1985[7] list of the world's 50 largest industrial corporations, drawn up on the basis of their turnover, there are seven state-owned companies (that is to say 14% of the total), six of which are multinationals?

If we look at the 1985 list of the 500 largest industrial corporations outside the United States — since in the United States the industrial public sector is virtually non-existent — we find 74 state-owned companies (that is to say nearly 15% of the total) of which 25 are multinationals (5% of the total).

In the directory of multinationals[8] which gives a list of the 500 major industrial multinational enterprises — these control over 80% of direct

    [7] According to *Fortune*'s classification, August 6, 1986.
    [8] J. Stopford, *The World Directory of multinational enterprises*, Macmillan, London, 1983.

investment abroad — there are 'only' nineteen state-owned companies. However, here again, if we discount American multinationals — almost half of the total — the proportion of state-owned multinationals amounts to 7.5%. One might well argue that Japanese multinationals should also be discounted, as they do not include any state-owned multinationals. Under these conditions, state-owned multinationals would represent about 10% of the total number of multinational companies outside the United States and Japan. In terms of unfair competition, however, Japanese multinationals are often regarded as no more than state-owned multinationals by American observers because of their evident collusion with MITI, despite the fact that the Japanese State does not hold a single share in their equity.

If the examination of the place occupied by multinationals today is revealing enough, what is most significant is the way this has evolved over the last 20 years. In 1965, of the world's top 200 industrial enterprises outside the United States, there were nineteen state-owned companies, three of which could at the time be regarded as multinationals. In 1975, the same group was found to include 29 state-owned enterprises, nine of which were multinationals. In 1985, the number of state-owned enterprises amounted to 38 including eighteen multinationals. Thus, the number of state-owned multinationals among the world's top enterprises has more than doubled every ten years since the mid-sixties and increased sixfold between 1965 and 1985. Tables 1.1–1.3 show this evolution and list the enterprises concerned.

We can explain this general evolution by bringing together three main phenomena:

— The increase in the number of state-owned multinationals between 1973 and 1983 is above all due to various recent waves of nationalization. Thus, in 1982 five multinational groups which were among the world's leaders were nationalized in France. In the United Kingdom, during the second half of the seventies, several major industrial groups such as British Leyland were nationalized. The revolution of 1975 in Portugal as well as the coming to power of a Conservative government in Sweden (paradoxical as the latter may seem) were accompanied by a series of nationalizations. The privatizations undertaken by the British Conservative government, and more recently by the French right-wing government are far from offsetting the effects of the various phases of nationalization previously implemented.
— The specific dynamism of the different sectors of activity provides the second explanation for the growing proportion of state-owned multinationals among the world's top companies. State-owned enterprises in traditional industries with little chance of extending their

Table 1.1   1965 — State-owned enterprises among the world's 200 largest industrial companies outside the United States

Rank	Enterprises	Sectors of activity	Country of origin
3	National Coal Board	Coal mining	UK
4	**British Petroleum**	Oil products	UK
18	**Renault**	Automobiles	France
29	Finsider	Iron & steel industry	Italy
32	Charbonnages de France	Coal mining	France
33	**ENI**	Oil products	Italy
38	Salzgitter	Iron & steel industry, machine tools	Germany
59	ERAP	Oil products	France
64	Pemex	Oil products	Mexico
88	Petrobras	Oil products, petrochemicals	Brazil
101	YPF	Oil products	Argentina
102	Richard Thomas and Baldwins	Iron & steel industry	UK
108	Hindustan Steel	Iron & steel industry	India
153	SEITA	Tobacco, matches	France
169	DSM	Coal mining, chemicals	Netherlands
171	Sud Aviation	Aeronautics	France
172	Voest	Iron & steel industry, machine tools	Austria
188	Iscor	Iron & steel industry	South Africa
198	Saarbergwerke	Coal mining	Germany

Note: The enterprises that appear in bold type are the ones that were really multinational in 1965 according to our criteria (cf Chapter Two).
Source: Fortune's ranking, August 1966.

Table 1.2   1975 — state-owned enterprises among the world's 200 largest industrial companies outside the United States.

Rank	Enterprises	Sectors of activity	Country of origin
10	**ENI**	Oil products, chemicals, textiles	Italy
13	**Renault**	Automobiles, tractors, machine tools	France
18	Elf-Aquitaine	Oil products	France
21	Petrobras	Oil products, petrochemicals	Brazil
27	British Steel	Iron & steel industry	UK
37	**British Leyland**	Automobiles	UK
52	National Coal Board	Coal mining	UK
62	Pemex	Oil products, petrochemicals	Mexico
63	Sonatrach	Oil products, petrochemicals	Algeria

Table 1.2 — Continued

Rank	Enterprises	Sectors of activity	Country of origin
65	**DSM**	Chemicals, fertilizers, plastics	Netherlands
70	**Salzgitter**	Iron & steel industry, machine tools, shipyards	Germany
73	Italsider	Iron & steel industry	Italy
94	**Voest-Alpine**	Iron & steel industry	Austria
95	Charbonnages de France	Coal mining, chemicals	France
105	Zimco	Mining, chemicals	Zambia
108	**Statsfortag**	Steel, mining, paper products, tobacco	Sweden
115	Indian Oil	Oil products	India
121	YPF	Oil products	Argentina
123	Enpetrol	Oil products, chemicals	Spain
128	Aérospatiale	Aeronautics	France
132	Pertamina	Oil products	Indonesia
162	Tabacalera	Tobacco products	Spain
164	Saarbergwerke	Coal mining, electricity, oil	Germany
181	Steel Authority of India	Iron & steel industry	India
183	Alfa-Romeo	Automobiles	Italy
185	**VIAG**	Aluminium, chemicals, electricity	Germany
187	OMV	Oil products, natural gas	Austria
192	Ensidesa	Iron & steel industry	Spain
200	Neste	Oil products	Finland

Note: The enterprises that appear in bold type are the ones that were really multinational in 1975 according to our criteria (cf Chapter Two).
Source: *Fortune*'s ranking, August 1976.

Table 1.3 1985 — state-owned enterprises among the world's 200 largest industrial companies outside the United States.

Rank	Enterprises	Sectors of activity	Country of origin
3	**IRI**	Iron & steel industry, aeronautics, shipyards, electronics, telecommunications	Italy
4	**ENI**	Oil products, chemicals	Italy
9	Pemex	Oil products	Mexico
10	**Elf-Aquitaine**	Oil products, chemicals	France
18	**Petrobras**	Oil products	Brazil
28	**Kuwait Petroleum**	Oil products	Kuwait
29	**Voest-Alpine**	Metals, machine tools	Austria
30	**Renault**	Automobiles	France

Table 1.3 — Continued

Rank	Enterprises	Sectors of activity	in
34	Petroleos de Venezuela	Oil products	V
35	Pertamina	Oil products	Ind
48	**Compagnie Générale d'Electricité**	Electrical, electronic engineering	Fran
51	Indian Oil	Oil products	India
54	**Saint-Gobain**	Glass, cast iron, building materials	France
57	**DSM**	Chemicals, fertilizers, plastics	Netherland
61	**Thomson**	Electrical, electronic engineering	France
63	Türkiye Petrolleri	Oil products	Turkey
72	**Rhône-Poulenc**	Chemicals	France
78	Statoil	Oil products	Norway
82	Neste	Oil products	Finland
85	Chinese Petroleum	Oil products	Taiwan
87	Sacilor	Iron & steel industry	France
99	Enpetrol	Oil products, chemicals	Spain
101	**Norsk-Hydro**	Oil products, chemicals	Norway
103	**YPF**	Oil products	Argentina
105	British Steel	Iron & steel industry	France
106	Usinor	Iron & Steel industry	France
112	British Leyland	Automobiles	UK
114	Charbonnages de France	Coal mining, chemicals	France
126	**Péchiney**	Aluminium	France
133	**Aérospatiale**	Aircraft industry	France
136	Petro-Canada	Oil products	Canada
153	Oil & Natural Gas Commission	Oil products, natural gas	India
168	**Salzgitter**	Iron & steel industry, shipyards	Germany
170	OMV	Oil products	Austria
171	**EFIM**	Metals, mechanical engineering, aeronautics	Italy
178	Steel Authority of India	Iron & steel industry	India
192	National Coal Board	Coal mining	UK
195	Saarbergwerke	Oil products, mining, coal mining	Germany

Note: The enterprises that appear in bold type are the ones that were really multinational in 1985 according to our criteria (cf Chapter Two).
Source: *Fortune*'s ranking, August 4, 1986.

activity abroad (coal-mining, shipbuilding), saw their position deteriorate because of the decline of the sector, whereas state-owned companies in expanding industries more likely to become multinational (automobiles, electronics, oil, aeronautics, . . .) were quick to develop.

— Lastly, in third world countries, particularly in what have been called new industrial countries, the rapid development of state-owned enterprises, some of which are actually showing signs of becoming multinational, contributed to the increase in the economic import- ance of state-owned multinationals and will continue to do so.

It is clear then that the multinationalization process of state-owned enterprises, limited during the sixties, has assumed surprising dimen- sions in the course of the last few years.

The reason why multinationalization at first mainly concerned private enterprises is that the first multinationals were essentially American firms and, as we emphasized, in the United States the industrial public sector has always been insignificant and its activities confined to public utilities. In the other developed countries where the public sector is more important, particularly in most Western and Northern European countries, the multinationalization of state-owned enterprises seems to occur together with the internationalization of the sectors of activity in which they operate. Thus, the multinationalization of Renault took place at about the same time as the other automobile groups in Europe, in similar circumstances, and at a time when the automobile markets themselves were rapidly spreading throughout the world. Also, the major European groups, either private or state-owned, became multi- national in much the same way. After having involved an increasing number of state enterprises in many developed countries, the process of multinationalization now seems to affect, as we have just stressed, certain state-owned enterprises in developing countries.

State-owned multinationals, whatever their country of origin, are found in a very large number of industrial sectors ranging from energy and raw materials (Elf-Aquitaine, ENI, Pemex, Kuwait Petroleum, Petroleos de Venezuela, Petrobras, Companhia Vale do Rio Doce, Office Chérifien des Phosphates, Norsk-Hydro, . . .) to chemicals (DSM, Rhône-Poulenc, . . .), nuclear power (Commissariat à l'Energie Atomique, Cogema, . . .), aeronautics (Aérospatiale, Embraer, CASA, British Aerospace until recently, . . .), automobiles (Renault, ENASA), the metallurgical industry (Salzgitter, Voest-Alpine, VIAG, Péchiney, . . .), electronics (Thomson, SGS, Matra, . . .), telecom- munications (CIT-Alcatel) or electrical equipment (CGE-Alsthom, Bharat Heavy Electricals Ltd, . . .), etc. . . . As can be seen, state- owned multinationals are far from being confined to a small number of industries. Belonging to one or another industry can nevertheless favour or slow down the multinationalization of state-owned enterprises, as well as that of private companies, depending on whether the activity of the sector in question puts it straight into the world market, as is the case with the automobile or aeronautics industry for instance, or whether it is limited to regional and compartmentalized markets like most public utilities (postal services, electricity or gas distribution, urban transport, railways, . . .).

If most state-owned multinationals are the consequence of an internationalization process started up by state-owned enterprises, some of them result from the nationalization of multinational groups belonging to the private sector. This is particularly true in the case of the five French industrial groups nationalized in 1982 (Compagnie Générale d'Electricité, Thomson, Péchiney, Rhône-Poulenc, Saint-Gobain)[9] but also in that of Norsk-Hydro nationalized in Norway soon after the Second World War, and of British Leyland nationalized in the seventies in the United Kingdom. Such differences in the origin of state-owned multinationals have a much greater importance than a simple historical anecdotal one as they largely condition, as we shall see, the corporate culture and identity of such groups as well as the way they formulate and implement their strategy. The state-owned enterprises which start a multinationalization process have to persuade their controlling authorities, with whom they have already been in contact for a long time, to leave them free to act and then progressively learn to run operations abroad. In contrast, nationalized multinationals have great experience in terms of international operations but must learn how to manage relations with the controlling body, whose preoccupations and reactions are quite different from those of the private shareholders of former times.

There is one other, rather special, category of state-owned multinationals: the companies whose equity is shared out among several national States. Still limited in number, they are generally created on the initiative of countries that come together to form an economic association and they develop an activity or a project of common interest to all the participating countries. European countries have thus collaborated in the creation of such 'transnational' state-owned multinationals. Amongst the most well-known, we might mention Airbus Industrie in the aeronautics field originally set up by France, Germany, the United Kingdom, and the Benelux countries, which were joined afterwards by other countries such as Spain. We might also mention Arianespace, whose purpose is to develop and market a space-launcher of European design, and Eurodif, which has perfected a uranium

---

[9] The victory of the right-wing party in the March 1986 elections led to the privatization of Saint-Gobain in December 1986 and of CGE in May 1987.

enrichment process available to member countries of the consortium. Enterprises of this kind have also been set up by developing countries. Thus, Mexico, Colombia, Jamaica, Nicaragua, Venezuela, Panama, Costa Rica and Cuba participated in the creation of the maritime transport firm NAMUCAR (Naviera Multinacional del Caribe), whose capital is divided up among the different countries. This operation originally came within the scope of what turned out to be an abortive project for economic association between various Latin American countries, SELA (Sistema Económico Latino-Americano). Right from the beginning, NAMUCAR experienced serious economic difficulties and is today almost bankrupt. Singapore, Indonesia, the Philippines, Malaysia and Thailand joined together to form an economic association, ASEAN (Association of South East Asia Nations), and decided to collaborate in setting up a network of industrial enterprises in priority sectors. These enterprises are installed in the different countries in turn and their capital is divided up among the five governments, each government owning the majority of the equity of the unit located in its own territory. Thus, a fertilizer factory was built in Indonesia, PT ASEAN Aceh Fertilizer, the major shareholder of which is the Indonesian State, the remaining four countries having a minority equity participation. In the same way, a copper-producing firm (ASEAN Bindulu) was set up in Malaysia and a third project is being studied in the Philippines. However, both the Singapore and the Thai projects are at a standstill or about to be cancelled, which shows, as does the NAMUCAR case, the difficulty of managing enterprises jointly supervised by several different countries. Experience seems to show that for such transnational state-owned firms to be viable it is essential that the various participating States are in total agreement concerning the enterprise's objectives as well as the means involved, and that they have a common political will to make the project succeed.[10]

All that has been said up to now shows that the state-owned multinationals phenomenon is not restricted to a few exceptional cases of enterprises with particular characteristics, but rather that for many and varied reasons and in very different ways, more and more state-owned enterprises have started, or are about to start, a multinationalization process. The reader will find mentioned and analysed in this book both true multinationals, defined according to the criteria most commonly accepted in this matter — which we will explain more precisely in Chapter Two — and state-owned enterprises which cannot be considered really as multinationals but which have started an inter-

---

[10] See M. S. Hochmuth, *Organizing the Transnational: The Experience with Transnational Enterprise in Advanced Technology*, A. W. Sijthoff, Leiden, 1974.

nationalization process that may ultimately turn them into multinationals. This book does not so much set out to present, at a given moment, an exhaustive list and a description of the world's state-owned multinationals, but rather to analyse the multinationalization process itself as applied to state-owned enterprises and to study its various forms as well as the phases it goes through in the course of its development.

Intrigued by all the contradictory rumour about state-owned multinationals and given the absolute non-existence of serious, and above all objective, research on the subject, we decided to clarify our own thoughts on this topic. We therefore carried out a thorough research into the question which resulted in this book.

Table 1.4 shows the state-owned companies which were given particular attention in the course of this research. They are divided into three major categories:

— In the first part of the table we list the state-owned enterprises which can be considered fully multinational.
— The second category is that of state-owned enterprises in the process of multinationalization; they are companies which, according to the formally accepted criteria (cf Chapter Two), are not yet really multinational but which, according to analysis, are likely to become multinationals sooner or later.
— The third category is that of engineering firms. Such enterprises are not, strictly speaking, multinationals insofar as they do not have industrial set-ups abroad. For a number of them, however, although their knowhow stems from their country of origin, most of their 'production' is carried out abroad. Moreover, it is quite clearly through the setting up of international engineering firms that a great many state-owned enterprises, in particular public utilities, start a multinationalization process.

The companies mentioned in Table 1.4 are the subject of a more detailed description in the Annex. The Index also contains a more exhaustive list of the enterprises looked at in this book: either real state-owned multinationals, or state-owned enterprises in the process of becoming multinational, or even recently privatized enterprises or state-owned companies which have separated from their foreign subsidiaries. Given that the available data are in short supply and tend to be biased, we felt that to get an idea ourselves of the essential character of state-owned multinationals, of the way they develop and of the questions and problems that the expansion of such a phenomenon could raise, it was necessary to go back to the primary sources of relevant information, that is to say to collect it ourselves from all the parties concerned. We thus met, in about 20 different countries, the managers

Table 1.4.

Enterprises	Sectors of activity	Country of origin
State-Owned Multinationals		
Aérospatiale	Aircraft industry	France
Agip (ENI)	Oil products	Italy
Assi	Paper products	Sweden
CIT-Alcatel (CGE)	Telecommunications	France
Cogéma (CEA-Industrie)	Nuclear industry	France
Compagnie Générale d'Électricité	Electrical, electronic engineering	France
DSM	Chemicals, fertilizers, plastics	Netherlands
Elf-Aquitaine	Oil products, chemicals	France
Embraer	Aircraft industry	Brazil
ENASA (INI)	Automobile manufacturing	Spain
Keppel Shipyard	Shipbuilding	Singapore
Norsk-Hydro	Oil products, chemicals	Norway
Péchiney	Aluminium	France
Petrobras	Oil products	Brazil
Renault	Automobile manufacturing	France
Rhône-Poulenc	Chemicals	France
Saint-Gobain	Glass, cast iron, materials	France
Salzgitter	Iron & steel industry	Germany
SGS (IRI)	Electronics	Italy
Thomson	Electrical, electronic engineering	France
VIAG	Metals	Germany
Voest-Alpine	Metals, machine tools	Austria
YPF	Oil products	Argentina
State-owned enterprises in the process of multinationalization		
Balmer-Lawrie (IBP)	Diversified	India
Bharat Heavy Electricals Ltd	Electrical engineering	India
CASA (INI)	Aircraft industry	Spain
Companhia Vale do Rio Doce	Metals	Brazil
Matra	Aircraft industry, diversified	France
Office Chérifien des Phosphates	Fertilizers	Morocco
Pemex	Oil products	Mexico
Petróleos de Venezuela SA	Oil products	Venezuela
Siderbras	Iron & steel industry	Brazil
Engineering firms		
Hydro-Quebec International	Electricity	Canada
ICCI	Public works	Indonesia
NIOG	Diversified	UK
RITES (Indian Railways)	Railways	India
Sofretu (RATP)	Urban transport	France

of all the state-owned enterprises which were either truly multinational or which we thought might eventually become so. We also met the state bodies that control these enterprises as well as, where possible, their customers or more generally their industrial and commercial partners, and even their competitors. Therefore, several hundred people in about 50 state-owned companies, either multinationals or in process of becoming so, in the civil service, etc. agreed to collaborate with us and spare us their time. Without their cooperation, this book could never have been written.

In Chapter Two we will start by taking a brief look at the theories about multinationals on the one hand and state-owned enterprises on the other, to then try to interrelate these two theoretical fields, bring out the resulting contradictions and see if a theory of state-owned multinationals emerges or, failing that, draw up lines for further reflection.

The third chapter will show where the state-owned enterprises run into more difficulties and have to overcome more obstacles than the private companies when they try to go multinational insofar as the 'owner-state' remains nationalist in most cases. Unlike their private counterparts, state-owned enterprises are often accused, however, of enjoying special, almost illicit advantages and of being unfair competitors.

In Chapter Four, we will try to clarify the question of unfair competition and to determine what specific advantages state-owned multinationals may have and also to judge whether such advantages make them an important threat to private enterprises.

In Chapter Five, we will show how certain state-owned enterprises know better than others how to develop arguments and implement particular strategies to overcome the difficulties they meet in their multinationalization process.

Then, in Chapter Six, we will see that what may really separate the state-owned enterprises which totally succeed in becoming multinational from those that fail to do so is indeed their 'corporate identity'. The ones which succeed are those which manage to reconcile a new and more multinational identity with the 'state-owned' identity.

In Chapter Seven, we shall try to draw up a typology of state-owned multinationals, according to the type of obstacles most often met in the course of the multinationalization process and thus according to the main strategic steps they may take so as to succeed in this venture.

Chapter Two

The Clash of Theories

INTRODUCTION

Although it is still not well known, the multinationalization process of state-owned enterprises is nevertheless, as we have seen, an important phenomenon in terms of its economic repercussions, and also because it calls the classical theory of multinationals as well as that of private companies into question. When they go multinational, do state-owned enterprises become more and more like private companies, or, are they rather transformed into a new species of enterprise which does not correspond either to the traditional pattern of state-owned enterprises or to that of private multinationals? This is the fundamental question that we shall try to answer in the course of this book through the analysis of the strategies adopted by state-owned multinationals.

Before actually studying the state-owned multinationals themselves and the process which led them to acquire this particular status, we must first consider the theories of multinationalization on the one hand and those of state-owned enterprises on the other. This short digression into theory will enable us to clarify the subject of our research and to highlight the main contradictions of principle that arise in the case of an enterprise which is both state-owned and multinational. In the course of this book, we shall try to analyse how such contradictions are, or can be, reconciled in practice by the enterprises concerned. Indeed, by confronting these two bodies of theory we shall be able to identify the first elements upon which a specific theory of state-owned multinationals may be based. This will be developed later and presented in a more comprehensive form in the last chapters.

THE THEORIES OF MULTINATIONALIZATION

We do not intend to conduct an exhaustive review of all existing theories of multinationalization, still less to develop an original theory. Our purpose is far more pragmatic. On the basis of the principal definitions and existing theories, we shall attempt to clarify the criteria used to identify the state-owned enterprises that we consider to be multinationals — or likely to become so — to which we have therefore devoted our attention. At the same time, we shall outline the key determinants of the multinationalization of private companies in order to establish whether the multinationalization of state-owned enterprises has the same strategic objectives, originates in a similar procedure and develops in the same way.

What is a multinational enterprise?

Most definitions of the multinational enterprise — also known as trans-national, supranational, plurinational (the different terms refer to the same notion) — that are to be found in the economic, political or managerial literature are based on economic and geographic criteria: generally the number of subsidiaries set up in different countries and the proportion of the activity carried out abroad. One can find very broad and purely qualitative definitions, for example: 'a company which has activities, other than selling, in more than one country,'[1] or 'a firm which makes direct investments abroad',[2] or 'any enterprise which carries out its main operations, manufacturing or services, in at least two countries'.[3] Other definitions are quantitative and more or less restrictive, for instance: 'any enterprise originating from one country, having stable activities under its control in n foreign countries which provide more than $x\%$ of its turnover'.[4] Michel Ghertman defines a multinational as an enterprise that operates in at least two foreign countries which account for 10% of its turnover, but he specifies that,

---

[1] M. L. Brooke and H. L. Renners, *La Stratégie de l'Entreprise Multinationale*, Edition Sirey, 1973.
[2] J. H. Dunning, *International Production and the Multinational Enterprise*, Allen and Unwin, London, 1981.
[3] As footnote 1.
[4] M. Ghertman and M. Allen, *An Introduction to the Multinationals*, Macmillan Press–IRM, 1984.

depending on the author, the definitions may involve anything between one and six foreign subsidiaries and the turnover they provide may vary between 5% and 50%. According to certain definitions any investment or subsidiary which gives the enterprise a legal status abroad — whether this investment is productive or not — constitutes a valid criterion. Other definitions, to really distinguish multinationals from mononational exporting enterprises, require that the foreign subsidiaries be industrial subsidiaries.

Thus, it is often the case that only industrial firms are considered to be multinationals, while it is noticeable that service companies tend to become multinational at least as much as industrial enterprises — though this is a later development. Furthermore, most analyses of the multinational phenomenon concern very large groups, whereas, according to all the previous definitions, multinationals[5] also include many small and medium-sized businesses.

In any case, these definitions are all extremely static and confined to establishing the 'multinational status' of an enterprise at a given moment.

Some definitions, less numerous but also less serviceable as far as identification purposes are concerned, underline the strategic character of the multinational phenomenon, stressing the overall policy of the multinational enterprise, which is conceived and carried out on a worldwide scale. This being the case, 'the group of enterprises whose activities, extending to many countries, are conceived and carried out on a worldwide scale' would be multinational.[6] Lastly, another approach to multinationals focuses on the legal aspect of the question, adopting as a criterion of multinationality the distribution of the authorized capital of the enterprise between shareholders of different nationalities.

The OECD, which has however drawn up guidelines and codes of conduct which it requires enterprises operating in its member countries to observe, considered that, given the problems this raised, it did not need to put forward a precise definition of multinational companies. It should however be borne in mind that the OECD emphasizes: 'generally, multinational enterprises are companies or other entities under private, public or joint ownership'.[7] Thus, the OECD explicitly contemplates the existence of state-owned multinationals.

For several years now, the UN, through its Economic and Social Council, has also been trying to work out a code of conduct which

[5] J. Savary, *Les Multinationales Françaises*, PUF–IRM, 1981.
[6] G. Y. Bertin, *Les Sociétés Multinationales*, PUF, 1975.
[7] OECD, *Guidelines for Multinational Enterprises, National Treatment, International Investment Incentives and Disincentives*, Consultation Procedures, Paris, 1976.

transnational firms — the term 'transnational' has been chosen in preference to 'multinational' — should respect.[8] The commission responsible for this has, however, not yet finished its work as it has come up against some difficulties, not least of which is that of finding a unanimously accepted definition of those multinationals to which the code of conduct should supposedly apply. In particular, the commission's work is baulked by the question of whether the definition should include transnational firms from developing countries, those from the Eastern bloc countries and those controlled by a state. The representatives of the Eastern bloc countries, as well as those of a number of developing countries, want only private enterprises originating from developed countries to be regarded as transnational enterprises. Needless to say, the representatives of those countries, especially in the United States, are opposed to this on the grounds that such a claim is based on purely political considerations.

Thus, at the UN, the question of whether or not there can be state-owned multinational enterprises has become a political issue, indeed a diplomatic one, giving rise to East–West and North–South confrontations.

Staying within the limits of the research which resulted in this book, it is not so much the multinational status, defined according to strict criteria and at a given moment, as the logic underlying the multi-nationalization of certain state-owned enterprises and the procedures involved that retained our attention. Therefore, we preferred to analyse the process whereby these state-owned enterprises become multi-national, the aims they pursue, the means they adopt and the obstacles they meet inside and outside the enterprise, rather than attempting to define and study the multinational status of any given state-owned enterprise. For this reason, we agreed on a formal criterion of multi-nationality, one which seems most commonly accepted, namely that the enterprises concerned should have industrial subsidiaries in at least two countries other than the country of origin and conduct 10% or more of their activity abroad. However, we also thought it necessary to consider a number of state-owned enterprises which did not entirely satisfy this criterion. The enterprises that appeared to be involved in a process (albeit at the embryonic stage) which would eventually transform them into multinationals should, we thought, be studied. The range of enterprises we chose to study includes both true multinationals, which satisfy the adopted criterion and generally originate from

[8] *Transnational Corporations in World Development: A Re-examination*, Report of the UN Economic and Social Council, March 20, 1978.

developed countries, and state-owned enterprises in the process of becoming multinational, which often originate from developing countries.

We also studied a particular category of state-owned enterprise which could be regarded as multinational from a strictly legal point of view. These are enterprises whose authorized capital is held by several states associated in the same project. Indeed, their case corresponds to our overall approach, inasmuch as they follow the logic of multinationalization and as their activity is divided between several countries and directed towards several national markets at once.

We chose not to study industrial enterprises exclusively but to include in our selection service and engineering enterprises. On the one hand, we decided not to look too closely at the case of airline companies or banks, although there are many state-owned multinationals in these two sectors. Even though the state-owned sector accounts for 85% of international air traffic, the multinationalization of such enterprises seems to follow a specific logic determined by the sector of activity. In the same way, we did not concern ourselves directly with banks, which are often both multinational and state-owned, because the specific nature of their activities is of overriding importance compared to the question of their state-owned character. We have, however, made exceptions in the case of state-owned financial bodies holding an equity participation in industrial companies likely to become multinational.

We also excluded from our research multinational enterprises originating from the Eastern bloc countries, which, by definition, are all state-owned.[9]

Why and how does an enterprise become multinational?

The answers to this question which can be found in the abundant literature on the subject are of two kinds:

1. The first relates to *economic theory*, every school of thought putting forward an interpretation of the multinational phenomenon in line with its own approach.[10]

---

[9] The question of 'red' multinationals is the subject of a specific research also carried out under the aegis of IRM; to be consulted on the matter:
E. Zaleski, 'Les multinationales des pays de l'Est', *Les Multinationales en Mutation*, PUF–IRM, 1983, Chapter X.
R. Gendarme, *Des sorcières dans l'Economie: Les Multinationales*. Edition Cujas, 1981, pp. 435–453.
[10] For a more detailed analysis of that interpretation see: R. Gendarme (footnote 9), pp. 42–69.

(a) Classical economic theory, particularly the theory of international exchanges, was originally based on the assumption that only goods could be exchanged in space and time, whereas factors of production were fixed. Later, mainly with the work of Samuelson, the theory announced the equalization in the prices of these factors on a worldwide scale through international exchanges. These assumptions explain why, for a long time, economic theory only accounted very imperfectly for the existence of multinational firms.

However, a consideration of what are called 'monopolistic advantages', that is to say the distinctive skills of the enterprises that set up abroad enabling them to assert themselves in the face of local competitors, has made the development of a more satisfactory interpretation of the multinational phenomenon possible within the theoretical framework of classical economy.

The work of Vernon,[11] in particular, falls within this school of thought and emphasizes the other parameters such as 'imperfect' competition, the product cycle, technological innovation, the uncertain fixing of costs, delocalization, monopolistic competition and direct investment. In the same way, Brems[12] explains direct investment in terms of inequality in capital resources in different countries and of the technical superiority of certain countries.

(b) In Marxist theory, whose exponents like Lenin or Rosa Luxembourg took a very early interest in imperialism and hence in the phenomenon of multinationality, three broad tendencies are to be found according to R. Gendarme.[13]

— The first, known as the theory of 'monopolistic state capitalism', explains the imperialism of developed countries (headed by the United States), as well as the multinationalization of the firms originating in such countries, in terms of the alliance between the State and capital, formed to offset the downward trend of profit rates. Increasing the total profit through an overexploitation of the outlying countries could provisionally maintain profit rates for remunerated capital — which tend to fall because of the phenomenon known as 'capital overaccumulation'. This thesis of 'monopolistic state

[11] R. Vernon, 'International investment and international trade in the product cycle', *Quarterly Journal of Economics*, **80**, May 1966.

[12] H. Brems, 'A growth model of direct investment', *American Economic Review*, June 1970.

[13] R. Gendarme (footnote 9), pp. 50–60.

capitalism', as far as imperialism and the multinational development of firms are concerned, remains very close to the theses of Lenin and Rosa Luxembourg.

— The second tendency, described as the third world tendency, of which Arghiri Emmanuel,[14] Samir Amin[15] and Gunder Franck[16] are the major exponents, is based on the notion of 'unequal exchange': the multinational firm is regarded as the instrument whereby rich countries exploit poor countries.

— Thirdly, the 'American imperialism' thesis, mainly developed by Nicos Poulantzas,[17] considers the United States as the centre of world capitalism. According to this view, American multinationals are the instrument whereby American capitalism dominates the world and are responsible for the spreading of the capitalist production system with its corresponding ideologies. Thus, the role of American multinationals is given much greater prominence than that of multinationals from other countries and this theory fails to account for the emergence of multinationals originating from developing countries[18] and of state-owned multinationals.

2. The second kind of answer to the question 'Why do certain enterprises tend to become multinational?' is provided by management science and seeks the explanation for the multinationalization of enterprises in the logic of their development, in their competitive environment and in the strategy they implement. From this point of view, the main driving forces of the multinationalization of enterprises fall into four categories:

(a) The search for cheaper and more abundant sources of supply. The most evident incentive for the multinationalization of firms is the need to look abroad for raw materials or natural resources which are scarce or simply unavailable in their own country. This type of multinationalization, which could be regarded as being imposed by the distribution of wealth throughout the world, is also one of its oldest forms.

(b) The search for less expensive factors of production. Setting up production units in countries where labour — or any other factor

[14] A. Emmanuel, *L'Echange Inégal*, Maspéro, 1972.

[15] S. Amin, *L'Accumulation à l'Echelle Mondiale*, Edition Anthropos, 1970.

[16] A. G. Franck, *Le Développement du Sous-Développement d'Amérique Latine*, Maspéro, 1970.

[17] N. Poulantzas, *Les Classes Sociales dans le Capitalisme d'Aujourd'hui*, Le Seuil, 1974.

[18] S. Lall, *The New Multinationals — The Spread of Third World Enterprises*, John Wiley & Sons, Chichester, 1983.

of production — is less expensive or more flexible is also one of the principal driving forces of multinationalization. Multi-nationalization which aims to lower transportation costs is in line with this approach. This form of multinationalization is imposed by the competitive dynamics of the sector of activity of the enterprises; it is imperative that they remain competitive. In this case the purpose of multinationalization is to optimize costs.

(c) The search for a production volume effect by winning new markets and the need to overcome protectionism in consumer countries. The search for new outlets, which make a production volume effect, hence a reduction of costs, possible is another standard element in the strategies of multinationals. While, from a theoretical point of view, the greater number of outlets and the conquest of foreign markets could also be obtained simply by adopting an export policy, protectionism, either open or disguised, practised by most countries, requires that at least part of the manufacturing be done locally. Some countries also demand that any import be compensated by equivalent exports. Moreover, a large-scale local set-up is often the only way of keeping in close touch with the local market and adapting the product to its specific needs.

(d) The desire to maintain an advanced technological level. In high-technology industries the increase of the research and develop-ment expenses requires that they be amortized over longer production series and that, consequently, the outlets be increased, which means, as we have seen, setting up plants abroad. However, in order to be in touch with the latest develop-ments and to incorporate them into its own product — or production processes — and thus remain among the techno-logical leaders, an enterprise must have industrial set-ups in the most developed countries, particularly the US and Japan but also in certain Western European countries or even Singapore.

The main driving forces of the multinationalization of enterprises that we have very rapidly examined are far from being mutually exclusive. On the contrary, the explanation for the multinationalization process of an enterprise should be sought in the combination of these different incentives. The following pages, and to a certain extent the third section of this chapter, will enable us to determine whether the logic of the multinationalization of state-owned enterprises is the same as the one described above, which is characteristic of private enterprises.

What are multinationals blamed for?

The theoretical approaches of multinationalization, especially the 'third world' and the 'American imperialism' theses we have mentioned, suggest the kind of criticism levelled at multinational firms and the 'ethical' problems raised when an enterprise goes multinational. The main criticism of multinational firms comes from either the 'left-wing' or the nationalist current of public opinion and concerns the economic, political and social role played by these companies in the countries where they are set up.

First, at the economic level, multinationals, as we have seen, are accused of being the prime instrument whereby rich countries exploit poor countries, of exporting to those poor countries the capitalist production system and of increasing the economic dependence of such countries, requiring them to specialize within the framework of the international division of labour. The incursion of multinationals into third world countries would thus be responsible for disrupting their traditional economic structure. Multinationals are also credited with imposing monoproductive systems mainly focusing on agriculture or natural resources, and thereby making the economy of such countries highly dependent on imports from developed countries, which are mainly profitable to multinational groups. According to this view, because of their size and their power (indeed some multinationals have a total turnover that is higher than the gross national product of small developing countries), multinational firms are able to impose their economic view in the host countries. They can take advantage of the assets of every country and are free to invest as they wish, setting up here, withdrawing there, according to circumstances; they employ the various legal and fiscal systems to their best advantage — making particular use of internal transfer prices. All in all, multinational firms are considered to be able to get around the controls of national states.

The governments of the host countries nevertheless have a number of means giving them at least partial control over the activity of the multinationals within their territory. Strict regulations concerning transfer prices, import or export of capital or repatriation of profits are by no means insignificant. Certain countries, like India and Mexico, require that any subsidiary of a foreign group be under majority control of national capital. Michel Ghertman points out in this respect that IBM and Coca Cola preferred not to set up in India if it meant accepting that local stockholders had a share of at least 51% of their Indian subsidiaries.

We do not propose to decide one way or the other and to take sides in the debate on the positive or negative role of multinationals in the economy of different countries, especially developing ones. However, whatever their reservations, most countries seek to attract foreign capital, and this would seem to imply that their governments consider that such investment has a positive economic effect or at least that they can hardly do without it. Moreover, in most countries the sectors which involve more multinationals seem to expand further than the other sectors. Nevertheless, we cannot infer that this is due only to the activity of multinationals themselves.

Multinationals, or at least some of them, are criticized even more severely from a political point of view. Certain enterprises have even been accused of direct intervention in the domestic policy of different countries in order to protect their own interests. Some multinationals are alleged to have helped finance the overthrowing of socialist or nationalist governments which threatened their interests, and the setting up of dictatorships or military regimes. Some analyses assert that, even when they do not intervene directly in the policy of the countries where they are set up, multinationals put pressure on the government of their country of origin so that it will act on their behalf. Thus, the CIA is accused of being the mailed fist of American multinationals throughout the world.

Lastly, in relation to social and cultural matters, multinationals are also accused of many sins; exploiting an underpaid labour force in developing countries, they avoid giving fringe benefits and promoting the overall improvement of living standards which working classes of developed countries have struggled for. Multinationals are said to be one of the driving forces behind the drift from the land to the cities and the overurbanization in developing countries. They are also accused of being largely responsible for destroying the traditional social structure by exporting the capitalist production system and the social relations that accompany it. Multinationals, through their activities, are said to lead to a worldwide standardization of culture, propagating American, or more generally western, tastes, culture and forms of consumption in every country in the world and shattering the specific local cultures. We do not intend to start debating the role of multinationals and the accusations levelled at them, but only to underline some of the current attitudes in this respect. As soon as they start a multinationalization process, state-owned enterprises must expect to be criticized in the same way as private multinationals and also to be compared with them.

THE THEORIES OF NATIONALIZATION

While the development of multinationals mainly started in the sixties, that of state-owned enterprises began earlier, since most of them appeared in the thirties and the forties. Paradoxically, for a long time there was no managerial literature on state-owned enterprises, whereas multinationals were the subject of much research and many published works. Historically, those who have shown most interest in nationalization, either praising or condemning it, are ideologists. State-owned enterprises were the subject of debate even before they existed. When they were actually created, the question was taken up by jurists, who described the circumstances of their creation and the way they functioned. Certain economists also started to study them, not making them the focal point of their theories but citing them as exceptions or as particular cases. Thus it was not until the seventies that their management was studied and publications on the subject began to appear.

Again, this book does not set out to review all the literature relating to the various subjects concerned since its origins. Above all, we shall try to give an overview of the main ideas found in this literature — any reader interested in more details should refer to our Bibliography. We shall do so by asking three essential questions which recur time and again and have fuelled research and speculation on the subject.

— Why are state-owned enterprises created?
— What difference is there between the way they are managed and the way private enterprises are managed?
— Is it possible to improve their management? If so, how?

By doing this we do of course tend to adopt the managerial approach, but we will see that this very approach involves economics, politics and law.

It is, however, necessary first of all to define what a state-owned enterprise is, and that is no easy matter as the answers given by the disciplines mentioned above are conflicting. From the legal point of view, there are several forms of state-owned enterprise whose point in common is to be an artificial person and to have statutory autonomy. But, the enterprises which are common law companies whose capital is partly or totally held directly or indirectly by the State should be distinguished from enterprises having a different status as defined by the statute by which they were created (public establishments in French law for example). This gives us a list, but certainly not a definition, of state-owned firms. From an economic point of view, the nature of the activity is more important than its legal status: legal status is not a necessary condition, the 'enterprise' need only produce and sell goods and services and have a profit and loss account. The state-owned character refers to the control of the management by the state, but not to the forms this takes. Lastly, from a political point of view, state-owned enterprises can be considered as the product of nationalization or *ex-nihilo* creations, a legacy from previous governments or government sanctions imposed on a company, etc. These distinctions are mainly based on the justifications for the existence of such enterprises. In addition, recognizing that an enterprise is 'state-owned' amounts to adopting a stance which has far-reaching consequences, especially at the social level — and this is not easy.

In this confused situation state-owned enterprises can assert their private character and private enterprises may be accused of being 'state-owned' (by competitors, for example). All this was not really central to our preoccupations and we have taken a state-owned enterprise to be an enterprise in the economic sense of the term, with most of its capital held by one (or more) states, directly or indirectly. Of course, there is still a grey area, although limited. If the State is the only large minority shareholder it exerts undeniable control, but the enterprise is not state-owned according to our definition. If there are a number of shareholders, federal states and local states for instance, or if these are state-owned enterprises (notably banks), we consider the enterprise to be state-owned when the public sector stockholders together hold a share of over 50% of the capital.

Why and how are state-owned enterprises created?

The question is a simple one, but the answers vary considerably in terms of form and content. We have maintained elsewhere[19] that there were only two very distinct reasons for creating state-owned enterprises — first, the *lack* of private initiative in sectors of activity regarded as being indispensable to the development of the country and the well-being of the population; secondly, the *inappropriateness* of this private initiative in sectors of activity where private control proves to be prejudicial to the consumers or to the country in general. It should be added that in both cases the acknowledgement of lack of initiative or inappropriateness is political in nature.

Other authors prefer to draw up a long list, as exhaustive as possible,

[19] J. P. Anastassopoulos, 'Entreprises publiques et pouvoir politique', in *Entreprises Publiques: Experiences Comparées* by the same author and J. P. Nioche, FNEGE, 1982.

of the reasons why state-owned enterprises are created, based on the examination of the greatest possible number of examples. It is this highly pragmatic approach which is adopted by Armeane M. Choksi[20] of the World Bank for example. This author, who is representative of an American school of thought, actually gives 25 reasons why a state creates state-owned enterprises, which are worth outlining here: '1. provide entrepreneurial support/substitution; 2. control monopolies; 3. control commanding heights; 4. provide public utilities; 5. earn profits for investment; 6. utilize resources efficiently; 7. prevent business failure; 8. offset externalities; 9. train skilled managers and technicians; 10. increase employment; 11. raise output; 12. reduce income inequality; 13. promote regional development; 14. stabilize prices; 15. subsidize necessary commodities; 16. set "modernization" example; 17. earn/save foreign exchange; 18. promote primary exports; 19. achieve socialism; 20. counterbalance power of domestic capitalists; 21. increase national self-sufficiency; 22. enhance national prestige; 23. implement government policy; 24. promote national security; 25. offset multinationals'. The author gives all these objectives without indicating an order of priority.

The drawback of this approach is that it simply provides a list with no reference to a theory or previously defined argument. That is why we prefer François Chevallier's approach, which we will now summarize briefly.[21] The author first notes, quite rightly, that the reasons why the State creates state-owned enterprises are 'obscured by the climate of ideological and political strife' which surrounds this issue. Then, he emphasizes, again quite rightly in our view, that while each of the explanations constitutes a necessary condition for the creation of state-owned enterprises, none of them is sufficient. He therefore distinguishes the 'underlying causes' of the setting up of the public sector from 'contingent factors'.

There are two kinds of underlying causes: ideological and economic. As for the former, Proudhon rather than Marx is the father of the doctrine of nationalization. It is because 'property is theft' that, according to this theory, production must be based on the autonomous organization of workshops under workers' control, formed into a federation under the aegis of the nation (not the State). Léon Jouhaux said: 'What we want from nationalization, is that collective ownership be

[20] A. M. Choksi, 'State Intervention in the Industrialization of Developing Countries: Selected Issues', World Bank Staff Working Papers No 341, Washington DC, 1978.

[21] F. Chevallier, *Les Entreprises Publiques en France*, Documentation Française, Paris, 1979. All the passages in quotation marks in this part of the text are taken from this book.

returned to the nation and that the means of production be controlled by the State through the cooperation of producers and consumers'. Marxist theory is very far from this position, advocating as it does in the phrase 'expropriation of expropriators' an increase in state power wrenched from the hands of the bourgeoisie by the workers. We may also cite as part of the ideological reasons the encyclical *Quadragesimo Anno* of 1931, in which the Pope wrote: 'There are goods which one can rightly claim should belong to the community, when their possession confers such power that they cannot be left in the hands of private individuals without posing a threat to the general good'. All these have contributed to the ideology of nationalization as expressed in France for example soon after the Liberation, in particular by the Conseil National de la Résistance, as well as in Norway at the same time.

In Great Britain, it was through the trade unions movement and the intellectuals of the Fabian Society that the Labour Party started to envisage nationalization. We must add that the trade unions have 'always been very suspicious of a system which would involve them in the management process and compromise the practice of collective bargaining. It was on the initiative of Sidney Webb and Beatrice Potter, first advocates of a 'municipal socialism', that in 1913, the Labour Party committed itself to the nationalization of a limited number of sectors entrusted to totally independent enterprises run by a tripartite board of directors. It was Herbert Morrison, Transport Minister under MacDonald's second Labour government (1929–1931), who won the party over to the cause of nationalization, advocating the theory of the autonomy of state-owned enterprises (of which more will be said). Marxism had no part in it. This is also true of course in the case of national socialism, which led to the creation of many state-owned enterprises in Germany, Italy, Norway and Spain. In contrast, in a great number of developing countries nationalization was inspired to a much greater extent by Marxism.

As far as the economic causes are concerned, that is to say the second set of underlying factors leading to the creation of the public sector, there are three theoretical tendencies: the Marxist tendency, the neo-liberal tendency and a third tendency which rejects any explanation based on economic theory. The two first schools of thought are sufficiently well known and we do not need to give a detailed account of them. For Marxists, the downward trend of profit rates together with overaccumulation of capital leads to the depreciation of capital. Since the sectors which experience this are still essential to the development of the rest of the economy, the State is forced to take them over. Thus, the capital that is depreciating is public capital, while private capital continues to be profitable. For the neo-classical or neo-liberal economists, there are goods produced in a way which precludes the existence of many individual competitors, and this leads to a monopoly situation. In this case, the monopolizer will make astronomical profits if productivity increases (the marginal cost increases more rapidly than the average cost) or will suffer structural losses if productivity decreases. Maximum 'social productivity' can only be obtained if the State intervenes to prevent superprofits or to cover particularly high deficits. Exponents of the third tendency are by no means convinced by these explanations. Indeed, there are sectors where the downward trend of profit rates does not necessarily entail nationalization, while the latter does occur in profitable sectors. The same is true of monopolies. For a number of economists mentioned by F. Chevallier, 'the very concept of the state-owned enterprise, does not lend itself to economic analysis', for 'the ultimate limit of economic analysis is the market and its mechanisms, whereas the action of the State and therefore its options are not confined to this limit. Thus, we must try to explain the creation of state-owned enterprises in terms of ultimate goals of the State, rather than in terms of economic analysis'.

We now come to the second part of the author's analysis, which is devoted to the contingent factors in the formation of the public sector. This part is closely related to what we have said above. First, there are economic motives (not to be confused with the causes which constitute *determining* factors) centring on the function of state-owned enterprises which are an instrument of national policies. Thus, this can involve implementing economic planning, particularly in upstream 'key sectors' in the industrial production cycle. It can also mean rationalizing the production system when the market mechanisms prove to be inefficient (as is often the case with electricity, transport and communications). More generally, as we have already noted, the aim may be to remedy a failure of private initiative such as is often found in the case of collective consumer goods and high-technology or research activities.

However, the above motives are all political. The most important of these is the determination of the State to reinforce its administrative structure. This would involve freeing itself from the large economic lobbies which dictate the government's policies without taking into account the exploitation of national resources and the national interest which it is incumbent upon the State to define and to pursue. This was the undoing of nationalization without state control in France as well as in a great number of countries which we shall term 'interventionist' as opposed to 'free market' as far as the role of the State in the economy is concerned. In this respect, nationalism is a powerful factor in the expansion of the public sector, particularly in developing countries.

What is special about the way state-owned enterprises are managed?

This was the second question that we asked ourselves. In our opinion, the answer to this involves two stages. First, we have to show the differences between state-owned and private enterprises in terms of objectives and performance; next, illustrate those differences through the individual analysis of the conditions under which such enterprises are managed. A great deal of literature has recently been produced on the subject, especially in developed countries which have a large public sector and where nationalization is a political issue: mainly Great Britain and France and to a lesser extent Italy. International organizations, such as the World Bank and the United Nations, are conducting research in this field. Certain countries in the process of industrialization, such as Mexico, Brazil and India, are also concerned with these questions and have started to produce some interesting studies. The United States is less fruitful in this respect, although some research was started a few years ago.[22]

All studies of performance based on standard criteria (profit, return on investment, etc.) agree that generally state-owned enterprises are less efficient than private companies. In this connection we can cite the conclusions of Mary M. Shirley, an economist at the World Bank:[23] 'a study of sixty-four state-owned enterprises in twenty-six countries in the 1960s found that when a normal depreciation was included and subsidies excluded, the companies showed a loss equivalent to 16% of total activity'. In developing countries, individual country studies also indicate 'that return on investment is often low or negative and self-financing of investment is close to nil'. These poor financial results mean 'rising debts and a growing burden on the treasury. Government subsidies to state-owned enterprises have reached more than 3% of GDP in a sample of 27 developing countries and 2% of GDP in seven developed countries in 1976–1979'. Finally, state-owned enterprises are important borrowers: 28% of all Eurocurrency borrowing in 1980. For Mary M. Shirley, although government policies are partly responsible for the bad financial performance of state-owned enterprises, it is clear that their operational efficiency is too low and should be improved.

What she says is certainly true of a great number of enterprises. But she makes assertions, reaches conclusions, which have to be explained.

---

[22] The organization of a symposium on state-owned enterprises at Harvard University in 1979 led to the publication of *State-Owned Enterprises in the Western Economies*, Croom Helm, London, 1981.

[23] See Mary Shirley, *Managing State Owned Enterprises*, World Bank Staff Working Papers No 577, Washington DC, 1983.

All the managerial theories of the state-owned enterprise deal with the analysis of the specific character of company management. They are still not very numerous and generally centre on the existing relationship between the State and the state-owned enterprise, as that is what substantially determines this specific character. We shall mention briefly here the analysis made by one of us based on research carried out in the 1970s.[24]

The relationship between the State and state-owned enterprises is characterized by the conflict of interests which sets them apart: it is therefore dialectical in nature. On the one hand, the company tries to achieve its own objectives implementing appropriate strategies and efficient management methods similar to those of the private enterprise. On the other hand, the State tries to use the state-owned enterprise as a simple instrument of its own policy, with its specific political–administrative methods. The objectives of one or the other may possibly be compatible, but this is hardly likely. The differences in their methods, each inspired by its respective logic, more often lead to an opposition rather than a convergence.

This dialectical opposition, which has to be overcome, emerges at three different levels of decision-making: economic, organizational and political.

— At the *economic* level, the oppositions first appear in the determination of the enterprise's general objectives. The enterprise tries to enhance its power and autonomy, while the State wants it to serve various conflicting objectives which hamper the enterprise's activities — job creation and greater public welfare, trade balance, town and country planning, stimulating the economy, etc. When an enterprise defines a market strategy (activities to be developed, initiated, abandoned) the State puts a spanner in its work in the name of is own industrial, energy and foreign policies, etc — to force the enterprise to make investments against its will or prevent it from carrying out those it wants to make. The State can impose national technology, suppliers and equipment on the enterprise; it can refuse to give adequate financial aid and prevent it from regulating its cash-flow by reducing prices. The State does not readily authorize large loans and obliges the enterprise to incur foreign debts from countries with strong currency. When the enterprise increases its productivity, the State prevents it from cutting its staff and, by giving employees a privileged status and yielding to union pressures for political reasons, it deprives the state enterprise of the means to manage its employees itself.

— At the *organizational* level there are other sources of conflict, as if all those we mentioned above were not enough. The fact is that the state-owned enterprise is strait-jacketed by a paralysing system of supervision and control. Many government decision centres are indeed involved in all the strategic options; of course, there is a controlling ministry to which the enterprise is attached, but there is also a ministry for economic and financial affairs which, as a matter of course, covers the work of the first and operates in various capacities through different official bodies: those responsible for state budget, credit, etc. Other ministries also try to use the enterprise as an instrument of their own policy. It should be borne in mind that the highest state authorities intervene when there is an important issue at stake, notably in the case of the appointment and dismissal of the top managers of the enterprises. Each of these official bodies has its own preoccupations which are quite different from those of the enterprise, and also its own power which theoretically is greater than that of the company.

— At a *political* level, everything seems to be in the hands of a few important figures: politicians and the high-ranking civil servants who work for them. Opposed to the latter, there is the company's chairman or managing director who must try to outsmart them, making use of his personal influence, his charm or his knowledge of the issues. However, the criteria underlying decisions are almost totally divorced from economic considerations: indeed, government representatives are concerned with public opinion, the media, forthcoming elections, the opposition, and above all with reinforcing their personal image and that of their allies.

The central question raised by this approach is that of the autonomy of the state-owned enterprise in relation to the State: how much is necessary, in what areas, and how can it be guaranteed? If the degree of autonomy is insufficient, everything we have outlined above shows that the state-owned enterprise cannot possibly be well managed. There will be too much state interference in its strategy and even its day-to-day management, and if badly used it would become a totally ineffective 'instrument' of the State. If, on the other hand, the degree of autonomy is too great, the justification for nationalization is called into question, as the state-owned enterprise will tend to behave exactly like a private company. Increasing the performance of state-owned enterprises without abandoning the idea that they have a key national role to play — this is the challenge the issue of autonomy[25] implies.

How can the management of state-owned enterprises be improved?

All experts agree that the relationship between state-owned enterprises and the State must be 'codified', that the 'rules of the game' should be clarified. Mary Shirley's suggestions cited above, for instance, involve four main points. First, the state-owned enterprises 'objectives must be defined by assessing and compensating the cost of all 'non-economic' goals imposed by the State. But some form of procedure is required for defining the objectives and she regards the French experience of the negotiated contracts between the State and the enterprises, taken up notably in Spain and Portugal, as promising in this respect. The planning contracts signed in 1983 between the French government and eleven large nationalized[26] industrial groups represent the most complete version to date of this type of 'instrument'. They comprise three main parts:

1. The major strategic orientations of the enterprise
2. The objectives of major national interest it will pursue
3. The financial relationship with the State.

The enterprise commits itself to reach a certain number of mid-term objectives (qualitative and/or quantitative, according to the matter in question) and the State approves its strategy and pledges financial aid (to be renegotiated at the end of each one-year period). Negotiations are based on the strategic plan of the enterprise and on the national policies defined by the government, which obliges the former to draw up this plan and the latter to formulate coherent policies. In the case of enterprises incurring public service costs, as in the field of transport for example, such contracts make provision for financial compensation by the State.[27]

There must then be 'control without interference', that is to say that the control must be organized. However, in this respect, the actual experience is much more disappointing, both in the case of a system of

---

[25] On this subject the *Rapport sur les Entreprises Publiques* drawn up by Simon Nora for the French government, published by La Documentation Française, Paris, 1967, is still relevant.

[26] Bull, CGE, CdF Chimie, EMC, Péchiney, Renault, Rhône-Poulenc, Saint-Gobain, Sacilor, Thomson, Usinor.

[27] As for SNCF (French state railways) and Air France.

holding companies used as a buffer between state-owned enterprises and the State and in that of a ministry or a public agency involving all the state-owned enterprises. The holding companies are the form of control adopted notably by two countries: Italy and Spain. In the former, there is the ENI, the IRI and the EFIM; in the latter the INI. Their *raison d'être* was found wanting: instead of serving as a buffer, they provided aid to lame ducks, taking in companies which since the mid-sixties had been finding it increasingly difficult to hold their own in the face of international competition. Furthermore, in the case of Italy, for a long time the appointment of the managers of these holding companies has been made on the basis of purely political criteria (the IRI, for instance, is a Christian Democrat stronghold, the ENI a Socialist one). This, in turn, influenced the way the managers of the firms involved in these holding companies were appointed; it is called the *lottizzazione*. The role these enterprises played in maintaining employment, cost what it may, was consequently greater. Other holding companies with technical characteristics, such as the National Enterprise Board in Great Britain and Statsforetag in Sweden, had similar experiences. The concentration of the control of the state-owned enterprises in the hands of one ministry, as is the case with Italy, always leads to confrontations with the ministry for economic and financial affairs. Even when a specialized bureau is set up as part of the latter, such as the Bureau of Public Enterprises in India, its role is limited to collecting information and serving as a think-tank. All things considered, it would appear that the best solution consists in giving real power to the board of directors of each enterprise, appointing a minimum number of state representatives to it, according to the British 'arm's length relationship' principle to which the British Minister Herbert Morrison was greatly attached. This principle, however, was called into question in its country of origin, where in 1976 the National Economic Development Office proposed to set up a 'council of strategic orientation' to mediate between the board of directors and the controlling ministry (which came to nothing). The solution of the Thatcher government to this problem is, as we know, privatization.

To go back to Mary Shirley, her third proposal consists in holding the managers of state-owned enterprises accountable for results. The problem here is that profit is not an adequate criterion for judging the results of an enterprise: indeed, many of them are monopolies and the profit does not have the same relevance for society as a whole as for private enterprise, many objectives of state-owned enterprises conflict with entrepreneurial profit maximization and market prices are often distorted in the public sector. However, there are some solutions to this problem. Where there is a monopoly, the prices must be set according to marginal costs, and if this is not possible the enterprise can still be required to minimize its costs. Profit can be judged otherwise, not so much in short-sighted financial terms as in terms of investment, research, etc. Conflicting goals can be compensated by government reimbursement of the extra costs they entail. Distorted prices can be rectified by using reference prices or opportunity costs to make a correct economic reassessment. Of course, these solutions are difficult to put into practice. The best way to improve the efficiency of state-owned enterprises might be to restore competition where this is feasible, especially in export activities. When this is not possible, state-owned enterprises can still be subjected to organized public pressure such as consumer councils or simply important clients.

Lastly, a fourth proposal consists in developing managerial efficiency and incentives. This can be done by giving the managers of state-owned enterprises greater autonomy when they have good results and vice versa.

Pecuniary incentives are traditionally more difficult to use in state-owned enterprises because of the prevailing spirit of egalitarianism. Indeed, the staff as a whole benefits from the available surplus with no substantial individual differences. All bonuses soon become established 'gains', considered as part of the salary, and can no longer be used to promote incentive. As for managerial skills, the solution to the problem is obvious: the managers of state-owned enterprises should resemble, as far as possible, managers of private companies rather than high-ranking civil servants. This seems relatively feasible in developed countries but is a serious problem in developing ones, where most managers of state-owned enterprises are recruited from the civil service and often from the army. In addition, there is a higher rate of turnover in the case of the latter, partly because of the shortage of competent people and partly because of political changes. Furthermore, in developed countries practice differs widely from one country to another. We have already said that in Italy the appointment of managers was politically influenced, but the same is true in France, where a great many managers are recruited from the civil service or even the government. In Scandinavian countries, Germany, the Netherlands and Great Britain, the heads tend to be managers recruited from the private sector.

So much for our brief review of the theories and reflections concerning state-owned enterprises. They all suggest that the very reasons which explain the creation of this type of enterprise also explain why it is difficult to run them efficiently. It is a totally different approach from that of the multinational enterprise, for which efficiency is the essential driving force of development and where the notion of national interest only figures as a local constraint. We shall now turn to the combination of these two currents of thought and find out what has been said — and above all what has been left unsaid — about state-owned multinationals.

AT A THEORETICAL CROSSROADS

While there is an abundant literature both on multinational companies and on state-owned enterprises, theoretical approaches and empirical studies dealing with the process of multinationalization of state-owned enterprises or with state-owned multinationals themselves are few and far between, and they are extremely partial. To date, no exhaustive analysis of this specific phenomenon has been made.

A few odd pioneers

The few authors who have considered the subject up to now have only done so in passing, as part of a larger endeavour centring on other matters of research. Thus, the few available references to state-owned multinationals stem from two main approaches:

— that of the theorists of the multinational enterprise who, in the course of their research, came across — perhaps to their surprise — multinationals which were also state-owned enterprises and consequently tried to incorporate them into their analytical framework;
— that of a few economists or political scientists, most of them American, for whom the actual existence of state-owned enterprises in a free market economy raises a problem. They have tried to assess the competitive threat — deemed unfair — that the foreign state-owned enterprises represent for American companies.

1. *The proponents of the 'imitation of the multinational model' theory.* The theorists of the multinational enterprise who first considered state-owned multinationals were the ones who were in close touch with them in their environment. Studying multinational companies in their country, these researchers realized that state-owned enterprises accounted for a significant part of their field of research and therefore could not simply be ignored. It is not surprising then to note that most of them originate from countries where the public sector occupies an important place in the economy. Thus, some European authors, notably

French[28] and Italian,[29] and experts from developing countries[30] have tackled the question of state-owned multinationals.

These theorists of the multinational company, however, tended to apply to state-owned multinationals the analytical framework that they had previously applied to private multinationals. The multinationalization of state-owned enterprises is then interpreted as a mere 'imitation of the model'[31] of traditional multinationals. Such authors infer from this, perhaps rather hastily, that the reasons for multinationalization are the same for state-owned enterprises as for private companies. The process occurs in similar circumstances and according to comparable procedures. Having established that in most cases there is a marked correlation between the size of the enterprises and their propensity to become multinational, they consider that state-owned enterprises, because they are often large companies, will necessarily tend to become multinational just like their private counterparts. This being the case, the classical theory of multinationalization, which we have examined in the first part of this chapter, should apply equally to state-owned enterprises as well as private companies.

The issue of state control or of the State's position on the multinationalization of state-owned enterprises is seldom touched upon, and even then only very superficially. The few authors who have considered this point give an analysis that confirms the generally held attitudes: the distinction between state-owned multinationals and private multinationals is not relevant. Thus, there are some analyses[32] which indicate that the multinationalization of state-owned enterprises is accompanied by the relaxation of the constraints imposed by the State: as they become more and more multinational, their state-owned character is less and less important. Other[33] authors put forward the hypothesis that by promoting multinationalization the managers of state-owned enterprises try to increase their autonomy in relation to the control of the State, with the latter giving state-owned enterprises relatively more

[28] R. Gendarme (footnote 9) and M. Delapierre, B. Madoeuf, C. A. Michalet, and C. Ominami, *Nationalisation et Internationalisation: Stratégies des Multinationales Françaises dans la Crise*, La Découverte–Maspéro, 1983.
[29] R. Mazzolini, 'Are state-owned enterprises unfair competitors?' *California Management Review*, Winter 1980.
[30] S. Lall, (footnote 18) and K. Kumar, 'Multinationalization of third world public sector enterprises', in Kumar and McLeod, *Multinationals from Developing Countries*, Lexington Books, 1981.
[31] R. Gendarme (footnote 9), pp. 420–435.
[32] B. Marois, 'Le comportement multinational des entreprises françaises nationalisées', *Revue Française de Gestion*, March–April 1977.
[33] S. Wickham, 'Biais marketing international des entreprises publiques', Communication in the first symposium of the *Politique et Management Public* journal, Paris, 26–28 September 1984.

freedom of action abroad than at home. According to this argument, state-owned multinationals can only really be state-owned at home and should otherwise be analysed in exactly the same way and using the same criteria as private multinationals.

Thus, the theorists of the multinational company are content to point out the state-owned character of certain multinationals without specifically analysing this phenomenon and its implications since they consider that the state-owned character is eclipsed by the multinational status of the enterprise.

In any case, there is no in-depth analysis of the possible, or indeed probable, differences of interest between the 'shareholder-state' on the one hand and the enterprise on the other. In other words, there is no analysis of the contradictions between the state-owned character and the multinational character of the enterprise. The way such contradictions are — or could be — reconciled is, of course, totally passed over.

2. *The proponents of the 'unfair competition' theory.* The analysis of state-owned multinationals made by certain American authors[34] is completely different. Indeed, unlike the other authors, they detect a very close link between the international development of such enterprises and the fact that their major shareholder is the State. Their position is quite clear: state-owned enterprises are accused, as we have seen, of being unfair competitors, of directly threatening private companies through their international development, especially the American ones, which naively respect the rules of free competition. Far from resembling other multinationals, state-owned multinationals are a special type of enterprise, as their collusion with the 'shareholder-state' undermines free competition. We shall return to these accusations of 'unfair competition' in Chapter Four to try to assess their validity. However, we would like to stress at this point the element of bias which this assumption introduces into the analysis of the multinationalization process of state-owned enterprises. Indeed, mainly concerned to prove the thesis of unfair competition, the authors fail to emphasize the diversity of attitudes held by governments in the face of the multinationalization of their state-owned companies. Perhaps more importantly, they neglect to bring out the logic of this multinationalization for the enterprises themselves. From this point of view, the 'militant' character of the analysis leads the authors to suggest that the sole motive that state-owned enterprises have for becoming multinational is to try and create problems for American companies. Furthermore, the study of

[34] D. Lamont, *Foreign State Enterprises*, Basic Books, New York, 1979; R. Monsen and K. Walters, *Nationalized Companies*, McGraw Hill, New York, 1983; H. D. Menzies, 'US companies in unequal combat', *Fortune*, April 9, 1979.

the way the multinationalization process is carried out by state-owned enterprises both inside (organizational structure, staff management) and outside (the relationship with the controlling bodies) is virtually non-existent.

Basically, in addition to the above-mentioned reservations, this approach to state-owned multinationals is not satisfactory according to the standpoint we have adopted, since it focuses less on the enterprises themselves and on the process which led them to their multinational status than on the nature of the competition they impose on American enterprises.

In conclusion, the very few existing references to state-owned multinationals are bedevilled by two conflicting poles of opinion:

— either they deny the specific identity of state-owned multinationals in relation to private multinationals and therefore they do not analyse them separately and in depth,
— or they consider state-owned multinationals as very special cases, in no way comparable to private multinationals.

We personally consider that the state-owned character of the multinationals which we are examining here justifies a specific and in-depth study of their particular situation but that, on the other hand, they should be compared with private multinationals, which some of them closely resemble. Lastly, state-owned multinationals do not have, as we have noted, the same characteristics, some perhaps falling into the category of 'unfair competitors', others behaving virtually as private multinationals. The approach we have decided to adopt should enable us both to bring out and to explain these differences.

This calls for a last important remark. To start a research on state-owned multinationals we thought it useful to mention briefly two theories, one concerning multinationals and the other state-owned enterprises. While the theorists of the multinational enterprise have mentioned the existence of state-owned multinationals, those of the state-owned enterprise seem to have passed over the existence of multinationals in silence.

Unknown territory . . .

The few existing studies which we have just reviewed do not represent a crossroads where the theories of multinationals and those of nationalized companies come together. The work of combining the two sets of theory remains to be done, and indeed this is essential if we are to go on to examine the true nature of state-owned multinationals and therefore proceed step by step. However, this is a vast undertaking and we must resist the temptation to be over ambitious! We will only try to highlight the most striking points of convergence without claiming to establish a new theory. Nevertheless, the following chapters should contribute to the formulation of such a theory.

First, there is a similarity between the two theoretical approaches. Both begin with a vital question: why are some enterprises multinational, why are some others state-owned? Two series of reasons, perfectly comparable, can be put forward. The similarity of the two approaches persists when they come to consider problems raised by the existence of each type of enterprise: what is wrong with multinationals, what is wrong with state-owned companies? Here again, answers are given and, as we shall see, comparing them is quite intriguing.

Secondly, what is striking is the recurrent element of antagonism in the answers to these two successive questions. This antagonism suggests that state-owned multinationals, if such entities really exist, are, to say the least, schizoid! It may well be fashionable to introduce psychological concepts into economic analysis, we are however interested not in the learned labels given to state-owned multinationals, but in their actual experience: what sort of enterprise are they really? how are they able to reconcile their own inherent contradictions? To start with, let us see what these contradictions are.

According to one theory, an enterprise becomes multinational to exploit advantages which have to do with the differences between countries: for example, differences in the level of technological development or in production parameters (costs and availability). Protectionist policies may also induce an enterprise to become multinational. In all cases it has to determine, on the basis both of opportunities and of threats presented by the world situation, where its best interest lies, whether in maximizing its profit, its growth or its power. According to another theory, the same enterprise is nationalized in order to be used as an instrument by a state which wishes to intervene in the economy of the country so as to preserve it from the excesses or the flaws of the market. The nationalization of an enterprise may also result from historical circumstances (government sanction on a company, 'legacy' from previous governments) which, although they seem to be of minor importance, are nevertheless treated with the utmost seriousness by the State. In all cases nationalization is a decision imposed on the enterprise and justified in terms of the national interest, which is different from, indeed opposed to, its own interest.

The differences are striking: the decision to become multinational is spontaneous, whereas nationalization is imposed. In the first case, the enterprise transforms itself from within, in the other it is transformed from without. The reasons for the respective decisions are totally conflicting: multinationalization places the highest value on the interests of the enterprise rather than on those of the country in which it operates, whereas nationalization subordinates the interests of the enterprise to those of the State which are considered supreme. Furthermore, when a state is not satisfied with the behaviour of the multinationals set up in its territory it nationalizes them. It is the best way for it to restore the primacy of the national interest. When a multinational company is not content with the behaviour of the host country, it leaves and sets up elsewhere. It is the best way to put its interests before those of the state.

Let us go one step further in the comparison of the two theories: what are multinationals blamed for, what is wrong with state-owned enterprises? In fact, the former are accused of being detrimental to the countries where they are set up, exploiting their natural resources and their labour force, both of which they obtain at low cost and without making provision for renewal or for realizing potential.

Multinational companies are even accused of repressing by all available means local reactions to this exploitation. As for state-owned enterprises, it is said that they cannot be run efficiently prevented as they are from adapting their production to their market and their staff levels to their production. In addition, they are accused of actually behaving as irresponsible economic agents since they want to serve all the national interests at once: lower prices, raise employment, increase investment and cut the trade deficit.

In other words, multinational firms are reproached with taking advantage of their multinationalization and behaving in line with the reasons which led them to become multinational. As for state-owned enterprises, they are accused of being the docile instrument of government policies, that is to say of justifying the reasons for their nationalization *a posteriori*. Here again the contrast is obvious: multinationals are well run and efficient, state-owned enterprises are badly run and inefficient. The former are selfish and are not concerned with the public interest, the latter are altruistic and benevolent. . . . Enough! you will say, that's all just ideology! But you are wrong: we are only comparing the theories which actually claim that, from the point of view of motivation and behaviour, multinational and state-owned enterprises are totally opposed.

Nevertheless, an enterprise can be multinational and state-owned at the same time. Such enterprises do exist; indeed we have come across many of them. This simple observation has the most surprising implications. We shall try, with due caution, to outline some of these. They should be considered as so many hypotheses which the book will set out to vindicate. These hypotheses are not in the least unusual; they are indeed in line with the statements most frequently made on the subject, which we have briefly mentioned above.

The first possible implication is that state-owned multinationals are 'fake' multinational companies. They became multinational before being nationalized or else they did so without their government's knowledge, in exceptional circumstances. In any case, their nationalization or their takeover by the State can only entail a slowing down, or even a regression, of their multinationalization process. In other words, given that these enterprises are truly state-owned, it is impossible to make them fully multinational in the long term. The state-owned character prevails over the multinational one, or else privatization occurs and the problem is resolved.

The second possible implication is that state-owned multinationals are true multinational companies but do not behave in the same way as private multinationals. Even abroad they are still the instrument of the policy of their state of origin. This is the standard accusation, namely that of unfair competition, which we have already mentioned. This hypothesis is hardly compatible with the previous one. It implies that in reality there is a harmony of interests between the state-owned enterprise which becomes multinational and its owner, the State. The latter gives it generous subsidies, enabling it to penetrate foreign markets, and this brings foreign currency back to the country of origin. Here it is the multinational character which prevails, since the constraints imposed by the state-owner status are more than compensated by the state's generous grants which, by their very nature, are not made to state-owned enterprises only.

How, at this point, can we not feel that it would be taking things to extremes to adopt one of the two hypotheses to the total exclusion of the other? On the one hand, we have the state-owned enterprise caught in the political–administrative system which prevents it from being successful in the international arena; on the other, the multinational company overwhelming its worldwide competitors with the generous subsidies of its 'shareholder-state'. 'Good sense' and our first observations suggest that there must be a middle course and that this, rather than the two theoretical extremes we have outlined, is what obtains in reality.

Actually, what emerges most forcibly from the combination of the two theories is that there must be areas of compatibility between nationalization and multinationalization. While their respective logics are at odds as far as their fundamental principles are concerned, a more searching analysis may well show that, in certain cases, they move close together and even converge. This is where the interests of the enterprise and the national interests of its country of origin coincide, not so much within the country itself (this is, of course, frequently the case) but rather in the enterprise's investments abroad. Nevertheless, this common interest must be appreciated by the official controlling body if it is to allow the enterprise to act freely. In other words, two coincidences are called for. However, these are probably not the only cases. It is not inconceivable that there should be particular circumstances which neutralize the opposition between the two logics: a lack of vigilance (or coherence) on the part of the controlling body for example, or the manoeuvring qualities of a manager, or even the shrewdness of a political leader. All may hinge on opportunity or skill . . . nothing is really impossible.

However, our first duty as we turn to the part of our study dealing with concrete facts is to give a proper account of the two conflicting hypotheses we have mentioned, for they are what make the headlines in the world. Once we have analysed at length the state-owned enterprise in the hands of its nationalist 'owner-state', and the multinational company, turned into an unfair competitor by its aid dispensing 'shareholder-state', we shall try to understand more complex phenomena. We shall then see that beyond the determinisms that the theories describe so well there is a place, by no means negligible, for freedom of action on the part of state-owned multinationals.

Chapter Three

The Nationalistic Tendencies of the Owner-state

INTRODUCTION

This chapter will deal with the first contradiction resulting from the clash of theories which we have just discussed. We shall try to demonstrate, by examining concrete examples, that state ownership of a company represents an almost insurmountable obstacle in its development as a multinational. This is mainly due to the nationalistic tendencies of the 'shareholder-state'. Indeed, we have observed that when the State intervenes in the management of the enterprises under its control, these enterprises are subjected to the requirements of national policies, which are designed to protect the interests of the nation rather than those of the enterprises, and, in fact, it is within the context of foreign expansion that these two interests diverge the most. Therefore state-owned enterprises are particularly handicapped by their state-owned character as far as the development of an international strategy is concerned.

However, this handicap varies widely from one country to another, and even from one enterprise to another. To study this phenomenon we must first examine the variables which determine it and, in each particular case, account for its impact as well as its distinctive characteristics. Therefore we shall go back over the history of the formation of state-owned enterprises in the various countries considered, since this seems to offer the best explanation for the latest trends in the development of such enterprises. Nevertheless, history is not the only explanatory factor; indeed, the history of state-owned enterprises can also be analysed as the result of the combination of two fundamental elements: ideology and economy. Ideology, as we shall see, conditions the policy and the doctrine of the government with regard to nationalization and the management of the industrial and commercial public sector. It is an interpretation of the situation which is not aimed at an accurate knowledge of the state-owned enterprise, but rather at a propaganda effect, for or against the existence of such an enterprise. In contrast, economic considerations cannot be contained by ideology: facts are more important than words and, in practice, compel governments to take measures of nationalization — or denationalization — which sometimes are not consonant with their official stance, as we shall see in a third section. Thus, we shall have prepared the ground for a better understanding of the behaviour of the 'owner-state' *vis-à-vis* its state-owned enterprises, particularly with reference to their multinationalization.

We shall next describe this behaviour and show why it constitutes a handicap for the enterprises. To simplify things, we shall divide it into four points which we shall present in turn. The first point will deal with the industrial and technological policy of the State: the search by all means for a 'national solution' to all problems which fall within the prerogative of the government is not likely to give the enterprises freedom of action in their international strategy. The second point covers all the constraints imposed by the State on these enterprises in the name of a short-sighted financial policy which checks their desire to expand abroad. The third point relates to what represents a burden for the enterprises, namely a social policy which tries to privilege the employees of state-owned enterprises and, at the same time, to impose an excessively large staff on these enterprises. The fourth and last point concerns foreign policy considerations resulting in a series of 'stop — go' orders in the operations of the enterprises which hamper their best plans to conquer world markets.

Before concluding, we must qualify our remarks; we were cautious in denouncing state control as an 'almost' insurmountable obstacle as far as the multinationalization of enterprises is concerned because some of them manage to overcome this obstacle and even to turn it to their advantage.

HISTORY, IDEOLOGY AND ECONOMY

Nationalization in the world in the twentieth century

There are two kinds of nationalization: one that is demanded and proclaimed publicly and the other which occurs without being announced. Nationalizations of the first kind usually involve a large number of companies simultaneously; they form part of a 'wave', marked at once by its brevity as well as its sweeping nature. In the second category, nationalizations are spread out over the years and are so isolated and sporadic that they are sometimes described as 'silent' or covert nationalizations. Most nationalizations tend to fall in this latter group. However, the nationalizations which are heralded with much fanfare are those which set the tone as they make the headlines, and consequently attract the particular attention — which usually proves to be most oppressive — of the government. Nevertheless, the causes and the circumstances of nationalization have a lasting influence over the future development of the enterprise concerned. Therefore, in order to understand the differences observed today between the major state-owned enterprises that we have studied, we must go back to their origin.

Let us start with the most well-known 'waves' of nationalization, which all occurred either a little before (apart from a few exceptions) or just after the Second World War. Two phenomena explain to a large extent the series of nationalizations which took place in the thirties: the economic crisis and the nationalistic surge throughout the world. A third phenomenon, the war itself and its consequences, explains the nationalizations of the forties. Then, as late as 1977 in the case of Portugal, Sweden and Great Britain and 1982 in that of France, two new 'waves' of nationalization occurred which, as we shall see, are anachronous in certain respects.

The economic crisis which shook the world after 1929 brought to power governments which were determined to intervene in order to offset the operating imperfections of the market, to boost activity and restore economic balance. The United States, though a stronghold of free market economy, saw the New Deal; Europe witnessed the parallel rise of socialist and fascist movements which were also interventionist; in large developing countries like Mexico and Brazil, which until then were the preserve of American firms, nationalist leaders like Lázaro Cárdenas and Getulio Vargas nationalized the means of production essential to their development: energy and mining, transport, part of the iron and steel industry and of banking. In France, the socialist *Front Populaire* government nationalized the railways, part of the arms industry and sea and air transport. In Germany, Italy, Spain and Norway, large state enterprises were created in the areas of energy, transport and heavy industry. They were associated with the rise of fascism and with figures like Goering, Mussolini, Franco or Quisling. In America, in a totally different context but equally under the impact of the economic crisis, Franklin D. Roosevelt himself created the famous Tennessee Valley Authority — TVA — (energy, regional development) within the New Deal framework.

This trend continued during the Second World War and even more so in the immediate postwar period. In France, General de Gaulle, and later his successors, nationalized to a large extent the coal-mining, nuclear and automobile industries, gas and electricity companies, aeronautics, aviation, banks and insurance. In West Germany and Italy, Spain and Norway, the enterprises which were the legacy of fascism were retained by the government under the form of companies with a total or majority state capital. In Great Britain, the Labour government nationalized transport, the coal-mining industry and the steel industry as well as, in part, the chemical and naval armament industries, aviation and aeronautics. In developing countries, the major state-owned enterprises were considered the driving forces of the economy. In such countries, the creation of state-owned enterprises often coincided with decolonization; independence resulted in the transfer to the new nations of the large enterprises, which until then had belonged to colonizers. This was the case with Keppel Shipyard and the group Sheng-Li in Singapore, as well as the Office Chérifien des Phosphates in Morocco. In India, the 'Industrial Policy Resolution', framed as early as 1948, asserted the dynamic role of the State in the development of the economy, a role which became increasingly important from 1956 onwards; the successive plans led to a wide expansion of the public sector. The United States was the only country where the rules of the market and free competition were restored (the TVA, however, was not privatized). A small country with a free market economy like the Netherlands nationalized the coal-mining industry, while in Sweden the socialist government nationalized energy, raw materials and transport.

How can the sheer scale of this phenomenon be explained? The common feature of all these different nationalization experiences, which again come within the scope of state intervention in the economy, is the inability of the *laissez-faire* policy to resist the successive upheavals of the economic crisis and the war. Partly because of the need for reconstruction, people and governments began to lose confidence in the system of free enterprise and to withdraw from the latter entire sectors of the economy which were to be controlled by the State — the emanation of popular power. These sectors were dominated by large units which exerted a determining influence on the other sectors. However, important capitalists were suspect from then on, for during the crisis they showed that they put their own interests before those of the country. As we have seen, in 1931 the Pope himself proclaimed this in the encyclical *Quadragesimo Anno*.

Very few of the enterprises nationalized at that time were multinational; however, their nationalization militated against their multi-national character. In developing countries, the subsidiaries of American multinationals which broke away from the parent company were signalled as marking a victory over foreign countries. Thus, the Herman Goering Werke were divided into several units which resulted in Salzgitter in West Germany and in Voest-Alpine in Austria. Maintaining their unity would have led to the multinationalization of the whole (through an original process, the division of the Hitler Reich into several independent countries!). The multinational character reinforced the 'stateless', antinational status which private capitalism was accused of, and was therefore inimical to the idea of a return to the nation underlying the nationalizations of this period.

The other kind of nationalization (or creation of state-owned enterprises) that we described as 'silent' or 'covert' is quite different. It has always existed. From the Egyptian pharaohs to Colbert in France, the State has intervened in certain situations to control directly the economic activities in which it was particularly interested. However, these interventions were sporadic and had no real impact on ideology and principles (except perhaps in the case of what was called 'Colbertism' in France). The industrial revolution occurred without any state intervention. In the twentieth century, however, state intervention progressively spread and became quite common. There was no objection when Conrail in 1976 or Amtrak in 1971 was created to save the jeopardized railways. Again, in 1984, the American government nationalized the Continental Illinois Bank without facing any adverse criticism. Most important European countries frequently resort to nationalizations for different reasons without raising larger issues of principle. Thus, for instance, in France in 1978 the right-wing president Valery Giscard d'Estaing created the Commissariat à l'Energie Solaire (Solar Energy Commission), while in Britain his Conservative counterpart Edward Heath took control of Rolls Royce in 1971. During the sixties and seventies, the conservative governments of Italy and Spain relied increasingly on the IRI and INI respectively to bail out all the lame ducks of their industries. Needless to say, socialist governments, whatever the country, were not lagging behind. The European countries which have associated to form Eurodif (nuclear fuel processing), Airbus Industrie and Arianespace are not too concerned about the source of capital, which for the most part comes from the State. In developing countries, the creation of state-owned enterprises is now a common occurrence despite the disapproval of the IMF and the World Bank. In such a context the multinationalization of the enterprises thus created or nationalized by a State does not raise a doctrinal issue. Multinationalization is a question of opportunity, as is the emergence of these state-owned enterprises. In fact, the aim of nationalization is to offset the lack of private initiative.

However, it was for ideological reasons that the new waves of nationalization were carried out in Europe:[1] in 1977 in Portugal (and to a lesser extent in Sweden and Great Britain) and in 1982 in France. These nationalizations are particularly interesting as most of the enterprises concerned were already multinational and this characteristic could not be changed. The example of Paribas Suisse is a good one in this respect, since the subsidiary of the major nationalized commercial bank returned to the fold of its parent company when it realized that it could not survive without the latter. A multinational group, in industry or in the banking sector, must function as a whole; if it is divided into several parts, it loses greatly in value, or even declines completely. This is true for all the groups nationalized by the French socialist government. At the same time, these nationalizations formed a wave which was used by the government as one of the principal instruments of its new policy. The contradiction consisting in nationalizing multinationals was simply evaded in public debate. Of course, this does not mean that it no longer exists, but only that these nationalizations were justified by the same doctrine as that of the Front Populaire in 1936, without any modification to take the multinational factor into account. These measures are anachronous in this sense, since the multinational factor appeared in the seventies and has become increasingly important.

What does the history of nationalization suggest? First, that the nationalizations which occurred openly for doctrinal reasons seem to be incompatible with the multinationalization of the enterprises concerned. Secondly, that nationalizations of the other kind, which were carried out for pragmatic reasons, are most likely to allow multinationalization. This is probably true. However, this type of interpretation is too static and does not take into account the changes of policy resulting from changes in government. The governments which run state-owned enterprises are not always — or do not remain for long — the same which created or nationalized them; therefore they do not share the same viewpoint on the matter. Admittedly, they must conform to the regulations and practices established by their predecessors, but they are allowed considerable leeway. Thus, to understand what conditions the multinationalization process of a state-owned enterprise, we must not

---

[1] In the same way, between 1972 and 1975 in Canada, the province of British Columbia conducted a great number of nationalizations which resulted in an industrial holding: British Columbia Resources Investment Corporation (BRIC). This policy of the New Democratic Party in power at the time was responsible for the name 'Chile of the North' given to the province in the local press.

only examine its origin but also the different phases of its development as well as its precise situation at the time of observation.

An enterprise which has been nationalized by a socialist government will be authorized to go multinational more readily by a more free market oriented government. On the other hand, an enterprise created by a 'free market' government will face greater restraints in a new, more interventionist government. But these are only assumptions: *laissez-faire* governments may not consider state-owned enterprises by standards of private industry, and interventionist governments may not systematically try to paralyse them. Doctrine and reality are two different things. There are particular circumstances in which a free market government may intervene (for example to prevent a state-owned enterprise from diversifying), and an interventionist government may allow state-owned enterprises freedom of action (when the interests of the enterprise and those of the government are convergent). All in all, a state-owned enterprise is undoubtedly marked by its past history. However, its submission to state control exposes it equally to the hazards of the present, arising from a difficult interaction of doctrine and practice, in other words of ideology and economic considerations.

Free market ideology vs interventionism

The ideology of the state-owned enterprise involves all arguments related to the justification for the appropriation of the means of production by the nation-state and to the forms this takes, as well as the use made of such means. This last element will form the subject of our study in this section as all the reasons for nationalization have already been examined. How must a state-owned enterprise be treated by the government? This is the fundamental question that arises in terms of ideology. To be more precise, what is the government policy regarding a state-owned enterprise that wants to go multinational? There are, as we have seen, two kinds of ideology in confrontation which we shall examine in turn. One is inspired by socialism, the other by capitalism. The first advocates the use of state-owned enterprises by the government for larger ends than those limited to the interests of the enterprise; the second favours their autonomy *vis-à-vis* the State and places the emphasis on their performance.

However, from the outset, one should try to avoid a Manichean vision of this issue. We are speaking of two kinds of ideology, which means that each of them allows the existence of a certain diversity of actual situations. For example, socialism does not necessarily mean

Marxism, and capitalism is not incompatible with nationalism. In fact there are two opposed tendencies: one advocating the increasing intervention of the State, the other giving greater importance to the entrepreneur with a corresponding diminution in the role of the State. Rather than confining them to two antagonistic schools of thought, these tendencies can be considered as linked within a continuum in which the predominance of one results in the correlative erosion of the other. Within this continuum, there is an infinity of specific ideologies. So much for Manicheism. Nevertheless, it may often be useful to schematize. Moreover, in practice, the options of governments amount to a simplistic choice: either impose their will on the state-owned enterprises or adopt a *laissez-faire* policy and give them freedom of action.

It is undeniable that in the world today there are states which have an established free market tradition that does not vary despite changes in government. Conversely, other countries are traditionally interventionist whatever the party in power; others again have no established tradition and undergo important political reversals with respect to the nationalization issue in the event of a change of government. Among the European countries, Great Britain belongs to the third category, Germany is the prototype of non-interventionist governments, France (or Italy) that of interventionist ones.

Non-interventionist ideology is well known. It considers market mechanisms as the sole guarantee for an optimum use of economic resources by ensuring the balance of supply and demand; state intervention therefore is confined to situations where market mechanisms do not function correctly. As we have seen, such situations are limited in number — so-called 'natural' monopolies, non-tradable goods and services, industries with negative 'economies of scale' — and have all been very well analysed by neo-liberal economists. However, most industrial and commercial state-owned enterprises likely to develop as multinationals do not fall within such categories. On the contrary, they are enterprises operating in world markets and are therefore subjected to serious competition, mostly that of private companies. When the State intervenes in their strategy, the rules of competition are disrupted with no theoretical justification and, since the State does not control foreign markets, its intervention may in fact jeopardize the activities of such enterprises.

According to non-interventionist ideology, it seems obvious that these enterprises should not be state-owned. In fact, they represent a kind of aberration which should disappear. However, ideology has its limits. In countries like Germany, Norway and the Netherlands, as well as Singapore, the United States and Brazil, all with free market ideologies, most state-owned enterprises inherited from previous governments have not been privatized. It is as though they had been accepted as belonging to the industrial landscape. Moreover, as we have noted, they are self-effacing and try to be indistinguishable from 'the others'. . . . Hence, how does a free trade government react to such enterprises?

The managements of VIAG and Salzgitter (West Germany), Norsk-Hydro (Norway), DSM (Netherlands) and Keppel Shipyard (Singapore) all have the same position on the issue. According to them, their respective governments require that these enterprises be as well run and as efficient as if they were private companies. The civil servants responsible for their control also adopt the same stance and add that they only intervene in the event of incompetent management . . . probably to instal new managers. It appears that the controlling agents and the enterprises under their control coincide in their views. Nationalization has been taken over by free market ideology, but an informed observer will note that the contradiction does exist and that it shows elsewhere. Governments cannot eliminate the results of nationalizations by simply asserting that they are chance mishaps.

A similar apparent harmony emerges when we examine the converse ideology, which upholds state intervention. This ideology is based on the grounds that the imperfections of the market are much more frequent than its normal functioning according to the rules of free competition and that these imperfections are used by a small group of individuals to exploit the great majority of people, consumers as well as employees. However, these individuals can have recourse to the government, through whom, as citizens, they exert their power. It is for their benefit that the State must ensure social justice, employment and improvement of living and working conditions. Nationalization is one of the means available for furthering these ends. The numerous and large state-owned enterprises must contribute to the pursuit of the above-mentioned objectives. Their attitude should be different from that of a private capitalist company (whose sole aim, it is assumed, is the maximization of profit) within the same sector of activity.

These state-owned enterprises may face competition, operate in a worldwide market and have an international strategy. There is a simple way to reconcile this situation with the stated national objectives. Every time the government intervenes to impose on a state-owned enterprise actions which fall outside the scope of its strategy the State can, indeed must, provide compensation for the negative consequences entailed in the form of adequate aid, termed 'additional revenue' rather than 'subsidies' in order to underline its true nature. This is what the French government did when it granted aid to Air France as a compensation for the extra costs resulting from the imposed running of Concorde. In

such conditions, state-owned enterprises are not debarred from multinationalization; if it proves to be contradictory to the objectives of the
government, the problem must be examined and settled according to
each particular case.

France and Italy, which we considered as examples of traditionally
interventionist countries, have both had state-owned multinationals for
a long time, such as Renault, Elf-Aquitaine, the IRI and the ENI.
Socialist governments do not check the worldwide expansion of these
enterprises. In fact, a French socialist government authorized Elf-Aquitaine to invest massively in the United States, whereas its predecessor,
supposedly free market oriented, had forbidden it to do so. Again, the
Italian government allowed the IRI to buy (or sell) equity participations
in subsidiaries abroad without the prior agreement of parliament. The
same attitude prevails in Sweden and Austria, which have similar ideologies. No Swedish government, either socialist or conservative, has
contested the fact that the natural market of Assi is Europe and not
just Sweden. The Austrian government will in no way prevent Voest-
Alpine from investing in the United States. If the Spanish state-owned
enterprises are still hesitant to venture abroad, it is not because the
government is opposed to their foreign expansion on principle but
rather because they are not prepared for it.

What conclusions can we draw up from all that has been said? Simply
that, once again, ideology must *inevitably* adapt to facts and always
manages to do so (while avoiding any explicit acknowledgement). If
nationalization invariably led to bankruptcy, interventionist ideology
would no longer exist. Therefore, some freedom of action should be
given to state-owned enterprises in order to enable them to continue
their development while maintaining the principle of their subjection
to the national interest. The best example of this point of view is the
watchword given in France by the socialist Laurent Fabius (Minister of
Industry at the time) to nationalized enterprises: 'Be profitable before
the end of 1985'. He was seeking to prove the success of nationalization
before 1986, when the legislative elections were due. Thus, we are
confronted with a paradoxical situation: management strategies used in
the private sector are now applied to state-owned enterprises in order to
legitimate their nationalization. This is another instance of the habitual
reversals of ideology. Great Britain is a particular case in point, though
there are other examples.[2] The alternance of Labour and Conservative
governments has resulted in dramatic switches of policy concerning

---

[2] In 1976, the Canadian province of British Columbia privatized BRIC, an industrial
holding company mentioned above, when the Social Credit Party returned to power; in
1986 the French parliament issued a law authorizing the government to privatize 65 state-
owned companies — Some of which had been nationalized just after World War II.

state-owned enterprises. The same company has been successively nationalized and privatized several times. British Steel in particular has been a victim of such changes; since 1979 denationalization is in fashion. However, apart from a change of status (state owned or privately owned), there have not been significant modifications in the management of the enterprises concerned. It is in the interests of the Labour Party that these enterprises perform reasonably well (as we have just seen in the French context) in order to legitimate their nationalization. This is also true for the Conservatives; in their case to better prepare the way for privatization. Once again, ideology must adapt itself to economic reality, sometimes with paradoxical results. Thus, a Conservative government may compel a state-owned enterprise to 'demultinationalize', for example by selling its assets abroad, in order to recover its financial balance, while the preceding Labour government would have encouraged the expansion of its multinational activities. Such is the case of British Leyland.

In conclusion, we may say that ideology, which expresses the formal point of view of the government, is often used to justify practices that are in reality incompatible with the official stance. Once again, this is due to the pressure of the economic situation, which we will now examine.

The economic imperatives

In a great number of countries, the presence of state-owned enterprises in certain sectors is often imposed by the economic situation and governments resort to these enterprises for operations which could not be carried out otherwise. We may say that, ideological considerations aside, it seems that no country can do without at least a few state-owned enterprises. The first factor which determines the need for a country to resort inevitably to the state-owned enterprise is obviously its level of economic development. However, there are other considerations, related to the nature of the economic activity of the sectors concerned; this activity can either involve public utilities or have a vital strategic interest for the country. Lastly, there are circumstantial factors regarding the enterprise itself; sometimes nationalization is the only way to avoid bankruptcy. We shall discuss all this in detail, bearing in mind that, over and above ideology which intervenes in their long-term vision of problems, governments in their day-to-day policies are probably most influenced by the economic situation.

It is commonly admitted, even within circles as remote from socialist ideology as the World Bank, that developing countries cannot do without state-owned enterprises. This is due essentially to insufficient private initiative and to the rejection of economic colonization by foreign multinationals. These countries have both inadequate private savings (private investors prefer to invest abroad or in real estate) and a low entrepreneurial potential at the individual level. Lacking capital and private entrepreneurship, the governments' only recourse is either the foreign company or the state-owned enterprise. Very often they try to limit the influence of the former for it is politically intolerable. Indeed, independence, which they won from a foreign power, is the focal point of their cultural identity. The state-owned enterprise thus appears prestigious and reassuring; it is financed by imposed taxes and by international loans and it is run by the elite, the product of public education (and/or foreign universities, thanks to government scholarships).

This need to resort to the state-owned enterprise is perfectly illustrated by the comparative study of two countries which are in the process of industrialization: Brazil and Mexico. The former is dominated by a *laissez-faire* ideology and follows the American model of free enterprise and a free market. In contrast, the latter is dominated by a 'revolutionary' ideology in which the State plays the part of the 'guardian' of the economy. Of the two countries, Brazil has long had the larger public sector, although Mexico is catching up. If we analyse the growth of the public sector over a long period, we realize that it was more extensive in Brazil than in Mexico because it started developing earlier in the former. This is simply due to the fact that in Brazil the economic boom occurred between 1965 and 1975 whereas in Mexico it only started around 1976–77. Thus, despite Brazil's insignificant oil resources, Petrobras was for a long time a far more important enterprise than its Mexican counterpart Pemex, even though the latter had the advantage of Mexico's fantastic oil reserves. Petrobras expanded as a multinational long before Pemex, which is only starting to set up abroad (but this is merely a partial explanation, as the failure to discover oil in Brazil was of course a determining factor in the internationalization of Petrobras activities between 1960 and 1980).

The level of development of the home country is also an explanatory factor for the degree of multinationalization of state-owned enterprises. The more 'multinationalized' state-owned enterprises are those of the more developed countries, for example Germany, Sweden, France, whereas the less 'multinationalized' ones originate from developing countries: Brazil, Mexico, India, Indonesia, etc. Countries like Canada or Spain which, though developed, have not yet fully exploited their 'domestic' potential, do not have true state-owned multinationals. Moreover, historically, the German and French state-owned enterprises began to expand abroad once the internal reconstruction was finished, that is to say in the sixties, and only became truly multinational in the seventies. The case of the United States is, to say the least, far from conclusive in this respect, since this country, which is the most developed in the world, does not possess a single state-owned multinational. In fact, it is precisely because of its level of development that the United States has very few state-owned enterprises. Moreover, it should be borne in mind that the United States did not need to rebuild its economy after the Second World War, unlike the European countries, which at that time could be qualified as 'underdeveloped'. Lastly, if ideology is constrained by economic considerations, the relation between the two can also be reversed and the United States is the champion of free market ideology.

Nevertheless, state-owned enterprises do exist in the United States. There are indeed many of them in the areas of municipal, social and health services, etc. As we have said above, the presence of state-owned enterprises in a sector of activity can be explained by the nature of this sector, regardless of ideology. When the activity involved falls under what is called in France a *'service public'* or in the United States 'public utilities' (although the two terms are not quite identical), the presence of a state-owned enterprise in the sector becomes far more probable. This is why there are so many state-owned enterprises in the field of transport, notably in the railways (as with Amtrak and Conrail in the United States), and of energy (the TVA, referred to earlier), which are in fact the two industrial and commercial sectors most controlled by the State throughout the world. The same is true for the sector of postal services, or of telecommunications.

Certain sectors do not fall within the category of public services but nevertheless, owing to their strategic importance, attract the attention of the government. This is the case with nuclear energy, the space industry and, more generally, all sectors related to national defence, which benefit from generous state budgetary programmes. In the land of free enterprise, NASA, which is a federal agency, was responsible for marketing its satellite launchers until its own mistakes led President Reagan to ban it from this activity in 1986.

State-owned enterprises are often entrusted with activities which require substantial investment and whose profitability is uncertain or can only be realized in the long run. In developing countries, a basic industrial sector may take on a similar strategic character as it conditions the whole development of the country. This is often the case, for example, with petrochemicals and the iron and steel industry. In this last sector we can cite Siderbras and Sidermex, belonging respectively to the two Latin American countries Brazil and Mexico.

However, in more developed countries, notably those of Europe, the existence of state-owned enterprises in such sectors is due to another factor, namely, the need to save large companies which, for various reasons mostly related to poor strategy, are on the verge of bankruptcy. This is the case with the iron and steel industry, that of coal-mining, the heavy chemical industry, shipbuilding and the automobile industry, as well as, it would seem today, the sector of financial credit to developing countries. British Steel, Usinor, Sacilor and British Coal are well-known examples. We have already mentioned Continental Illinois in the United States and we can also cite Creusot-Loire in France, British Leyland in Great Britain, ENI Quimica in Italy, RUMASA in Spain and many other examples. For these enterprises, known as lame ducks, nationalization offered the only solution for their survival.

Apart from public utilities, strategic activities, lame ducks, etc., . . . there are probably other sectors where state-owned enterprises tend to proliferate. In such conditions, what is their propensity to go multinational? Will the State, which nationalized them, force them or prevent them from doing so, and under the pressure of what economic necessities? Since public utilities are domestic in nature, they have no need to expand abroad. Some of them however, as we shall see, manage to do so indirectly, but they are limited in number. As for strategic sectors, the determining factor is their relation to national defence; the more 'sensitive' the technologies used, the more their manufacturing will be restricted within the limits of the territory and the less the enterprises will set up abroad. On the other hand, the greater the expenses incurred, the more urgent is the need to amortize costs on a large market, thus favouring multinationalization. Hence, governments prefer to monitor the whole system by signing bi- or pluri-lateral agreements with other governments to multinationalize the research and development programmes. This is the case in the arms industry, but it is equally true of important civil programmes like Arianespace, Airbus and Eurodif, already mentioned. In this instance we do not have a multinationalization of the enterprises in the usual sense but rather an association of several governments. In developing countries, PT ASEAN Ace Fertilizer in the field of fertilizers and NAMUCAR in the field of transport offer two examples of this form of multinationalization. These two sectors are strategic only in the context of the level of economic development of the countries concerned.

As for the lame ducks, there are many possibilities. The State can force them to turn to the domestic market (as in the case of British Leyland); on the other hand, it can decide that multinationalization offers the only solution, even if it leads to a subsequent privatization. In conclusion, we can say that in all cases, whatever its ideological preferences, the State must take into account the economic situation of the enterprises under its control.

Nevertheless, the appraisal of the economic situation, which is after all also influenced by ideology, may result concretely in a wide range of actions not necessarily consonant with the economic imperatives. Governments evaluate the economy in relation to the national policies which remain their primary concern. We shall now examine four of them: the industrial and technological policy, the financial policy, the social policy and the foreign policy.

GOVERNMENT POLICIES AND BUSINESS STRATEGY

The industrial and technological policy

Most nationalizations are carried out in the name of the industrial and technological policy of the government. It is also in the light of this policy that governments evaluate the strategies of nationalized enterprises, giving them the go-ahead or imposing their veto. Unfortunately for these enterprises, the industrial policy proceeds from a logic which is totally different from that of their strategy, particularly at the international level. The objective of an industrial policy is to find a 'national solution' in all the sectors where problems arise. To caricature things, the ideal solution would be the existence, for all the activities concerned, of one or more national enterprises using domestic technologies and proving to be competitive on a worldwide scale. State-owned enterprises represent the chosen instrument of this kind of policy for a certain number of reasons.

First, state-owned enterprises often use advanced technologies and the State can influence them to choose a technology conceived in their own country in preference to a foreign one. The choice depends on the quality and the price of this domestic technology. If the enterprise is forced to buy less efficient and/or more expensive equipment than the best on the market, it is evident that at the international level it will be handicapped in relation to its competitors, which have no constraints as far as their equipment is concerned. The French government, for example, obliges its entire public sector to buy one-third of its computer equipment from the Compagnie des Machines Bull (ex CII-HB). The

British government imposed on British Airways the purchase and operation of the Concorde aircraft. Air France was subjected to the same treatment and had to wait a long time before being allowed to replace its old French-built Caravelles by Boeing 737 aircraft. The great majority of countries in the process of industrialization have regulations obliging their state enterprises to be supplied by the local manufacturers whenever these exist, even if their products are far inferior to those of foreign manufacturers (which is generally the case). Thus, BHEL (Bharat Heavy Electricals Ltd) in India and DINA (Diesel Nacional) in Mexico, for example, enjoy a monopoly for the supply of their respective products (electrical equipment in the case of the former and lorries and railway equipment in that of the latter).

Generally, the companies which benefit from such monopolies of supply are state-owned enterprises. However, this protection does not necessarily help them to be competitive abroad; on the other hand, the firms which are forced to be supplied by such companies are also state-owned enterprises for whom this constraint proves to be a handicap. Moreover, when they ask for compensation they come up against a series of difficulties of which not the least is the assessment of the detriment sustained. The collective benefit of this kind of policy is also very difficult to evaluate. Hence, the governments which implement this policy do not have reliable indicators and cannot be assured of the validity of certain obligations that they impose on the enterprises. Neither are they able to envisage alternative and possibly better solutions to attain the same objectives.

Nevertheless, the industrial policy does not solely consist in dictating to state-owned enterprises the technologies they should adopt and the manufacturer they should choose as their supplier. Indeed, the government can 'restructure' entire industrial sectors, that is to say compel a particular enterprise to abandon a particular activity or, conversely, to take over another activity. This amounts to depriving the enterprise concerned of most of its strategic autonomy, in other words the management of its business portfolio. The consequences of this policy can be serious, particularly as far as the international activities of the enterprise are concerned: the latter may be deprived of its foreign assets or handicapped in its domestic market by activities which prove to be burdensome.

This kind of practice is best exemplified by the French government with regard to the company Saint-Gobain. This enterprise, which was multinational before being nationalized, had diversified its production into computers, electronic components and office automation systems. However, the government forced it to abandon its new development activities since these were incompatible with the official 'sectorial policy' (*politique de filière*), which aims at creating industrial leaders in each of the fields mentioned; thus, computers have been concentrated on the firm Bull, electronic components on Thomson and office automation systems on the Compagnie Générale d'Electricité. So, in the end, after wasting a lot of time and money, Saint-Gobain was compelled to revert to its previous business portfolio. It is interesting to note that the fact that Saint-Gobain was by far the best managed among all the group nationalized in 1982 did not make the government hesitate; on the contrary, it probably allowed the government to feel free to act according to its wishes.

Far from being isolated, this example is quite common. Thus, in Italy, the IRI and the ENI have frequently been forced, on behalf of the State, to take over enterprises in difficulty. These were often 'sold' by private groups happy to get rid of them (for instance, the transfer of Montedison's chemical industry which was in deficit to the ENI). This is also true in the case of Spain, where the INI seems to have the same role. In Great Britain, British Leyland was forced to sell Jaguar at the moment when the famous car manufacturer started to earn money after having been in deficit for some time. The privatization programme of the British public sector is based on the following system: as soon as a segment of the activities of a state-owned group is seen to be profitable, the government sets it apart and sells it to private shareholders, sometimes with surprising results. The company British Shipbuilders comprises two main divisions of which the first manufactures and sells merchant ships to international private clients and the second specializes in warships, with the British government as its sole customer. Strangely, the latter profit-making division will be privatized, whereas the former division, which will still be in deficit in the years to come, will probably remain in the public sector. Evidently this is rather a case of the absence of any coherent industrial policy; however, the end result is the same. In developing countries, the State often resorts to the existing major state-owned enterprises either to take over firms in difficulty or to start new activities. Indeed, these large enterprises are the ideal instrument for this kind of operation since they have significant technical, financial and managerial capacities. In Singapore, the important group Temasek (which includes Keppel Shipyard) plays such a role. Thus, the State can require it to create an indispensable economic activity (like Singapore International Airlines) and to keep the enterprise running in the event of the inability of the private sector to take it over. On the other hand, when an activity is profitable, the group must sell it in order to assign its available capital to other priority sectors. However, it cannot choose the latter; for example, the government excluded the group from the telecommunications and robotics sectors, which were allotted to the Singapore Technology Corporation.

Lastly, an industrial policy signifies a direct intervention of the State with regard to the internationalization of the activities of the state-owned enterprise. So far we have mentioned policies which only had an indirect influence, however important, on the state-owned enterprise's chance of succeeding abroad. We are now concerned with a direct action of the controlling State. This action takes the form of prohibitions, or at least reservations, on the part of the government whenever the development of the domestic activities of a state-owned firm is considered a priority, even if they are less profitable than the international activities or if it means preventing the enterprise from seizing opportunities which may not occur again. Naturally, this attitude is much more common in developing countries, where the internal development is of crucial importance and where the idea of investing abroad is almost an aberration.

Thus, an open conflict a few years ago opposed the managing director of Pemex to the Mexican government regarding the expansion of this large enterprise, the leading one in the country. The issue was the volume of exports, which could easily be increased and hence yield greater resources. But the government claimed that such resources would lead to inflation, for the Mexican economy was incapable of using them for productive purposes. Pemex argued that the extra resources could be invested for productive and profitable ends abroad. President López Portillo finally settled the matter without taking into account the opinion of the enterprise. The internal development of the country was considered a priority and it was felt that the national wealth which oil represented should not be utilized outside the country. Moreover, Pemex was probably considered too powerful; it was dangerous to let it become a true multinational.

The governments of countries like India, Indonesia and Brazil have the same attitude regarding their own state-owned enterprises (unlike the Middle East oil-producing countries). We have mentioned that Canada and Spain, for similar reasons, do not encourage their state-owned enterprises to invest abroad. In contrast, the governments of France, Italy and Great Britain, as well as those of countries with traditional free market economies, do not have the same reservations. It must be admitted that in such countries state-owned enterprises are important and have technological skills which enable them to implement an international strategy, whereas this is seldom the case in developing countries. Nevertheless, even when these enterprises have the possibility to expand abroad and when the government is not opposed to this on principle, they still have many obstacles to overcome, namely, the financial, social and foreign policies of the government.

The financial policy

When a state-owned enterprise can plan its international strategy relatively unhampered by questions of principle, the first obstacle that it must face from the government will be of a financial nature. Investing abroad requires substantial financial resources which usually are not available to the enterprise in its normal cash-flow. Moreover, the latter is determined to a great extent by the structural constraints imposed on the enterprise by the State, which should be borne in mind although we will not discuss them again here. All enterprises have a certain number of resources at their disposal for augmenting their finances. They can call on their shareholders for increasing their capital, on private investors for selling them bonds, or on banks for obtaining long, medium or short-term credit. In the particular case of the state-owned enterprise, another expedient is provided by the granting of equipment or research and development subsidies, although it does not have exclusive rights on them. However, as we will see, in terms of financial resources state-owned enterprises are at a considerable disadvantage in relation to private multinationals.

The shareholder of a state-owned enterprise is by definition the State. Therefore, the only way that such an enterprise can increase its capital is by obtaining specific budgetary grants. Although not impossible, these grants are nevertheless seldom easily available since in most countries the state budget is in deficit and governments try to cut public spending. Moreover, in the case of grants intended for investments abroad, even if they are approved (or tolerated) by the controlling authority, the financial sanction — which depends on financial bodies such as the treasury — is difficult to obtain. In addition, it must be remembered that the state-owned enterprise is not alone in demanding this kind of financial help. In fact, there is keen competition among the different state-owned enterprises for government financial support. The government is often forced to assign the greater part of its resources to a few monsters which inevitably suffer from sizeable deficits. For example, in France, 59% of state aid to state-owned enterprises goes to the SNCF (the French railways) and to Charbonnages de France (the French National Coal Board). Thus there is not much left for the most efficient companies, which are precisely those aiming at multinationalization.

In Great Britain, the White Paper of 1978 on public enterprises recommended that the external borrowing requirements of these enterprises should be included in the borrowing requirements of the entire public sector (the state budget and that of the local authorities, which are all in deficit). All these taken together form the 'public sector borrowing requirement'. The Thatcher government was forced to grant larger financial aid than foreseen to ailing industries like the iron and steel industry, the railways and British Leyland. At the same time, it wished to reduce the public spending deficit. It therefore imposed extremely harsh financial constraints on other state-owned enterprises, precisely those which invest in growth sectors. Faced as they are with financing problems, which have proved to be a bottleneck, it is not surprising that British state-owned companies are not able to go multinational despite the prevailing free market ideology.

In France, where the ideological climate was quite different, the situation was practically identical. The enterprises with growth potential such as Thomson, CGE, Rhône-Poulenc and Saint-Gobain could not obtain the necessary financial support from the State because the iron and steel industry or the coal-mining industry took up most of the available resources. To invest abroad such firms must make a cash-down payment of the corresponding sums. If we compare the way in which Renault took control of American Motors and of Mack Trucks with that of Peugeot when it bought Chrysler Europe, we realize that the former incurred heavy debts and later was obliged to sell the most profitable of its new acquisitions (the military activities of AMC). Peugeot, on the other hand, simply used the system of exchanging shares: Chrysler Corporation took 16% and in exchange transferred all its European subsidiaries. In order to invest in new plants in Canada, Péchiney was forced to sell the aluminium concern of its American subsidiary Howmet. CIT-Alcatel, the leading manufacturer of digital switching equipment, finds it difficult to penetrate the US market because the required financial contribution is far too burdensome for its own resources. Thus, financial constraints impose a considerable check on the international expansion of enterprises which have the technological and managerial potential for becoming world leaders.

When the State as the shareholder cannot be of help, the enterprise can always resort to borrowing in the home country or even abroad. However, it will face a series of specific problems. In free market economies like those of Germany or the Scandinavian nations, the government requires the state-owned firms to be self-financing in return for its non-interference in their management. The systematic resort to borrowing leads to an imbalance in the financial structure of such enterprises. In the end they are compelled to renounce their autonomy and appeal to the government for help. The government then changes the management and demands a greater rigour. Two such examples are provided by the Swedish holding company Statsforetag and the German firm Salzgitter. However, in this context multinationalization becomes more difficult. On the other hand, interventionist countries like Italy and France arrive at the same result by a reverse process. In their case, state intervention leads to an imbalance of the financial structure of state-owned enterprises.

Moreover, when a country has a sizeable foreign debt, as is the case with all developing countries — and also with developed countries in time of crisis, such as France in the eighties — the access of state-owned enterprises to the international financial market is considerably reduced. Borrowing becomes practically impossible. This was the problem faced by Petroleos de Venezuela when it tried to set up a joint venture with VEBA in Germany. Since Venezuelan oil is particularly heavy in quality, it requires a special kind of refining which is extremely expensive and easier to carry out in cooperation with an industrialized country. Before accepting this cooperation, the Venezuelan government had long hesitated owing to lack of money and the fear of further increasing its external debt (which was the fourth largest in the world). In Brazil and Mexico, state-owned enterprises are responsible for a third of the foreign debt. Therefore it is not surprising that in such countries the state-owned firms which manage to set up abroad can only do so by relying on their own resources. Balmer-Lawrie, the subsidiary of the Indian group Indo-burma Petroleum, offers an example.

A joint venture like that between Petroleos de Venezuela and VEBA is obviously a means of obtaining additional financial aid since in principle the partner contributes half of the funds. In the same way, the creation of a subsidiary in a country with an open and abundant money market, such as the United States, can provide an extra boost. The funds given by the home country allow the enterprise to borrow locally. Finally, this kind of subsidiary can even be introduced in the stock exchange in order to draw on capital. Surprisingly, the major obstacle for such forms of financing is the same in all countries, whatever their prevailing ideology (*laissez-faire* or interventionism). Governments refuse to allow state-owned enterprises to dilute the capital of their subsidiaries. The reason is evident: they fear that it would mean a loss of government control. Their position is that the enterprises can become multinational in their activities but not in their capital.

Therefore, governments prefer, as we have already pointed out, to split the financing by using their capital to create multinationals among themselves. When one of the governments is the major contributor, this form of intergovernment association is particularly profitable to the state-owned enterprise designated as the leader of the consortium, as is the case with the Commissariat à l'Energie Atomique in Eurodif, where France is the majority shareholder.

The social policy

An enterprise which aims at investing abroad and which has managed to overcome the two impediments of the government industrial and financial policies is still confronted with a third obstacle as forbidding and as difficult to surmount as the two previous ones: the government's social policy. The social policy only concerns the activities of the enterprise in its home country; however, as we shall see, it has a direct influence on the operations carried out abroad. It aims at three principal objectives: the improvement of the satisfaction of the employees, the development of employment and a better geographical distribution of jobs. Applied to the enterprise, these become *ipso facto* priority objectives and are totally inconsistent with the multinationalization of its activities. The government improves the satisfaction of the employees above all through high wages. In most developed countries, the wages in state-owned enterprises are comparable with those paid by the most efficient private companies and are much higher than the country's average. Private firms are more generous only at the executive level. The same phenomenon occurs in developing countries. Apart from foreign companies or the few important private businesses, state-owned enterprises offer much higher salaries than other organizations. However, what is remarkable in all cases is the greater number of fringe benefits that the employees of state-owned enterprises enjoy in comparison with those of private companies. Moreover, these fringe benefits do not only concern the employees themselves but also their families. In France, the famous book by François de Closets *Toujours Plus* (more and more) revealed some of the privileges of certain employees in the public sector. Yet, such privileges are not specific to a particular enterprise or country.

We may cite as an example the conflict which opposed the management of Voest-Alpine to the Austrian government in 1984 precisely concerning the fringe benefits accorded by the enterprise to its employees. After having incurred a loss of 2.5 billion schillings in 1983 and having started a vast programme of modernization and strategic redeployment (aimed at services and trade), the important metallurgical company of Linz had decided to cut its allowances by 600 million schillings. Voest-Alpine had to abandon the idea under the pressure of the government. To crown it all, at the same time Alfred Dalinger, the Minister of Social Welfare, mentioned the possibility of reducing the working week to 35 hours, a proposal which was categorically turned down by all the managers of the nationalized industry. In this respect, the criticism of the managing director of Voest-Alpine, Herbert Apfalter, regarding the 'politicization of the economy' in Austria expresses their fears for the future.

As far as multinationalization is concerned, the costs incurred by state-owned enterprises owing to a generous social policy do not particularly favour their competitiveness on an international level. For these costs are far from being compensated by a greater dynamism among the employees, who are used to good treatment, consider their allowances as a right they are entitled to and are above all concerned with egalitarianism and with eliminating the management's 'despotism'. It is precisely at the level of those who can lead the others, in other words the top executives, that such enterprises cannot raise their salaries in line with their private counterparts. Sometimes, in addition, the rigid regulations concerning the staff, inherited from nationalization, may hinder the expatriation of personnel. Confident as they are in the progression of their career regardless of their performance and rightly convinced that an assignment abroad for several years would not bring any change in their career, or could even slow it down, the employees are not motivated to expatriate themselves. Thus, the ones who agree to do so fall into two categories: they are either attracted by an expatriation bonus (which can easily increase their salary threefold — at a very high cost to the enterprise) or they are bored in their present post and want to discover other countries (but such an attitude is often characteristic of those who are somewhat on the fringe and do not particularly have the required character to struggle in a hostile and foreign environment).

Underlying all this is a dual factor which must be borne in mind, for it indicates the measure of the constraint specific to state-owned enterprises. For the State these are the ideal instruments of its social policy, and for the trade unions the chosen setting for better purchasing power and claiming improved working conditions. There is thus a coalition of two extremely powerful forces which leave state-owned enterprises with practically no choice: they must be the strongholds of social welfare. It is too bad if they are thus handicapped in their multinationalization. This is true even in *laissez-faire* economies, despite the denial of the controlling authorities as well as that of the management of the firms. In fact, it would seem that the social role played by state-owned enterprises is the principal reason why governments in such countries cannot privatize them, or at least not as much as they would wish. The attempts made since 1979 by the British government are particularly significant in this respect. Certain state-owned enterprises cannot find a buyer precisely because the potential private shareholders are not too convinced about the capacity of such firms to be run efficiently owing to the practices they have long operated under. In fact, private buyers do not suspect the government, as a minority share-holder, of continuing to exert a bad influence but rather the trade unions, which would remain after privatization and would be likely to negate its impact.

The development of employment, which is the second major objective of social policy common to the government and trade unions, represents an even greater handicap for state-owned enterprises. We will not examine in detail the deplorable consequences of overstaffing as far as competitiveness is concerned. Since such enterprises cannot easily lay off personnel, their employees represent a long-term immobilization for them. However, it is mainly with regard to multinationaliz-ation that the protection of employment is an almost insurmountable obstacle. Unemployment is a major concern of the government and the trade unions; the former must convince the latter, who are always critical of its efforts, that it intends to combat this problem by all available means. In such a situation, it seems impossible for the state-owned enterprises to make the unions accept the creation of jobs abroad while few, or none at all, are created in the home country — in fact some are even suppressed. The conquest of foreign markets does entail new jobs in the home country, but how many and for how long? The logic of multinationalization, on the contrary, is that jobs must be localized where they are more profitable, on a worldwide scale. In the vocabulary of the unions (and governments), investments abroad are often termed as 'delocalization of jobs'.

Thus, in France, the most virulent opponent of the multinationaliz-ation strategy of Renault, the nationalized car manufacturer, is the country's leading trade union, the powerful communist Confédération Générale du Travail (CGT). The CGT officially refuses to consider that the French automobile industry has an excessively large staff (whereas an official report indicates that 50 000 jobs should be suppressed) and demands vociferously that all models sold by Renault in France be produced in the country. Many of these models are manufactured in Spain, Belgium and in Portugal. The creation of jobs by AMC in the United States is also considered as an anti-French policy. The CGT regularly obtains more than 50% of the votes in the elections for staff delegates.

Generally, this kind of pressure is not in itself strong enough to prevent investments abroad; however, it exerts an important negative influence on the strategy of the enterprises. The latter find it more difficult to close down plants and lay off personnel, at a time when they are creating jobs abroad. Therefore they are inclined to tolerate over-staffing to a certain extent and as a counterpart tend to moderate their expansion abroad. There is another danger underlying the multination-alization of state-owned enterprises though it is only potential at the moment, namely the possibility of the trade unions of the different countries coming together and exchanging their views on grievances, thereby tending towards the standardization of their situation through-out the world. The advantages acquired in one country would be generalized in all the others. This would be a nightmare for the manage-ment. The managing director of Voest-Alpine recently complained that in his firm there were 284 staff delegates working full time to defend the social advantages of the employees and only 118 directors!

Moreover, trade unions have a considerable support from another source: regional authorities. The third social mission of state-owned enterprises is to develop regional employment. For example, the Swedish municipalities were most opposed to the closing down of plants in the country by Assi while the firm was investing in the EEC at the same time. In West Germany, the Länder frequently acquire equity participations in the enterprises to favour employment. The important state-owned enterprises often fulfil a role of regional development. Thus, Salzgitter is considered as an essential factor in the development of a border region near East Germany. In Berlin, the creation of DIAG (which includes the industrial participation of the Bund of the city) was intended to allow the survival of the mechanical engineering industry. The Howaldwerke (shipyards) are the most important employer in the Schleswig-Holstein area. Enterprises like the IRI and the ENI in Italy were the principal agents in the development of the Mezzogiorno. Even in the United States, the regional role of the TVA is incontestable.

All these factors add to the constraints of state-owned enterprises which aim at multinationalization, as they are thus solidly attached not only to their country but also to their town of origin. This constitutes an additional handicap, but there are others.

The foreign policy

When it is set up abroad, a state-owned enterprise inevitably more or less represents the State which is its shareholder. Therefore the activities of such an enterprise abroad can never be disconnected from the foreign policy of its country of origin. This has two consequences for the enterprise. First, its government will tend to use it as the instrument of its own policy. Secondly, the host countries where the enterprise wishes to invest will perceive it as the emanation of a foreign State. In most cases these two aspects are important handicaps in the international expansion of a state-owned enterprise.

As an instrument serving the foreign policy of its country of origin, a state-owned enterprise is subjected to all kinds of pressure, indeed orders, which are opposed to its interests. It can thus be pressurized in the choice of the foreign country where it will, or will not, do business. The oil sector is characteristic of this kind of interference between politics and economic considerations as it is in itself very politicized. Thus, the ENI set up in Libya because the Italian government required it to do so. On the other hand, Elf-Aquitaine was obliged to freeze its activities there by the French government which was supporting Chad against Colonel Gaddafi. Again, the French government forced one of its state-owned enterprises, Gaz de France, to sign a supplying contract with Algeria on extremely disadvantageous terms (the purchase price was one-third above the world price). In another sector, at the time when General de Gaulle was in power, Renault for long bore the brunt of the French–Quebec friendship, being obliged to maintain non-profitable operations in Canada. DSM abstains from investing in South Africa, an extremely rich mining country, because the Dutch government disapproves of apartheid. Thus there are a great many examples of state-owned enterprises which, following conflicts and tensions, are subjected to a series of stop–go orders making their multinationalization on a healthy economic basis more difficult. Even in the absence of exceptional circumstances, such enterprises can be obliged to respect a list of 'priority' countries according to the foreign policy of their government (either because they are allied countries or because their currency is particularly attractive . . .).

Moreover, in certain cases, governments negotiate projects involving their respective state-owned enterprises which they later try to impose on them. One of these mythical monsters which is regularly the subject of talks but has not yet been realized is the 'Petrolatin Trinacional'. This is the name for an association of three important Latin American oil companies: Petroleos de Venezuela, Pemex and Petrobras. Needless to say, the companies in question are totally opposed to this project. However, the threat is still alive; Petroleos de Venezuela and Pemex have already been forced to sign an agreement concerning the distribution of their oil supplies in nine Central American countries

('Acuerdo de San José'). The Contadora Group thus uses their oil, hence their state companies, as political instruments.

Finally, for an enterprise wanting to invest abroad, being a political instrument implies one last inconvenience: that of appearing as the more or less direct agent of its country of origin. Although this reaction is not always very marked, it is a serious obstacle in the various countries which represent attractive markets. Such is the case in the United States, which is the world's greatest market in many sectors and which is therefore of interest for the enterprises aiming at multinationalization. In fact, the United States is dominated by an anti-state ideology which is extremely unfavourable to state-owned enterprises. There is much to say about the links between the American government and the business establishment but it is not relevant to our present subject. When they feel threatened within their own territory, the Americans often resort to legal action against unfair competition. In this respect state-owned enterprises are an ideal target. As we shall see in the following chapter, generally these lawsuits are not justified. They are nevertheless filed and give a bad reputation to foreign state-owned firms. This reputation created by aggressive competitors has an influence on the local partners of such enterprises — customers, suppliers, bankers, etc., and even the general public. It is the reason, as we have noted above, why state-owned enterprises are reticent about their attachment to a foreign government when they set up in the United States. Generally speaking, all the countries reputed to be free market economies (whether they deserve this reputation or not) constitute an unfavourable environment from this point of view. Thus, the French firm Thomson was banned from taking over Grundig in West Germany. The local press echoed the reservations of the authorities about letting a company nationalized by a socialist government dominate the German household electronics market. The French group also had the reputation of being a 'job-killer' because it had laid off personnel in its Videocolor subsidiary in Germany. This was considered to be enough justification for supposing that the French government would incite Thomson to 'repatriate' all possible jobs to France, thus leaving Grundig weak and drained. Such is the price to be paid for being a state-owned enterprise abroad.

NATIONALIZED AND NEVERTHELESS MULTINATIONAL

All things considered, the nationalization of an enterprise is not favourable to its multinationalization. Nationalization brings extremely

burdensome historical, ideological and economic constraints. It exposes
the enterprise to the successive interventions of the State in the name
of its industrial, financial, social and foreign policies which are not
particularly congruent with the strategy of the enterprise. The State
deprives it of its most effective activities, obliges it to take over lame
ducks, cuts its subsidies while at the same time requiring it to develop
employment and to be the standard-bearer of social welfare, and lastly
decides where it can, or cannot, set up, often changing its mind without
prior warning. In such conditions, how can an enterprise possibly
succeed in the formidable task of multinationalization?

Nevertheless, many have successfully attempted to do so. Does the
State as the shareholder of a state-owned enterprise really play the role
of the villain? Some assert that, on the contrary, its role is beneficial.
In their view, the government's industrial policy is meant to help state-
owned enterprises to build empires and its financial policy mainly
consists in giving generous subsidies without ever asking for dividends.
They also think that, rather than implementing a social policy, state-
owned enterprises set up abroad behave like slave drivers. Moreover,
the government puts at their disposal diplomats and the political and
economic pressures of the State to help them penetrate foreign markets.

What is the real situation? It is true that being state-owned does not
prevent an enterprise from being multinational. On the other hand, as
we hope to have shown in this chapter, nationalization does not make
things easier. However, can it sometimes possibly be of help? This is
the question we shall examine next.

Chapter Four

Unfair Competition?

INTRODUCTION

Are state-owned enterprises unfair competitors which pose a threat to private companies? The question arises for all enterprises which do not constitute strict monopolies. They are so numerous that one can wonder whether there still exists, in the capitalist world, a single state monopoly which has not been attracted by diversification, albeit marginal, and hence which has not joined the competitive market. Diversification can take many forms: for example, the postal services can branch out into banking, the national coal boards or state oil companies into the chemical industry, the national railways into road transportation, etc. In most countries, the chairmen of private industries periodically protest against the 'covert' nationalizations that these diversifications represent. However, whether they are unfair or not, the competitive activities of state-owned enterprises, carried out within the national territory, are legitimized since they are decided and controlled (explicitly or implicitly) by their governments.

The question is quite different in the case of state-owned firms starting activities abroad; indeed, is not this considered to be a glaring example of unfair competition? According to the classical theory of international trade, if every nation produces the goods for which it has a competitive advantage and exchanges them for the goods from other nations, the general well-being will be maximized. This was the idea that, in the eighteenth century, Adam Smith opposed to mercantilist governments. Today it is the same idea that Hayek propounds against the development of protectionism throughout the world. In fact, today, all countries, including the strongholds of a *laissez-faire* economy, protect themselves against imports while at the same time subsidizing their exports. Undeniably this phenomenon has developed with the surge of state-owned enterprises. On the one hand, the State tries to protect such enterprises from the entry of competitive products in the national territory; on the other, it can utilize state-owned firms as a source of foreign currencies or even as an instrument of economic expansion by forcing them to export, indeed to set up abroad. However, state-owned enterprises, as we have seen in the previous chapters, are not subjected to the same rules as private companies (they need not earn profits, they have privileged access to financing and to preferential markets, etc.). In a purely free market system, state-owned enterprises are unfair competitors. In the first section of this chapter, we will discuss a number of examples of these accusations of unfair competition. Next, in the second section, we will examine the different forms of support provided by governments, including those with a prevailing free market ideology. This will lead us to prove, in a third section, that the state-owned enterprise is only a particular case of unfair competition among many others. A fourth section will deal with the foreign subsidiaries of state-owned firms which observe the same rules of the game abroad as their private competitors. Thus, in conclusion, we will maintain that state-owned multinationals can hardly be differentiated from other multinationals.

THE ACCUSATIONS OF UNFAIR COMPETITION

Accusations of unfair competition are based on three principal arguments which, as we shall see, recur time and again in the official rhetoric of the enterprises claiming to be its victims.

— First, the state-owned enterprises concerned are accused of receiving, in the form of subsidies for research and development, massive aid from their 'shareholder-state'; in addition, they invariably benefit from orders placed by the government. Thus, they can offer foreign countries high-technology products at a price which does not take into account the initial investment. In contrast, a private company can only count on its own resources and has to face competition in its domestic market. We have thus a flagrant example of inequality.

— Secondly, in the event of this indirect aid being inadequate, state-owned enterprises can receive direct subsidies to cover operating losses. They can therefore sell at a loss in foreign markets, since the State can always compensate their deficit. In contrast, a private firm cannot implement this kind of strategy in the long term because it would lead to bankruptcy.

— Lastly, the support of the State can be of a more general nature, the specific form that it takes being determined by the particular circumstances. Apart from the two forms just mentioned, the government may for example carry out the complete restructuring of a sector of activity, sign bilateral agreements with other countries, exert economic or diplomatic pressure, etc. An independent enterprise rejecting government interference obviously cannot benefit from these different forms of support.

The criticisms levelled at state-owned enterprises concern mere export operations as well as the setting up of industries abroad. However, they are particularly aimed at a certain number of state-owned multinationals which we have studied, as we shall see from the examples taken from aeronautics, chemicals and the iron and steel industry.

Of course, it is in the United States, which is the stronghold of free market ideology, that foreign state-owned enterprises are most accused of unfair competition. Such accusations mainly affect the sectors of aeronautics (particularly Aérospatiale, Rolls-Royce, Airbus and Arianespace) and the steel industry, where European firms, joined over the last few years by Brazilian companies, have borne the brunt of criticism. When AHC (American Helicopter Corporation, the US subsidiary of Aérospatiale) signed an important contract with the US Cost Guards (215 million dollars for 90 helicopters), Bell Helicopter filed a lawsuit against Cost Guards contending that both the performance specifications of the tender bid as well as the 'Buy American Act' (50% of the components had to be American) had been violated. Since the Government Accounting Office decided the operation was in order, the case was dismissed and Bell resorted to political lobbying. However, the action was rapidly abandoned owing to the problems it could entail in diplomatic relations between France and the United States. The case inspired two American authors (J. Monsen and K. Walters in *Nationalized Companies: A Threat to American Business*, McGraw Hill, 1983) to write: 'the day that the French government buys foreign helicopters rather than those of its domestic supplier will be the day the President of France serves California wine at state dinners'. The authors chose to ignore the fact that the French market represents roughly one-tenth of the American market, and that neither Bell nor Sikorsky are willing to make the required investment to obtain a contract with France for only nine helicopters.

In the same way, in December 1983, the American Business Aircraft Committee addressed a letter to the managers of 5000 American enterprises (potential buyers of business aircraft and helicopters) denouncing unfair competition from 'subsidized' foreign companies. The chief target was Aérospatiale together with a Brazilian state-owned firm Embraer, whose main product (the 'Bandeirante') sells more in the United States than in its country of origin. Philippe Orsetti, executive vice-president of AHC, replied in the internal review of his firm (*Update*, March 1984) that for the last few years Bell had received 186 million dollars from the American government for its research and development and 275 million dollars from the Canadian government to produce a model which was to be imported in the United States despite the fact that almost all its components were manufactured abroad.

The situation is even more difficult in the steel industry. In 1980, in spite of the recommendations of the federal government, which wanted to avoid a deterioration in the relations with allied countries, US Steel filed 23 anti-dumping cases, mainly against a great number of state-owned (mostly European) enterprises but also against private companies 'subsidized' by their government (many of them Japanese). A survey conducted in 1982 by the American Department of Commerce showed that, for example, the French state-owned Firm Sacilor sold its steel 27.7% below a fair value. In 1983, the Brazilian state-owned enterprises of the Siderbras Group (CSN, Cosipa, Usiminas) sold their steel products at a record 50–75% below the US domestic prices (depending on the category of the product). Using the 1974 Trade Act, at the end of 1983 Bethlehem Steel put forward a demand for quotas on imports and the fixing of a minimum price for the Brazilian carbon steels. However, Pinopole Point Steel, one of the accused importing companies, won its case by proving that CSN was the only firm which could supply it with the specific quality of steel it needed and that Pinopole itself sold the transformed product at a higher price than its competitor, US Steel. At the 1983 meeting of the US International Trade Commission on December 7, Henrique Brandao Calvacanti, chairman of Siderbras, asserted that 'for Brazil, steel is an instrument of economic policy, which explains the prominence of the state-owned enterprise in the Brazilian iron and steel industry'. It should be remembered that in most cases such enterprises benefited from American government funds for their creation and development investments. Despite the Reagan ideology, protectionist measures in the iron and steel industry are most likely to proliferate in an attempt to check the dramatic cutback in employment in this sector in the United States (570 000 jobs in 1979 and only 335 000 remaining in 1983) and limit the financial outflow of the enterprises. Hence, the Brazilian state-owned enterprises have implemented new strategies. In 1984, Vale do Rio Doce bought 25% of the steel-making firm Fontana belonging to US Pacific Steel and set up in California, while the Japanese Kawasaki, with which Vale is associated for the production of semi-finished steel in Brazil, took another 25%. Thus Fontana transforms more than one-third of the production of the huge Tubarao plant recently installed by Siderbras on the Brazilian coast.

Nevertheless, the extent of these accusations should not be overestimated. In more than half of the European state-owned enterprises we studied in the United States, including Renault-AMC, DSM, Péchiney, Rhône-Poulenc, SKW and Voest-Alpine, the management denied ever having been accused of unfair competition. 'The individual reaction of the red-neck cowboy against anything that has to do with the government does not really affect our business', declared one of the managers we interviewed. Others, however, admitted that they were greatly concerned by this problem and convinced that it fuelled the position of their competitors, thus indirectly hampering their development. Generally speaking, most top managers acknowledge that they avoid emphasizing the state-owned character of their firm.

In fact, this situation is not specific to the United States. Several European firms in the chemical industry bitterly reproach the Italian government with saving the ailing subsidiaries of Montedison and Montecatini and granting massive subsidies to the whole sector. The same criticism is levelled at SEAT (Spain) in the automobile industry. It is interesting to note that in both cases most of the accusations are made by other state-owned enterprises which consider themselves to be fair competitors. Thus, DSM condemns most vehemently the setting up of ENI-Quimica by the Italian government on the ruins of the private and public chemical sector; the government contributed with capital as well as tax relief, subsidies for the purchase of raw materials and other forms of support which seriously disrupted the European chemical market. The development in Europe of Kuwait Petroleum Corporation provides a similar example; following the takeover in 1983 of the assets of Gulf in several countries, its European subsidiary KPI accounts for 3000 service stations and three refineries. The distribution networks of KPI in Sweden and the Benelux countries are accused by competitors of slashing prices, since they benefit from privileged purchase rates offered by the Kuwaiti government. It seems that at the moment KPI is considering setting up in most European countries. Such observations lead us to question the validity of the idea that state-owned multinationals are necessarily unfair competitors compared to private companies. We must therefore analyse more thoroughly the different categories of special advantages and privileges that state-owned enterprises enjoy and try to determine whether private companies benefit from similar advantages.

ADVANTAGES FOR STATE-OWNED . . . AND FOR PRIVATE ENTERPRISES

'Free market' governments also put a wide range of aids (tax exemptions, direct subsidies, preferential loans, etc.) at the disposal of all categories of enterprise. For instance, it is interesting to note that the American government does not publish complete tables of the federal aids to industry, preferring to concentrate on its campaign against 'subsidized' foreign firms and wishing to avoid providing counter arguments for its adversaries. A study conducted by the Kennedy School estimated such aids in 1982 for all sectors 196 million dollars, without taking into account the increasing aids given locally by the states. These federal aids essentially comprise tax exemptions and special loans intended in particular to promote investment, research and development, support to certain sectors, regional development and exports.[1] In addition, the impact of the military budget on industry must also be taken into account; in this respect, we must bear in mind the findings of J. K. Galbraith on the functioning of the military–industrial complex. In 1984, for example, the research and development funds in the US defence budget alone amounted to 29 billion dollars. Thus, all governments, including those advocating a free market economy, intervene massively to distort the free play of market forces, and the consequences of such interventions are not limited to their national territory. The set-up abroad of state-owned enterprises is only a variant of this kind of action, whether it means supporting national technology, helping an ailing sector, protecting an industry or awarding public orders to domestic competitors. This is what we shall examine next.

Aid to high-technology sectors

One of the missions with which the state often entrusts state-owned enterprises consists in protecting the country's technological independence, especially in leading sectors. This is particularly true in the case of Western European countries where private industries are often tempted, for evident reasons of immediate economic efficiency, to buy foreign licences rather than develop their own technology. This, for example, was the reason which led to the creation of Cogéma, a

[1] See J. M. Saussois, *Les Aides Fédérales à l'Industrie Américaine*, FNEGE-ESCP, Paris, 1984.

subsidiary of CEA in France, and SGS, a subsidiary of STET (IRI group) in Italy. More generally, all European leading sectors (computers, electronics, aeronautics, nuclear power, etc.) include many state-owned enterprises. In France, the companies nationalized in 1982 were also entrusted with technological development targets. However, as we have noted, the private firms of such sectors also benefit from considerable research and development public aids. In general, in most western countries, more than 50% of research and development is financed by public funds. Japan represents a remarkable exception with only 30% (*The OECD Observer*, March 1979). Nevertheless, apart from financial aid, the MITI gives great support to Japanese enterprises; thus, in American industrial, financial and academic circles it is fashionable to assert that all the major Japanese firms are in fact state-owned enterprises.

The example of the space industry is particularly significant; in such a context the issue of fair or unfair competition may no longer be relevant. In 1984, however, the American company TCI (Transpace Carrier Incorporated, a private company that sells the Thor-Dela launchers) took action against Arianespace, which it accused of having received special subsidies in order to increase its export sales, notably to the United States. TCI requested the government of the United States to take measures against the European governments backing Arianespace and their agencies (ESA and CNES). Negotiations were started between the United States and European countries. The European countries which control the consortium Arianespace had decided to pay 25% more than the price of its American competitor in the starting-off phase of Ariane. In an interview, the general director of Arianespace wondered whether TCI's main target, through the intermediary of Arianespace, was not in fact the American space shuttle, which was another of its competitors. Indeed, in 1984 a shuttle flight cost between 300 and 350 million dollars and the revenue obtained from its customers amounted roughly to 40 million dollars. Even in the long run, the financial aid from the State will be considerable since it is reckoned that when the shuttle is launched 24 times a year, the cost of each launching will be between 160 and 175 million dollars whereas the revenue obtained will not exceed 100 million dollars (today a full flight yields a revenue of 71 million dollars).[2] Let us make a rough assessment. The turnover of Arianespace for the years 1987–1988 is estimated at around 500 million dollars a year. If we consider that during the same period the shuttle will fly 20 times a year with a

---

[2] The space shuttle accident which occurred in January of 1986 has obviously completely modified the situation.

subsidy of 75 million dollars per launching (a figure which is probably underestimated), the revenue will amount to 1500 million dollars a year, that is to say three times the total turnover of Arianespace. How many private enterprises (customers, suppliers, subcontractors) indirectly benefit from such a windfall? Thus in high-technology sectors there is little to choose between private and state-owned enterprises, even though the financial flow partly goes through different channels.

Indeed, the dividing line between public and private ownership is becoming increasingly blurred as agreements between nationalized and private firms tend to proliferate. One of the latest was signed in September 1984 between IBM and the Italian nationalized group STET (which controls the telecommunications activities of the holding company IRI). According to the terms of the agreement, a common plant (51% STET, 49% IBM) in Genoa will manufacture productics equipment, joint research will be carried out in the field of telecommunications and telematics, and IBM will buy most of its chips from SGS (a subsidiary of STET). Apparently, there is nothing to prevent the collaboration between a private multinational like IBM and a state-owned enterprise, in this case STET (a previous agreement was signed with British Telecom), any more than in the case of its cooperation with a private company, for example Olivetti. Moreover, STET had started negotiations with General Electric and later signed an agreement with the French nationalized firm CIT-Alcatel and also with the private company Ericsson. This shows the extent to which the private and the public sectors tend to interpenetrate. Thus IBM will benefit at least as much as the local partners from government generosity and will modernize the British and Italian telecommunication networks. Evidently a judicious agreement is much more profitable than a bad trial.

Support to ailing industries

The objective of state intervention is sometimes to support an entire ailing economic sector. In the shipbuilding industry, no government can really accuse any other of unfair competitive practices. The French government accords more than one and a half billion francs a year to the enterprises in this sector. Thus, in 1984, the recently formed Normed group alone received a credit of about two billion francs. Can it still be considered as a private enterprise? In 1977, the Swedish government nationalized all the shipyards and injected six million dollars over a period of four years (that is to say ten times more than the aid accorded over the four preceding years) into the group Svenska

Varu thus formed, in order to cover deficits and start a rationalization process. It is interesting to note that in Sweden the 'bourgeois' government which came to power in 1976 carried out more nationalizations in four years than the socialists in 40 years. In Germany, most shipyards, including HDW and Vulcan, are controlled by the Länder and benefit from privileged loans and substantial subsidies. In Spain, the state-owned enterprises Astano and ACIA, whose resources amount to only six billion pesetas, show a deficit of 150 billion pesetas, compensated by the State. In Denmark, the shipbuilding industry is private. However, the government allocates long-term loans without interest to developing customer countries and considerable tax exemptions to private investors who invest in ship 'participations' or in leasing in the sector. The EEC has created an Intervention Fund (article 92) which also subsidizes the European shipyards. Unable to assess the importance of the aid accorded by each member country, the EEC cannot conduct a coherent policy. It has therefore decided to intervene whenever a ship is sold, using Japanese prices as a reference. A disenchanted manager of British Shipbuilders whom we interviewed told us: 'Our business is employment, nothing to do with commerce . . .'.

The situation is very different in South Korea, whose private shipbuilding industry is one of the world's leading exporters (25% of world orders in 1983, that is to say the equivalent of all the European shipyards together). Part of their development investment as well as the price of steel is subsidized, imported equipment is exempted from taxes, the Seoul import–export bank allocates low-cost loans and favourable terms of payment, and finally the South Korean government imposes what in practice amounts to a cartel policy (market sharing, price fixing, . . .). Surprisingly enough, in the sector of shipyards, the concept of absolute unfair competition no longer exists. However, a new concept (which neo-classical economists had not envisaged) can be put forward — that of relative unfair competition. Each country claims that its competitors are more unfair than itself. Thus the Japanese accuse the South Koreans, the Danish accuse the other member countries of the EEC, the Germans accuse the French. This situation, which has become commonplace today, shows that, for the enterprises playing a significant role in the economy, the distinction between 'public' and 'private' ownership is not significant. Moreover, the Finnish shipbuilding industry, which is poised to become the leading one in Europe, includes both private companies and one state-owned enterprise (all suppliers to the USSR) and the former do not complain about the latter. This is a good example of peaceful coexistence which confirms our thesis.

Shipbuilding is only one among many other ailing sectors of activity.

The attitude of the American federal government during the crisis which shook the automobile industry in the early eighties can only be interpreted as massive support for the sector. The bailing out of Chrysler constitutes a case in point. In addition, the fixing of quotas on Japanese imports together with unprecedented political pressures for the passing of protectionist legislation by Congress greatly contributed to save the ailing American automobile industry. Thus, the average price of a car increased by 2000 dollars in one year, domestic manufacturers rapidly recovered their margins and Japanese competitors were forced to associate with American firms to produce locally. The economic recovery of course largely contributed to the total reversal of the situation, but so did the government policy. The official position, however, was careful to disguise this fact, proclaiming instead with great fanfare the virtues of competition. After all, this attitude on the part of the land of free enterprise is not really surprising if one recalls the difficulties faced by Concorde in 1975 in obtaining landing and take-off rights on American territory, and the imposition in 1983 of customs duties on motorbikes of over 700 cc under the pressure of Harley-Davidson. The powerful International Trade Commission regularly recommends that, according to the terms of the 1984 Trade Act, the federal State allow a particular industry a period of adaptation ('breathing time') in order to prepare it to face foreign competition. This is nothing short of protectionism that dares not acknowledge itself.

All-out protectionism

All countries try to protect their enterprises, either state-owned or private, by practices aimed at limiting international competition. The quotas on Japanese car imports in France are meant to protect Peugeot as well as Renault. The obstacles the two firms meet concerning the approval (homologation procedure) of foreign vehicles in Germany are the same. The newly industrialized countries (India, South Korea, Taiwan, Brazil, etc.) have developed a strategy to support their enterprises whether state-owned[3] or private. First, foreign set-up in the sector is banned and the government helps local private firms to acquire and develop the required technologies. In the event of the private sector being too poor or too dependent on foreign countries, a state-owned

---

[3] See S. Lall, *The New Multinationals: The Spread of Third World Enterprises*, John Wiley & Sons, Chichester, 1983, and J. P. Anastassopoulos and G. Blanc, 'Entreprises publiques et développement', *Revue Politiques et Management Public*, No. 1, Winter 1983.

enterprise is created. Secondly, when the products have been developed, the government favours their export. Thirdly, once the enterprise has become self-sufficient, it naturally enters into the phase of setting up abroad. Embraer, the aeronautics enterprise created by the Brazilian government in 1969, offers a good example as it managed to overcome the obstacles which this kind of operation usually meets:

1. By retaining the control of the enterprise while collecting private capital through shares with no voting rights but with tax exemptions;
2. By manufacturing certain products under foreign licences (Piper) and imposing heavy taxes on imported products;
3. By making a great effort in training and research: training technicians abroad, creating a well-equipped research centre, inviting foreign engineers;
4. By stimulating the domestic market (which is the third in the world as far as regional airlines, air taxis and important landowners are concerned) and guaranteeing regular military orders;
5. By ensuring the long-term stability of the management and technical teams, in particular protecting them from political changes.

These efforts have enabled Embraer to export 50% of its production (mainly in developed countries) as well as, since 1980, to set up two important subsidiaries in the United States and in Europe which are responsible for sales, maintenance, stocking of spare parts and the training of pilots. A decree of the President of the Republic was necessary for the creation of these subsidiaries as they each represented a ten million dollar investment. The Brazilian government is now adopting a similar strategy in the field of microcomputers, where it tries to protect the development of a domestic technology. In this case, however, it relies on private enterprises.

Another favourite instrument of state protectionism is the awarding of government orders to domestic enterprises. Besides direct aid for research and development (which is sometimes presented as prototype orders), government procurements are a key element in the functioning of the 'military–industrial complex' as described by J. K. Galbraith. According to the 'Buy American Act', 50% of any product bought by a government agency must be manufactured in the United States. Foreign enterprises, both state-owned and private, are thus encouraged to set up production facilities in the United States when government markets are an important target. All countries with an industry to protect have, tacitly or explicitly, established similar regulations. In this context, the multinational firm often resorts to the setting up of a joint venture which allows an easier local adaptation of the product. In the case of important state-owned organisms appealing for foreign cooperation, a state-owned enterprise of the cooperating country might be preferred. Thus, for example, within the scope of the Andean Pact, Yacimientos Petroliferos Fiscales (YPF), an Argentine state-owned enterprise, set up a petrochemical complex in Bolivia in which it has a 45% equity participation, the remainder being held by the Bolivian Oil Company. This industrial complex is meant to produce pesticides, a field in which several firms in the countries of the Andean Pact could claim to have greater experience than YPF. However, they were private enterprises, subsidiaries or licensees of multinationals.

Generally speaking, in agreements between two governments, a marked preference for state-owned enterprises is noticeable. The reason may be that the representatives of the two governments feel they can thus control the implementation of their policy more directly. On the one hand, in the case of developing countries, the host nations are often tempted to choose a foreign state-owned enterprise in preference to a private one, and even more so in the event of setting up a joint venture with a local state-owned firm. Thus, to make an important industrial investment in 1983, Pescados de Chiapas of Mexico preferred Alsthom, which belongs to the French nationalized group CGE, to its private competitors.

On the other hand, governments wanting to help foreign countries in the process of industrialization might have a tendency to favour their state-owned enterprises rather than their private ones. Before 1981, when the French head of state or one of the ministers went abroad on an official visit, his programme would include negotiations on behalf of Dassault, Matra or Aérospatiale. The nationalization of Dassault and the state participation in Matra do not seem to have altered things. It is widely known that when travelling abroad, all government representatives, even from a free market government, take with them a great many industrial and commercial projects which include those of state-owned enterprises as well as private firms with a view to exporting and setting up abroad. The management of private enterprises, whether French, Italian or Swedish, for instance, is very particular about this equality of treatment with the public firms. In Brazil, fierce debates opposed the managers of private trading companies to the government, which was accused of favouring Interbras, a subsidiary of the state-owned group Petrobras. As we have seen in the previous chapter, according to its foreign policy, the government may encourage a state-owned enterprise to invest (or on the contrary prevent it from doing so) in a particular foreign country, regardless of the dictates of a purely managerial logic. However, once again, the French nationalizations of 1981 offer an interesting counter example. None of the managers of the firms we interviewed in France or in the foreign subsidiaries declared having noticed a significant change in the foreign investment policy of their enterprise since 1981. Anyway, as far as a set-up abroad is concerned, whatever the prevailing ideology, a government favours the enterprise which it assesses as technically the best, provided it is a national — but not necessarily state-owned — firm.

It might be argued that state-owned enterprises are unfair competitors owing to their permanent and subsidized deficit. This has been clearly pointed out by J. Monsen and K. Walters.[4] Between 1972 and 1981, of the 25 largest European state-owned enterprises, only four earned profits. In contrast, in the same period, among the 25 largest European private companies, only one firm, Rhône-Poulenc (which has since been nationalized), recorded losses outstripping profits. Even if Fiat and Dunlop were added to the list of private enterprises in deficit for a considerable part of the same period (the information presented in their table is incomplete), the gap still remains significant. Evidently, at least in this field, there is an essential difference between the strategies of state-owned firms and those of the major private enterprises.

However, Table 4.1, which includes *all* the state-owned multinationals that we have identified among the 200 largest enterprises outside the United States, indicates that state-owned enterprises are not invariably money-losers. Of the eighteen enterprises studied over a five-year period (1981–1985), only three show losses every year, six report profits every year and the others have variable results. Over the total five-year period, nine of the enterprises studied have run at a loss while nine others have made overall profits. Moreover, an important point remains to be discussed — is not the state-owned enterprise compelled to seek profits in all its activities abroad? This will be the subject of the third section of this chapter.

THE LIMITS OF COMPETITIVE ANALYSIS

As a conclusion to the analysis conducted in the preceding section, we may say that, at least within the national territory, the state-owned enterprise enjoys greater 'special advantages' than its private counterpart. However, it is very often just a question of degree. At the most it can be said that, compared to a private company, a state-owned enterprise tends to indulge more in practices of unfair competition, to use the standard economic jargon. In fact, this criterion has possibly lost

[4] In *Nationalized Companies*, McGraw Hill, New York, 1983, pp. 98–99.

Table 4.1   Profit or loss of the largest state-owned multinationals, 1981–1985 ($000).

Enterprises	Rank (1985)	1981	1982	1983	1984	1985
IRI	3	NA	NA	NA	NA	(664 000)
ENI	4	383 234	(1 206 970)	(928 925)	(50 119)	427 180
Elf-Aquitaine	10	682 316	536 336	488 451	742 576	708 069
Petrobras	18	831 215	579 170	485 088	633 164	1 790 566
Kuwait Petroleum	28	1 690 312	1 053 585	1 055 827	958 377	693 200
Voest-Alpine	29	(9 356)	(14 948)	(2 062)	27 117	(189 247)
Renault	30	(124 916)	(194 796)	(206 769)	(1 435 861)	(1 215 915)
CGE	48	74 607	68 475	52 611	67 533	84 752
Saint-Gobain	54	83 180	39 032	53 135	58 761	81 803
DSM	57	40 888	(70 222)	57 328	144 289	121 094
Thomson	61	(13 625)	(136 029)	(140 776)	(2 402)	14 023
Rhône-Poulenc	72	(61 995)	(128 344)	12 857	227 473	257 318
Norsk-Hydro	101	71 698	24 162	66 839	130 399	241 875
YPF	103	(3 820 963)	(3 669 510)	(4 643 995)	(3 592 682)	(697 129)
Pechiney	126	NA	(455 285)	(60 771)	62 398	81 469
Aerospatiale	133	29 343	14 637	(46 903)	37 969	60 434
Salzgitter	168	(175 708)	(15 785)	272 863	(153 279)	16 259
EFIM	171	NA	(287 798)	(509 307)	(323 694)	(238 806)

Source: Fortune's Annual Directory of Largest Industrial Corporations Outside the United States 1982, 1983, 1984, 1985, 1986.

its relevance in today's economic context. Today the strategy of enterprises, whether state or privately owned, must incorporate, as we have
discussed elsewhere,[5] a new dimension which we have termed the
'relational' dimension. It is admittedly crucial for the enterprise to
produce the best quality at the lowest price. However, it is strange
that all strategic analysis models ignore the important aspect of the
relationship between the enterprise and the government. The study of
the possible means of incorporating state intervention in the prospects
of the enterprise should not be relegated to a secondary position in
competitive analysis. It should rather be one of the principal elements
in the analysis, like the key factors of success in the industry and the
distinctive skills of the firm. To a certain extent this is taken into
consideration by French enterprises, which sign planning contracts with
the government, and even more so by Japanese ones. In fact, the latter,
in collaboration with the MITI, draw up what amounts to a joint
industrial strategy in order to coordinate the objectives and constraints
of the private sector and the government.

The classical theories of competitive analysis are no longer adequate
for explaining the complexity of contemporary economics and need to
be replaced by a true relational theory. Moreover, this theory should
not be confined to the relationship between the firm and the government. It should also include the relations with all the other partners of
the enterprise, and above all the alliances with other enterprises, which
seem to be proliferating. A large number of American industrialists
today demand a greater flexibility of anti-trust laws. For example, the
iron and steel industry has demanded that the Reagan administration
authorize the setting up of joint ventures in order to rationalize
production. In the same way 'customer–supplier' agreements have been
increasing in number, as we saw in the case of Vale do Rio Doce –
Kawasaki – Pacific Steel. In more general terms, the relational theory
can include agreements with banks and even the trade unions (for
example agreements for cutbacks in wages and in personnel). In this
context, state ownership is just one of the forms that the extremely
complex relationship that exists between the government and the enterprises can take. Therefore state ownership is not necessarily the most
relevant criterion for defining the close links between the State and the
enterprise. In fact, a large number of 100% privately owned companies
(in ailing industries, high-technology industries and sectors of strategic
importance) have far closer links with their governments than for
example DSM (a 100% state-owned Dutch company), Norsk-Hydro (a

---

[5] J. P. Anastassopoulos, G. Blanc, J. P. Nioche and B. Ramanantsoa, *Pour une
Nouvelle Politique d'Entreprise*, PUF, 1985.

51% state-owned Norwegian firm) and Volkswagen (in which the Lower Saxony Länder and the German federal government each have a 20% equity participation). By opposing the principle of free competition (with, as its corollary, the condemnation of unfair competition) to, on the one hand, state intervention and, on the other, cartels, the debate is reduced to simplistic terms and fails to take into account the complexity of the real situation. We therefore propose that theoretical business strategy models inspired by free market ideology should include a new dimension as defined by Cyert and March[6] more than 20 years ago — namely, the search for security. Security is obtained through all kinds of agreements with the firm's economic partners (customers, suppliers, banks, competitors, all forms of state authority, trade unions). Classical business strategy models, particularly those widely diffused in the seventies by the Boston Consulting Group and Arthur D. Little, are based on two analytical dimensions:

— one characterizing the sector of activity (of each strategic business unit of the enterprise) by its growth rate, its maturity or by a combination of criteria investing it with a certain 'attractiveness' or 'value' for the enterprise;
— the other defining the competitive position of the enterprise in the sector in quantitative (market share) and qualitative (mastery of key factors of success) terms.

Today, limiting strategic analysis to these two dimensions amounts to a serious misinterpretation of economic reality. The two dimensions are certainly essential, but it is necessary to add the third one, in other words the security which is determined by the importance and the quality of the alliances between the enterprise and all its economic partners. A state-owned multinational will not adopt the same position, in terms of security, *vis-à-vis* its various strategic business units. In most cases, it is in a much more secure — and often totally protected — position in its own country. In contrast, abroad, the rules of the game are almost the same for state and privately owned multinationals, as we shall examine next.

THE RULES OF THE GAME FOR SUBSIDIARIES ABROAD

A state-owned enterprise, especially if it is vested with a mission of public service, enjoys certain privileges within its own country; once it

[6] *A Behavioural Theory of the Firm*, Prentice Hall, 1963.

ventures abroad, after overcoming all the obstacles imposed by the government which hinder its multinationalization, it becomes an enterprise like any other. Its mode of functioning is identical to that of private companies, notably when it comes to defining the objectives of multinationalization. In the course of our research, we found that the managers of foreign subsidiaries of state-owned multinationals talk essentially in terms of profits, market share and growth. More generally, most of the strategies developed abroad are comparable with those of standard multinationals. The means utilized to implement such strategies are identical with regard to the sources of financing as well as the legal status adopted, although very often the state-owned multinational is subjected to a stricter control. Lastly, in the field of social relations, there is little similarity between the policy of the parent company and that of its foreign subsidiaries. We shall now examine each one of these different themes.

The search for profitability in the strategies of foreign subsidiaries

'We are here to do business,' declared the chairman of the American subsidiary of a well-known French state-owned enterprise. All the other managers of subsidiaries in the United States whom we interviewed shared the same viewpoint; given the size of the market and the high-technology environment in the United States, all enterprises are obliged to assert their presence, both to earn profits and to keep up with international competition. This is true in the fields of chemicals (DSM and its subsidiary Nipro), of automobiles (Renault and AMC), of the mechanical engineering industry (VIAG and SKW), of aeronautics, of telephone switching equipment, etc. Thus, since 1982, the entire strategy of Renault has been aimed at restoring the profitability of American Motors. However, the United States is not the sole El Dorado for state-owned multinationals. Indeed, both the French subsidiary of the Italian firm SGS in the sector of electronic components and the British subsidiary of the Swedish company Assi in the field of cardboard packaging earn profits. The situation of French multinationals nationalized in 1981 is also worth noting; despite their nationalization, the objectives assigned to their foreign subsidiaries, either in developed or in developing countries, have been maintained: profitability continues to be the primary aim. Interestingly, this is also true of enterprises whose major preoccupation would not *a priori* be to earn profits, such as, for example, the state-owned enterprises of countries in the course of industrialization, whose most important mission is national development. Even for the foreign subsidiaries of such enterprises, profitability is the foremost concern and all losses give rise to severe criticism. This was the case for Interbras in 1983 when it recorded losses for the first time since its creation. The essential mission of this firm is to sell Brazilian products abroad and to be a source of foreign currency, a mission that can very well lead to selling at a loss. However, it is clear that, at least as far as the official stance is concerned, priority must be given to profits.

In the same way, the multinationalization strategies of state-owned enterprises are very similar to those of their private counterparts.[7] On the one hand, cost leadership strategies (based on volume effects, economies of scale and the experience curve) can either apply to a wide range of activities (as is the case with CGE and ENI) or focus on certain particular products (for instance a car model adapted to global markets, a specific type of steel, or 'caprolactam' manufactured by DSM). Such strategies imply defending a sizeable, indeed dominant, share of the world market (as in the case of DSM) by keeping prices down with concentrated and technologically sophisticated means of production. On the other hand, the logic of differentiation strategies requires that subsidiaries in foreign countries focus on a specific segment in terms of products, of particular services offered or of a limited category of customers. Most of the state-owned enterprises that we analysed rely on differentiation strategies, which is not at all surprising as few of them can compare in size with giant multinationals and successfully implement cost leadership strategies. Differentiation strategies are often based on privileged relations that exist between two countries with particular affinities. Thus, for example, ENASA (a Spanish firm) manufactures and sells lorries in Latin America, RITES (an Indian enterprise) equips and modernizes the railways of several African countries, Keppel Shipyard (from Singapore) has set up and successfully operates floating docks in the Philippines. Lastly, internationalization often originates in the desire of the parent company to control its outlets. In 1982, the Moroccan Office Chérifien des Phosphates (OCP), which owns almost 75% of the world resources of phosphates, took partial control of one of its important customers — the Belgian company Prayon, specialized in downstream technologies, which was undergoing serious financial problems. In the same way, Pemex and Petroleos de Venezuela invested in Spain and West Germany respectively in order to secure outlets for their oil and Assi invested in Great Britain, Denmark, West Germany and Switzerland to sell the paper pulp it produces. Similarly, like their private counterparts, the state-owned oil

---

[7] See M. Porter, *Competitive Strategy*, The Free Press, Macmillan, New York, 1980.

companies (Elf-Aquitaine, ENI, BP, VEBA, etc.) invested massively in oil-producing countries. We can also cite the considerable investments of two German firms in the US coal-mining sector: Saarbergwerke, which took 25% of Ashland Coal, and RWE, which took 24% of Consolidated Coal. Since Brazil has no high-quality coal, the Compania Vale do Rio Doce acquired a coal mine in Western Canada and Siderbras set up a joint venture with a Colombian company to exploit coal mines in Colombia. Thus the development strategies of state-owned multinationals abroad — cost leadership, differentiation, vertical integration — are comparable with those of private multinationals.

Financing investment

As we have seen in the previous chapter, state-owned enterprises do not always have the same facilities for investing abroad as their private counterparts. Even those which maintain flexible relations with the government and pride themselves on being run just as private enterprises — as is the case with the Scandinavian, German, Dutch and the French companies nationalized in 1982 — acknowledge that their decision-making processes concerning financial operations are often slower and more complex owing to state intervention. The waiting period for the approval of a project after it has been submitted to the authorities may vary between one and two years, which leaves enough time for competitors to react and for the project to lose its relevance. However, state-owned enterprises sometimes have privileged access to certain categories of special loans accorded by governments to boost their foreign expansion (exports or set-ups abroad). Sometimes these can be loans granted to customers of the enterprise (for instance what are called in France '*crédits sur protocole*'). These loans are in principle intended equally for public and private enterprises and in fact, in most cases, private multinationals make a better use of them.

To avoid the institutional problems posed by direct investment abroad, foreign subsidiaries also seek local financing, especially in industrialized countries. However, being a subsidiary of a foreign state-owned enterprise does not give the firm a particular advantage in the eyes of local bankers, even though the risk involved is virtually nil. In the United States, admission to quotation on the stock exchange offers considerable possibilities for financing; this is the case with Certain Teed, the subsidiary of Saint-Gobain. But it can also entail heavy constraints concerning the rights of the minority shareholder; for example, Péchiney, long before its nationalization, had chosen to take total control of Howmet after a few years of majority shareholding experience. In fact, very few subsidiaries of state-owned enterprises are quoted on foreign stock exchanges. Most of them are totally controlled by their parent company while many others set up joint ventures with local firms. Thus, in most cases, the subsidiary finds itself in a situation where the advantages and drawbacks counterbalance one another: on the one hand, state-owned parent companies do not usually require their foreign subsidiaries to pay dividends; on the other, these seldom benefit from increases in capital as the State is very reluctant when it comes to investing abroad.

Moreover, in the United States, being a nationalized enterprise creates an unfavourable impression on the local money market as investors are suspicious of the 'shareholder-state'. In the autumn of 1984, Renault was demoted from an A+ to a simple A rating as a borrower on the US financial market, not only owing to its poor results but also because the French government seemed to have difficulties in supporting its recently expanded industrial public sector. In general, a firm undergoing financial problems cannot expect a better treatment because it is state-owned.

This is the reason why a great number of state-owned enterprises abroad look for a local partner, either public or private, which has a good image and inspires investors with confidence. During the last few years, there has been a considerable spread of joint venture operations parallel to what is observed in the case of private multinationals, in line with the relational theory presented above. Joint venture often results from a direct agreement with another industrial partner, which can be a state or privately owned enterprise. Sofretu, which has been building underground transport systems in many countries for over 20 years now, has gone into joint ventures with a number of public and private partners, which are either French or indigenous. In October 1984, the chairman and managing director of Sofretu signed an agreement with the president of Lummus-Crest, a large American private engineering firm, to create a common subsidiary (50% each) whose activity will cover the entire field of urban transport engineering in the United States. Its first important contract will be that of Orlando in Florida. However, the state-owned enterprise spontaneously tends to seek a joint venture with a local state-owned company. For example, GIOL, which is the largest Argentine enterprise for the production and distribution of wine, set up an industrial joint venture in Colombia with a state-owned local firm, although there are a great number of private enterprises in the business.

The autonomy of the firm in investment decisions

The financial commitment that the setting up of certain joint ventures represents often leads governments to intervene to such an extent that state-owned enterprises can be relegated to the role of operator. It is sometimes difficult to determine who really has the initiative and conducts the operations. In 1984, the setting up of Latinequip, a company trading in industrial equipment, formed by the bank of the province of Buenos Aires, the bank of the state of Sao Paulo and the Mexican bank Nacional Financiera, was entirely conducted by the managers of the enterprises concerned with no real active intervention of the different governments. When Petroleos de Venezuela (a state firm) agreed with VEBA on installing a joint refinery in West Germany (56% Petroleos de Venezuela — 44% VEBA), the Venezuelan Congress claimed that the operation had not been submitted for its approval and that it had been entirely conducted by the board of directors of the enterprise with the support of its controlling ministry. However, on the other hand, when government representatives of Mexico, Venezuela and Brazil meet, they invariably discuss the Petrolatin project mentioned in the preceding chapter. Yet, the managers themselves are little inclined to study the project, which they consider to be unrealistic. The extent of the impact of state intervention also depends on the prosperity of the investing country.

Evidently, foreign investment of a state-owned enterprise originating from a poor country is an exceptional operation in which the government of the investing country plays a crucial part. This was exemplified by all the cases we observed: Embraer and Vale do Rio Doce investing in the United States, Petroleos de Venezuela in West Germany and the Office Chérifien des Phosphates in Belgium. The fact that, in most cases, the chief executive of the enterprise is a former minister, or even a minister in office, facilitates the control by the government. As for the Office Chérifien des Phosphates, the King of Morocco himself made the decision to invest in Belgium, despite the criticisms of a number of ministers. When later a similar case occurred in the Netherlands, the management of the enterprise alone decided to abandon the project although the investment was in line with the long-term strategy of the firm. In more general terms, the controlling authorities always intervene at the crucial moment in the decision of the state-owned enterprise to invest abroad. State intervention is extremely burdensome for the enterprises of developing countries and far less oppressive for those of developed countries, the greatest entrepreneurial autonomy prevailing in Northern European countries (the Scandinavian nations, the Netherlands and West Germany). The French and Italian governments do not intervene in operations abroad, which are mainly decided by the management of the enterprises, except in the event of an investment with important repercussions on national policy. In the course of our research, it was a representative of the Norwegian government who expressed himself most clearly on the issue: 'State-owned enterprises are run exactly like private companies. We appoint directors who are eminent figures in the economy and well-known and respected managers, not mere civil servants. Once they are appointed, they are totally free. There are no government representatives in the board of directors; members of Parliament have no right to participate or intervene in the management. In the event of an important economic issue, which is seldom the case, a commission of inquiry is appointed. However, investment abroad does not fall into this category'.

The management of human resources

It is undeniable that, as far as social policy is concerned, there is a marked difference between the policy of the enterprise in its home country and that of its foreign subsidiaries. In the social field, the attitude adopted by the latter is practically identical to that of foreign subsidiaries of private multinationals. Despite the takeover of their company by Renault, the employees of AMC continue to work according to American standards; the UAW, their leading trade union, considers AMC only in comparison with the other American car manufacturers and has no contact with Renault's French unions. Moreover, AMC's new board has not altered the existing forms of relationship with the staff. In the same way, for several years, Aérospatiale's US subsidiary, like any American private firm in the same situation, has been trying to avoid the setting up of a trade union (in the United States, a union can only be set up at the request of over 50% of the personnel). In fact, state-owned multinationals and their private counterparts alike content themselves with observing the 21 June 1976 OECD declaration stipulating that the terms of employment and industrial relations should not be inferior to those of comparable employers in the host countries. However, a difference in nuance can be detected. The managers of several subsidiaries acknowledged that the state-owned character of their parent company led them to adopt a greater 'social morality', although not at the expense of a possible sacrifice of profit. The nationalization of Rhône-Poulenc produced a few changes in the social policy of its foreign subsidiaries, though possibly more owing to a spontaneous modification in the policy of the local management rather than to the application of explicit instructions from the parent company. The Dutch management of DSM does not easily accept lay-offs in its subsidiaries in the United States and requires more detailed justifications from the local managers than a private company would. In other words, the foreign subsidiaries of state-owned enterprises are required to be 'fair with people' far more than their private counterparts. In this respect, however, the difference is more one of nuance than of written rules. In fact, it seems that very often the managers of foreign subsidiaries, either because of habits acquired in the parent company or owing to a desire to avoid shocking the principles of the latter, spontaneously adopt social policies which are very similar to those of the parent company. Therefore, these policies can noticeably differ from those of the country where the subsidiary is set up. When this is the case, how can this not be considered as a handicap that such firms impose on themselves compared with their private competitors, which do not bother about such scruples? In such conditions, can there still be any unfair competition?

IS THERE ANY DIFFERENCE BETWEEN STATE-OWNED AND PRIVATE MULTINATIONALS?

It is therefore an overstatement to consider the state-owned multinational as an enterprise whose logic of development is totally different from that of the private multinational. It is revealing that, up to the present, all cases filed against them in the United States for unfair competition have been dismissed. Moreover, all countries, whatever their ideologies, tend increasingly to support their state or privately owned enterprises, thereby directly or indirectly favouring their international development. The American federal government concentrates its aid on research and development. The MITI in Japan directs the strategy of the major private enterprises. A great number of European countries or countries in the process of industrialization rely on state-owned firms. The smaller the market of the country of origin, due to its size or its level of economic development, the more difficult it is for local private enterprises to use this market as a springboard for international activities. In most cases, only state-owned companies, which sometimes enjoy a protected monopoly, have the means for internationalization. Over the past ten years, owing to the slackening of economic growth, the difficulties in the way of internationalization have increased, thereby giving rise to strategies of reinforcement of the acquired position and hindering the emergence of new multinationals. Moreover, as we have seen, the controlling authorities of state-owned enterprises often oppose decisions concerning setting up abroad, especially in the case of countries with limited financial resources.

Nevertheless, a great number of enterprises manage to overcome these obstacles. In fact, in certain cases, they appear to have turned the impediments to their advantage. In this chapter we have tried to prove that private companies can enjoy similar advantages. However, this is only a general assessment; in some cases, the state-owned enterprise is clearly disadvantaged compared to its private counterpart when it tries to multinationalize while in others both have equal opportunities, either because in reality they both profit from the same exorbitant advantages in relation to the normal rules of competition, or because neither is in a specially privileged position compared to the other, or even because these advantages, though different in nature, are well balanced. There are probably other cases where state-owned enterprises are in a favourable position but it is always extremely difficult to produce concrete proofs of special favours, for the arguments can be reversed and pertinent counterexamples are easily available.

But our principal objective is to show in what way state-owned multinationals are different from other multinationals. In the first place, it must be stated that generalizations are not possible: all state-owned enterprises are not in the same situation. Some state-owned enterprises multinationalize more successfully and more extensively than others. While some do so by following methods of private enterprises, others adopt a more original strategy. However, these discrepancies do not seem to depend either on their sector of activity, or on the nature of the State which controls them, or even on the level of the economic development of their country. How, then, can all these differences be explained? More particularly, how can we account for the successful multinationalization of certain state-owned enterprises? We shall see that, in reality, the key factor in the multinationalization of state-owned enterprises is their ability to manage the paradoxical situation of belonging to one state and setting up in another. Not all of them succeed in this venture, but within the same country some succeed better than others. Consequently, their success or their failure is linked more to the ability of their management to develop complex strategies, in which the state-owned character, rather than being a burden, constitutes an additional advantage in the multinationalization process, than to the attitude of their controlling authorities. This is why the entire following chapter will deal with the study of such strategies.

Chapter Five

Managing the Paradox: A Matter of Strategy

INTRODUCTION

In the two preceding chapters we have shown that in most cases the state-owned enterprise which manages to go multinational:

1. succeeds in overcoming the obstacles which are often imposed, directly and indirectly, by its own government;
2. develops in the host countries a strategy comparable with that of private multinationals.

Admittedly, there are countless exceptions. First, in a large number of cases that we analysed, the State in fact helps its state-owned enterprises to go multinational. On the other hand, certain host countries, particularly developing countries, tend to prefer the set-up of a foreign state-owned enterprise to that of a private multinational. However, such examples are relatively isolated. Evidently, for a state-owned enterprise wanting to go multinational, the attachment to the public sector — usually a handicap for multinationalization — must be transformed into an asset. Many state-owned enterprises have succeeded in this venture while others have failed. Such successes or failures cannot always be explained by insurmountable differences in each firm's political, economic or technological environment. In our opinion the real explanation is twofold. In the first place, the strategy implemented by the enterprise, as we will show in this chapter, is an essential factor of success. Secondly, the corporate identity of the firm is also a key element that must be taken into account, as will be discussed in the following chapter.

It is possible to identify three principal strategies which allow the management of state-owned enterprises to succeed in multinationalization.

1. The best strategy consists in fully exploiting all situations where the

national policy and the foreign expansion projects of the enterprise converge.

2. In the event of the market being, or becoming, worldwide, the government must be persuaded that multinationalization is essential for the economic health of the enterprise, and hence that of the country itself.

3. Lastly, in countries with a limited private sector, state-owned enterprises must show that they alone are competent enough to implement a multinationalization policy which is indispensable for the economic balance of the country.

A fourth case remains to be examined, that of the strategy of enterprises which were multinational before being nationalized.

THE CONVERGENCE OF NATIONAL POLICY AND MULTINATIONALIZATION

The imperatives of diplomacy

In Chapter Three we discussed the negative repercussions of the government's foreign policy in the decisions of state-owned enterprises to set up abroad. However, experience has shown that diplomatic relations between governments can lend a helping hand to business, the state-owned enterprises being the primary beneficiaries. Nevertheless, in a difficult economic context, as for example the current economic crisis or the situation of third world countries, strictly diplomatic considerations have to give way to more direct economic motivations. In a certain number of circumstances the multinationalization of state-owned enterprises can appear as a direct consequence, or even as the chosen instrument, of the government's economic policy; this will be the subject of the second part of this section.

International diplomatic relations, though inevitably disrupting the normal economic planning of state-owned enterprises, often prove to be beneficial for their development. The diplomacy of General de Gaulle did not have solely negative consequences for the French enterprises, though it often upset their projects. His *'Vive le Quebec libre'* proclaimed at the townhall in Montreal, and his famous *'La mano en la mano'* declaration of solidarity between France and Mexico during his memorable visit to Latin America, in both cases led to the opening up of these countries to French firms, notably French state-owned enterprises. He was thus directly responsible for the agreements concerning the building of the underground transport systems of Montreal and Mexico City by Sofretu, a subsidiary of RATP, and indirectly for the remarkable expansion of the firm as a consequence of these projects. Though Elf-Aquitaine has cause to complain about the vetos passed against one of its big projects in Libya, it has also recently often benefited from solid government support for its investments abroad, particularly for its important plans in the United States over the last few years. In the immediate postwar period, the international development of the ENI under Enrico Mattei was totally compatible with the Italian government's desire to reestablish itself on the international scene. In the sixties, the ENI in Italy and the ERAP (the predecessor of Elf-Aquitaine) in France were pioneers in signing contracts with oil-producing countries (notably Middle Eastern ones) for the joint exploitation of newly discovered oil fields. This was a deliberate strategy carried out in agreement with their governments, with a view to upsetting the hegemony of the 'Seven Sisters' — the multinationals, for the most part Anglo-American, which dominated the market. In the same way, the Brazilian government was largely responsible for the set-up of Braspetro in Italy, a country with which it maintains especially close diplomatic relations. More generally, the strategy of oil companies, especially state-owned ones, has always been greatly influenced by the dictates of diplomacy. In this connection, we may recall the San José agreement whereby the supply of oil to nine Central American countries is shared by Pemex and Petroleos de Venezuela. The two companies sell their oil at OPEC commercial prices, but at the same time the governments of Mexico and Venezuela grant low-interest loans to these countries in order to cover 30% of their fuel bill.

The international strategy of Kuwait Petroleum Corporation is greatly influenced by the Kuwaiti government; although it primarily aims at strengthening the company's presence on European markets, it also serves the country's long-term financial interests by securing revenues from sources other than oil.

In another context, Hydro-Quebec ventured abroad partly owing to the encouragement of the Quebec government wishing to affirm its independence from the rest of Canada on the international scene. A good example of the link between the imperatives of diplomacy and multinationalization is provided by Mazzolini,[1] to whom a manager of

---

[1] 'Are state-owned enterprises unfair competition?', *California Management Review*, **23**, No. 2, Winter 80.

an important French state-owned enterprise explained: 'France had poor relations with the host country and had no embassy there. So we were encouraged to invest there because this was an opportunity to establish semiofficial, yet unobtrusive, ties with the foreign country, which might be useful to develop new relations with local authorities. . . . This was the only mechanism that enabled us to go international. . . . It should be clear, however, that proceeding in this fashion seriously hinders the pursuit of a profitable expansion strategy overseas.' This is an extreme example of a situation where the first, and most difficult, step towards multinationalization results from exclusively diplomatic motives, economic considerations being totally excluded. Nevertheless, a competent management may always use such a situation as a springboard to further multinationalize the enterprise.

The search for synergy

Apart from 'a-economic' (and even anti-economic) policies, the management of a state-owned enterprise is fortunately able to benefit from existing synergies between the economic policy of its government and the multinationalization strategy of the enterprise. The state-owned enterprise can integrate a wide range of government economic policies in its strategy, notably in the following cases:

— By supporting state-owned enterprises on their domestic market, the government indirectly provides them with the base for foreign expansion.
— State-owned enterprises can play an essential role in the development of important plurinational economic projects.
— The multinationalization of state-owned enterprises is often necessary for the technological independence of the country, a priority for governments of developed nations.
— Third world countries in the process of industrialization rely on their state-owned enterprises for reinforcing their commercial and technological balance.

In all these cases, the State plays an important role in the strategy of the enterprises, which are often the chosen target of criticism for all crusaders against unfair competition. Certain enterprises are merely the instrument of government industrial policy, whereas others are able to skilfully utilize government support to further aims which are identical to those of private multinationals.

1. The concerns of politicians, ministers or members of parliament alike are mostly local and short-term since voters must be made to perceive the positive consequences of government decisions. Such short-term and local concerns are incompatible with the long-term logic of a multinationalization strategy. Nevertheless, placing priority on the resolution of immediate regional, industrial and social issues has sometimes made the development of multinationalization strategies easier for state-owned enterprises. Thus, at the end of the sixties, DSM, which ran the Dutch coal mines, was confronted with decreasing competitiveness and receding markets, seriously jeopardizing employment in the whole Limbourg region. Political and financial support from the Dutch government enabled the enterprise to make a considerable effort to transform its activity by the progressive closing down of coal mines, the setting up of a chemical industry — partly based on organic chemistry but mainly on natural gas from the north of the country — and a complex programme for the retraining of miners. Within a few years, DSM's foundations for international expansion were laid; its healthy financial situation as well as its technological dynamism have permitted the firm to set up in several European countries and in the United States over the last ten years. In 1983, the Swedish company Assi (which produces wood, paper and cardboard and manages about 20 plants in Europe outside Sweden) was granted an increase in capital of two billion crowns from the government, which allowed it to restore its financial equilibrium and to recover its profitability, owing to a reduction in financial costs. Without this aid, the enterprise would have had to envisage disinvestment — probably in its foreign subsidiaries rather than in Sweden, owing to national employment concerns. Above all, it would not have invested abroad as it has been doing since, particularly in the Netherlands. This is only one among the numerous cases where government aid which was in principle intended for regional development indirectly allowed enterprises to start or maintain multinational activities.

2. However, state-owned enterprises are sometimes directly requested by their government to participate in the realization of important bi- or plurinational industrial projects which the government cannot carry out on its own. International organizations such as UNIDO, UNCTAD, etc., underline the importance of such joint ventures,[2] particularly for developing countries. This is the means used by Latin American countries which are trying to establish their economic

---

[2] Purists will object that this is a different case in point. In fact it raises exactly the same problem, namely that of a state investing in a foreign country.

unity, especially in opposition to the United States. In this respect, we have previously mentioned GIOL and YPF, both state-owned Argentine enterprises which have set up joint ventures, the former in Colombia, the latter in Bolivia, with state-owned firms of the host country. In the same way, Brazil and Paraguay have jointly installed an important binational enterprise to build and operate the world's largest dam in Itaipu. In October 1984, when the first turbines were started, the investment it represented amounted to 14.5 billion dollars. Countries in South East Asia have also engaged in cooperation of the same kind. For example, in 1979, PT ASEAN Fertilizer, a chemical plant, was created in Indonesia and production started in 1984. Other similar ventures are projected in Malaysia and in the Philippines. In Africa, Benin and Ghana set up a joint venture — the firm CIMAO — to exploit calcareous deposits in Togo, using the energy supplied by Ghana. CIMAO supplies the Ghanaian cement works with the raw material and these sell part of the finished product to Togo and Benin. The Andean Pact, the Assocation of South East Asian Nations, agreements between African and Middle Eastern countries, agreements between countries bordering on the North Sea to exploit oil and gas, the association between European countries for manufacturing, putting into orbit and operating satellites, etc. — we can cite countless examples of state-owned enterprises which form the ideal instruments for multinational cooperation in the fields of energy, industry and technology, where considerable investments are required.

A closer look at these joint ventures reveals various kinds of government strategy. Sometimes the alliances are concluded on a more or less egalitarian basis between countries which lack sufficient resources for carrying out an important project on their own. Often, however, a more powerful country is in a dominant position *vis-à-vis* weaker neighbouring countries to which it offers support. This is illustrated by Mexico's strategy with regard to the smaller countries of Central America, but similar examples can be found in the policies of Argentina, Brazil, Indonesia and even Ghana, as we have just seen.

These strategies developed by governments apply either to zones defined on a regional basis or to zones of cultural affinities. Thus, Brazil encourages the set-up of its state-owned enterprises in Portuguese-speaking African countries, as seen by the agreement concluded at the end of 1984 between Furnas and the Angolan government for the construction of a large dam. Moreover, the Brazilian state-owned enterprises compete with those of Portugal in this field. Profabril, an engineering company belonging to the

Portuguese industrial group IPE (Investimentos E Participações do Estado), carries out important industrial projects in Angola, Mozambique and Guinea–Bissau — but also has activities in other developing countries in Africa and the Middle East. In the same way, the Spanish state-owned enterprises set up mostly in the Spanish-speaking countries of Central and South America. For example ENASA, a subsidiary of the INI, has plants for the manufacture and assembly of lorries in Chile and Ecuador. These 'affinities' can be more wide-ranging. The Indian state-owned enterprises set up mostly in East Africa (for example RITES), thereby asserting Indian presence and trying to supplant the former British influence in the Middle East (for instance Balmer-Lawrie) and more generally in all countries belonging to the non-aligned movement in which India seeks to play a leading role. On the other hand, Canada tries to emphasize the fact that, being an ex-colony, it cannot be accused of imperialism. Canadian enterprises — especially state-owned firms like Hydro-Quebec or CDC — are able to persuade Central American and African countries that their set-up is a form of cooperation, quite different from the aims of US private multinationals.

3. In all countries, particularly the more developed ones, state-owned enterprises are considered as ideal instruments for national technological development. Today, a technology can only succeed if it becomes worldwide, for two essential reasons. First, in order to prove its quality and its value and therefore to contribute to the technological progress of its country of origin, a technology must compete on open international markets. This was the motive behind the setting up of SGS and Matra in the United States (notably in California) and in Japan, since it is essential for all leading high-technology firms to have a foothold in these two regions. Thus, in the United States, Matra Datavision, a computer aided design company, was formed by Matra (65%) and Renault (35%). This firm aims at establishing itself as one of the leading US enterprises in this field and at capturing eventually a 10% share of the world market, of which the United States alone accounts for 50%. These technological considerations have even led the INI to create a specialized state-owned enterprise ENISA, with the explicit aim of studying and purchasing foreign technologies to be transferred to Spanish companies. Secondly, state-owned enterprises often resort to a constant search for an increasingly sophisticated technology in order to compete with their private counterparts, which tend to take the upper hand as far as prices are concerned. Rather than attempting to descend rapidly along the 'experience' curve, state-owned enterprises rely on their technology to compete, and, because

of the extremely high research and development costs entailed, must aim at world markets. We have defined this strategy as the 'armament model'[3] since it was first utilized in this sector before being extended by a certain number of countries, notably France, to most high-technology industries: aeronautics, radars and satellites, telephone switching equipment, nuclear power stations, data processing, etc. In this model, on the one hand, the high research and development costs are largely financed by the State while on the other hand, owing to exorbitant prices, the customer — especially in the case of a poor country — is accorded preferential loans and different sorts of guarantee by the selling government. The high-technology enterprise helped by the State at all levels is often state-owned, or at least considered as a 'nationalizable' firm, depending on the country and the political climate. The customer country, for its part, often demands the setting up of a local manufacturing unit with a view to saving foreign exchange and preparing the ground for eventual transfers of technology. Such a situation offers the ideal conditions for the multinationalization of the state-owned enterprise. In many cases governments are closely involved in such operations — for example, the contracting of CIT-Alcatel in India was the consequence of President F. Mitterrand's visit to Mrs Indira Gandhi. For the management of state-owned enterprises, the best strategy consists of a judicious mixture of politics and technology.

4. In third world countries in the process of industrialization, the state-owned enterprise not only permits a certain technological independence, but also represents an ideal instrument for reducing the deficit of the balance of payments and, above all, provides the essential means for the economic development of the country. Thus, the 1978 UNIDO report shows that in the ten-year period 1966–1976, the public sector accounted for more than 60% of all industrial investments in India and more than 50% in Venezuela. Certain countries rely mainly on a single important natural resource, as for example Morocco on phosphates. Thus, the OCP plays a crucial role in the country for developing phosphate-producing regions and for obtaining foreign currency, especially since the country has to import coal, gas and oil. As we have shown elsewhere,[4] Brazil and Mexico have adopted a 'tripod model' in which the economy depends on three kinds of enterprise: foreign multinationals, local private enterprises and state-owned enterprises. The latter account for roughly

---

[3] See J. P. Anastassopoulos and P. Dussauge, 'French "savoir-faire" in selling arms: a new way of doing business?', *Long Range Planning*, October 1985.

[4] J. P. Anastassopoulos and G. Blanc, 'Entreprises publiques et développement', *Revue Politiques et Management Public*, No. 1, Winter 1983.

one-third of the annual gross fixed capital formation in these two countries. In all fields, their strategy is compatible with the policy of their governments, despite occasional inevitable differences of opinion. In the preceding chapters, we have shown through various examples that the synergy of the government and state-owned enterprises favours multinationalization. The essential objective, either direct or indirect, is always to contribute to the independence and the economic growth of the country:

— by better marketing domestic natural resources abroad (Pemex in Spain and Vale do Rio Doce in the United States) thereby consolidating exports;
— by developing indigenous technologies according to the following process: (1) purchase of patents for production within the country, (2) development of a specific technology for export, (3) setting up abroad (see Chapter Four for the example of Embraer);
— by improving the situation of the balance of payments through these exports and substitutes for imports (as testified for instance by Brazil's balance of payments in 1984 and 1985).

The role of strategy

It must be remembered that it is not always easy to exploit the convergence of the state-owned character of the enterprise and government policy with a view to multinationalization. Some enterprises, though placed in similar circumstances, are far less successful than others. Given the specific nature of each individual case, comparisons are difficult to make. However, when comparisons are possible, the results are often surprising. Thus, among the French 'Sofre' companies (which are subsidiaries of public utilities aimed at exporting the knowhow of their parent companies), some have prospered considerably on an international scale while others have been less successful. Though initially Sofretu and Sofrerail possessed comparable assets, the latter has far outdistanced the former in its operations abroad. How can the success of RITES be explained if we consider the technological level of the Indian railways? Why have the British National Coal Board and its French counterpart Charbonnages de France taken so long before following, albeit timidly, the example of DSM? Why has British Leyland remained mostly insular whereas Renault has become truly multinational?

In each of these cases, the political and economic conditions vary little from one enterprise to another. The difference lies firstly in the vision and strategic objectives of the management teams and secondly, as we will see in Chapter Six, in the organizational culture — the corporate identity, which is at once a factor and a consequence of the strategic behaviour of the management. Thus, certain enterprises have been able to abandon their native traditions and adapt themselves to foreign countries, using their state-owned nature according to the circumstances. The example of Sofretu can be cited in this respect; in the United States and Singapore it is considered as a private company, whereas in Algeria and in Malaysia it is seen as a state-owned enterprise. The management and the executives must practise a chameleon-like strategy, adapting their rhetoric, their mode of functioning and their daily attitudes to the particular environment. However, some state-owned enterprises, though fully benefiting from government support, are unsuccessful in implementing a multinationalization strategy, whereas others, on the contrary, are obliged to prove to their government that multinationalization would serve the general interest before being able to set up abroad. This will be the subject of the second section of this chapter.

WORLDWIDE MARKETS VS DOMESTIC PRIORITIES

A large number of industrial and commercial state-owned enterprises which sell their products in a highly competitive market appear far removed from the control of the State. The researcher studying their diversification and internationalization strategies is generally more welcome than one who questions them about their subjection to the government. 'We are no different from other enterprises' is their stock reply. In general, these enterprises can skilfully exploit, when necessary, the synergy of the government policy and their own strategy, as we have seen in the first section of this chapter. Functioning like private enterprises, in a market where most of their rivals are private multinationals, they tend to follow strategies of multinationalization to the utmost, according to the dictates of entrepreneurial logic. Governments do not often see eye to eye in this respect; the enterprises must do their best to persuade them, sometimes even exerting pressure. In order to do so, state-owned enterprises must abandon their traditional entrepreneurial arguments, trying instead to convince the government and high-ranking civil servants, members of parliament, trade unions and finally the general public that their multinationalization contributes to the interest of the nation. We will examine three cases in turn, each of which poses increasingly difficult problems of justification for the state-owned enterprises:

— The domestic market of certain developed countries is too limited (Scandinavian countries, the Benelux countries, Austria, etc.) In order to attain economic efficiency, it is necessary to export, but exporting in favourable conditions requires a set-up abroad.
— Today, owing to their specific characteristics, some industries can only be developed on a worldwide scale. This is the case with the automobile and the aeronautics sector, where even the United States does not have an adequate domestic market.
— In a number of sectors, the only way to remain competitive is to exploit the international cost differentials (energy, raw materials, labour).

The above arguments are typical of private companies. The management of state-owned enterprises like General Motors in the United States must prove that what is good for their enterprise is also good for their country.

Limited domestic markets

Limited domestic markets tend to induce state-owned enterprises to go multinational. In Austria, the largest enterprises have been under state control since 1946 (after having been directly controlled by the Nazi regime for many years) without the populist or socialist governments in power in turn bringing any structural changes; today, of the nine largest Austrian industrial enterprises, five are totally state-owned, one is under major control of the State, two others are state-controlled through nationalized banks and only one is privately owned. It was logical for a major enterprise in the metallurgical industry like Voest-Alpine to try to export in order to achieve the required economies of scale. Later, to optimize the use of the advanced technologies it had developed, Voest-Alpine set up abroad; it now owns plants in Virginia and a steel-making complex in Louisiana. In the United States, its turnover is 220 million dollars; however, its direct exports from Austria which are marketed by its trading company in the United States amount to 500 million dollars. The case of Norway is even more revealing, since the public sector roughly represents 40% of the industrial investment compared to less than 20% fifteen years ago, before the North Sea boom. In this context, Statoil (in the oil sector) and Norsk Jernverk (iron and steel industry) have not yet set up abroad. In contrast, Norsk-Hydro, despite the 51% equity participation of the Norwegian government, behaves like a standard multinational; its controls subsidiaries all over the world including Vinatex, the third British PVC producer, Norsk-Hydro Alu — which manufactures aluminium automobile parts in the United States — bauxite mines in Brazil, a large petrochemical plant in Qatar, and sells its technology throughout the world. In the same way ASV, which was taken over from Alcan by the Norwegian government, manufactures primary aluminium and transformed products not only in Norway but also in Sweden and Denmark. Even smaller state-owned firms like Konsberg Vapenfabrik (military equipment) or Sydvaranger (iron and steel) control industrial subsidiaries abroad, the former in Great Britain and the latter in West Germany. Other Scandinavian state-owned enterprises like Assi (Sweden) and Valmet (a Finnish enterprise) have followed the same line of development. More generally, firms like Cockerill (a Belgian company) or DSM (the Netherlands) as well as many other state-owned enterprises in a Europe which, though technically advanced, remains fragmented both politically and economically, have multinationalized because of their limited domestic markets. Certain state-owned enterprises like Keppel Shipyard and Taiwanese Fertilizer (Taiwan), originating from small countries in the process of industrialization, could also be included in the preceding group of firms.

However, the process followed by these enterprises is not necessarily 'logical' or 'natural'. Many state-owned enterprises placed in comparable circumstances have contented themselves with exporting without really envisaging setting up abroad — notwithstanding the salutary effect of such a decision for the company. For example in the sector of paper, Assi, which is well integrated in downstream activities, sets up plants in Western Europe, the 'natural' market for Sweden. Portucel (a Portuguese firm), on the other hand, despite its advanced technology and the fact that it has to import most of its raw material, contents itself with exporting paper pulp in large quantities. In the same way Donohue (which is controlled by the province of Quebec) produces newsprint in Canada but sells most of it to the United States. In the field of metals, as we have seen, Voest-Alpine has set up industrial plants abroad following the example of its main private German competitor Mannesman. In contrast, LKAB, a Swedish state-owned enterprise of the same sector, is confined to exporting a sizeable part of its production. Therefore it appears that Assi and Voest-Alpine on the one hand, and Portucel, Donohue and LKAB on the other, though placed in similar economic and technical conditions, have adopted radically different strategic options. Furthermore, Assi and LKAB find themselves in identical political situations. The Swedish government (like the Norwegian and the Austrian governments) tries to give its state-owned enterprises great leeway. Indeed, even the governments of Portugal and Quebec would probably approve a well-conceived project of international expansion for their state-owned enterprises. Thus, although multinationalization requires particular economic and political conditions, these alone are not sufficient. The pressure for foreign expansion must originate in the enterprise and its management, even in countries where the domestic market is evidently too small to allow an adequate industrial development.

Worldwide industries

In a certain number of sectors, notably automobiles and aeronautics — but also in those of computers, electronics, the iron and steel industry, nuclear power, etc. — it is very difficult for an enterprise to survive if it does not have a worldwide scope or aims at a specific segment, as for example BMW or Embraer (even in this case, the enterprise can hardly remain confined to its domestic market). Unless the survival of the enterprise is ensured by increasing subsidies, which may eventually become politically intolerable, especially since in such industries the enterprise is not a public utility, the state-owned firm is obliged to go multinational. Renault, Aérospatiale, SGS, Finsider and Salzgitter as well as their private counterparts followed this line. Eurodif and Airbus were conceived as multinationals from the very beginning. In all these sectors, it seems difficult to amortize the burden of technological investments in only one country, whatever its economic potential. On the other hand, it is almost impossible for an enterprise to depend solely on exports owing to the protectionism of governments, which in most cases require that the products sold to the country be partly locally manufactured, especially in the case of government contracts and advanced technologies. Thus, in the example of Airbus, the consortium is aimed at associating the knowhow of all participating enterprises but its main objective is to ensure access to the market of each member country. Nevertheless, some state-owned enterprises in the industries considered to be 'worldwide' are much less multinational than others. SGS became truly multinational only recently, thanks to the dynamism of its new chairman. Among the major European state-owned holding companies, IRI, INI, OIAG, Statsforetag, there are a great number of enterprises belonging to sectors termed 'multinational' (electronics, the iron and steel industry, heavy mechanical engineering industries, etc.) which are not multinational firms. The most flagrant examples, however, are those of British companies. Analysis of the objectives of the state-owned enterprises, as defined in the Acts of

Parliament which, since the end of the Second World War, have governed their creation, shows that it is practically impossible for them to go multinational. Moreover, when British Leyland in 1974 and British Aerospace in 1977 were nationalized, most of their foreign industrial assets were sold. British Leyland sold its plants in Italy, Belgium and Spain. Only its Land Rover division has maintained a few assembling plants in Africa and still controls L. R. Santana in Spain. The management of British Leyland considers that the Austin Rover subsidiary, though limited to the domestic market, may become profitable if its production process is made more flexible and if its agreement with Honda proves to be successful. In the same way, when it was created in 1977, British Aerospace sold its foreign plants, notably Hawker Siddeley Canada, retaining only a small electronic components factory in Australia. Will the gradual privatization undertaken since 1981 favour multinationalization? In any case, in this field it is increasingly difficult to export without accepting that a significant part of the product be manufactured abroad; this has led British Aerospace to set up joint ventures especially with French (Matra), Finnish (Valmet), Swiss and Egyptian firms. In the same way in France, the iron and steel producing enterprises Usinor and Sacilor, which have always exported more than one-third of their production and have only recently been nationalized, never did set up significantly abroad. On the other hand, state-owned enterprises in different European countries such as Finsider and Salzgitter have successfully ventured abroad. Lastly, it is noteworthy that within the same sector relatively small state-owned enterprises (as in the case of Sydvaranger cited above) have managed to go multinational. In the coming years, it would not be surprising to see an enterprise like SEAT[5] (the Spanish car manufacturer) multinationalize successfully owing to its newly obtained independence from Fiat as well as its dynamic management.

Thus, it is evident that even in the case of enterprises belonging to an 'international' sector, multinationalization is not always easy to achieve. The management has to draw up a sound strategy and defend it against the adverse criticism of the State, the unions and even public opinion. State intervention is much greater in certain European countries like Austria, Italy, France and Spain (and even more so, as we have seen, in countries in the course of industrialization) than in Northern European nations like Norway, Sweden, the Netherlands and West Germany. In Sweden for example, despite the large number of major state-owned enterprises, the controlling authority in the Ministry of

---

[5] In fact SEAT was taken over in 1986 by the Volkswagen group and was thus integrated in a multinational automobile firm.

Industry comprises only a seven-member team. An important official declared: 'All decisions for setting up abroad are taken solely by the management of the enterprise concerned without any intervention on our part. I read in the newspaper that one of the enterprises has just bought a British company — which is perfectly normal. Unions as well as local politicians try to influence us but such issues are not our concern. They should discuss the matter with the management of the enterprise.' According to the management of Assi, it is not their firm's state-owned character but rather its poorer financial situation which explains why its international expansion has been less rapid than that of its private counterparts like Swedish Cellulose. 'Setting up abroad only raises problems if we are obliged to call upon the State for financial support. In fact, our inability to appeal to the stock market is a far greater handicap than state ownership.'

However, in other European countries the situation is more complex. Ministers and high-ranking civil servants expect to be consulted on all decisions concerning foreign expansion, and the unions claiming to defend local employment exert a far greater pressure. In such cases, the competence and the negotiating ability of the management becomes crucial. Not all chief executives have the skill of a Chalandon (Elf-Aquitaine), a Pistorio (SGS) or an Apfalter (Voest-Alpine). Not only must the government be persuaded that multinationalization is necessary for international competitiveness, but the unions and the general public must be convinced that a set-up abroad will eventually lead to the creation of jobs in the home country. This is seen in the following text taken from the 1984 report on Renault's activities in the United States and entitled significantly: 'American activities of French plants'.

The exports of the Renault group (in the automobile branch) from France to North America (including Mexico) went up from 2 billion francs in 1981 to 4 billion francs in 1983. The 1983 exports to the United States alone amounted to 3.5 billion francs. These figures correspond practically to a net balance since the imports from the United States (the Jeep range) are negligible.

This spectacular growth results in a significant boost for production and in a marked increase in employment in Renault's French plants as well as in its subsidiaries and subcontractors. Though the Alliance and Encore models are manufactured in a 70% proportion in the United States, for each car, 300 parts are sent from France, including engines and gear boxes. Moreover, the Maubeuge, Sandouville and Flins factories in France assemble built-up vehicles (Renault Fuego, Renault 18 i 'Sportwagon' and Renault 5 'Le Car') which are exported to the United States and Canada. In all, in 1983, American Motors supplied work for 8500 workers in France: 3200 in the Renault plants

(2000 for the 'Alliance' and the 'Encore', 1200 for 'built-up' vehicles),
5300 in the supplying enterprises and Renault's subsidiaries (3500 for
the Alliance and the Encore, 1800 for 'built-up' vehicles).

However, this kind of detailed argument is not always possible. Very
often the strategies of multinationals are far removed from the aim of
national interest which, in principle, is the justification for state ownership. The contradiction is even more flagrant when these state-owned
enterprises try, through multinationalization, to profit from cheaper
raw material and labour compared to those of their country of origin.

The search for cheaper factors of production

As we have previously discussed in the theoretical section in Chapter
Two, the search on the one hand for cheaper sources of supply and on
the other for lower labour costs are the two main motives behind the
multinationalization of private companies as well as of state-owned
enterprises in developed countries. In these cases the competitive
dynamics is the sole factor which determines this type of decision; the
entrepreneurial dimension predominates over the state-owned
character and the enterprises are thus indistinguishable from other
multinationals.

For example in the seventies, the German group VIAG (through its
subsidiary SKW) set up in North America in search of cheaper electricity. It aimed at reimporting in Germany iron alloys manufactured
in the United States and Canada. In fact, VIAG was soon obliged to
change its strategy, since competitive products from Scandinavia were
supplied to Germany at a lower price than those from North America.
Faced with this problem, instead of disinvesting, SKW, concentrated
on making its investments profitable on the Canadian, US and Japanese
markets. For products like iron alloys where low prices constitute the
key factor for success, the managing director of SKW in Canada
adopted the strategic principles proposed by the Japanese. 'A third
should be produced in the country (in order to master the technology
and be able to improve it), another third should be bought on the
international market (in order to benefit from low prices at the right
time) and lastly, a third should be produced in the country where the
product is sold (in order to comply with nationalistic demands).' There
are countless examples of state-owned enterprises which set up abroad
in regions where supplies are cheapest. All the major oil companies,
from Elf-Aquitaine to Petrobras, have also installed refineries and even,
in certain cases, petrochemical plants (Norsk-Hydro in Qatar) in oil-

producing countries. The same tendency is observed in enterprises in the sector of minerals. Thus, Cogéma, a subsidiary of the French CEA, has set up uranium processing plants in Niger, Gabon and Canada. Péchiney sold the aluminium activities of its American subsidiary Howmet since it considered the rise of energy costs in the United States to be unprofitable. Instead, it invested in Canada and in Australia without meeting any opposition from the French government.

For a state-owned enterprise, the strategy of setting up abroad in order to exploit low labour costs is far more paradoxical. This was the strategy adopted by Renault, perhaps for unavoidable reasons in the context of the cut-throat competition which it had to face. FASA, Renault's Spanish subsidiary which has always reexported a large part of its production to France and other countries, for long served this purpose. The same motive impelled Renault to set up a plant for the manufacture of engines in the north of Mexico with the major portion of the production being exported to the United States. A similar strategy is also prevalent in the electronics industry, as testified by the subsidiaries of SGS set up in Malta and in Singapore. The labour costs for assembling electronic components have led most multinationals in this sector to build plants in South East Asian countries. However, it is somewhat surprising to see a state-owned Italian enterprise like SGS set up a second factory in Singapore while at the same time it has laid off part of its staff in its Catania (Sicily) factory, using the Italian system of the 'Cassa Integrazione'.

The extent of the paradox is underlined by the fact that most of the European state-owned multinationals tend to think on the same lines as Renault and SGS. When labour costs and social security contributions rise steeply, companies invest elsewhere. This reasoning is more typical of private multinationals. The state-owned character is totally ignored and in the end the enterprises seem to consider that being state or privately owned is merely an accident of history.

THE USE OF SKILLS

In the course of our research we observed one recurring factor: all state-owned enterprises which, owing to a sound economic strategy and a rigorous internal management, achieved good financial and/or technological resuls, invariably exploited their success to obtain a greater freedom of action with respect to government policy and the bureaucratic constraints of the controlling authorities. In general, they use this freedom to implement a policy which is more entrepreneurial and less state-owned in nature, in the context of a country with a free market ideology. Internationalization, together with diversification, represents a line of development which can give an impetus to the enterprise without encountering any check from the government; in contrast, in developing countries following free market principles, the most efficient enterprise is considered as the best qualified for venturing abroad. However, if the enterprise incurs losses, is no longer self-financing or carries out non-profitable operations, it loses its acquired liberty of action and has to restrain its multinationalization schemes.

This is true of Latin American companies (Petrobras or Giol) as well as Asian ones (Keppel Shipyard or Balmer-Lawrie). In these countries, few private enterprises possess the managerial capacities necessary for multinationalization.[6] Thus the field is left clear for the best managed state-owned enterprises, especially since the latter can often draw on a more extensive financial and human base. In Brazil, the comparison made in 1984 by the '*Exame*' *Review* between the country's 50 largest state-owned enterprises and the 500 top private companies shows that:

— the turnover of the 50 state-owned enterprises together amounts to almost half of the total turnover of the 500 private companies;
— the total profits earned by the 50 state-owned firms are comparable to those of 500 private companies;
— total assets of the 50 state-owned enterprises are 75% greater than the total assets of the 500 private companies;
— between 1973 and 1983 the participation of state-owned enterprises in the country's economy has increased twofold.

Thus it is not surprising to see that among the world's true or potential state-owned multinationals, Brazilian enterprises are in a favourable position. We have already mentioned the foreign investments of Petrobras, Vale do Rio Doce and Embraer. In the same way we can cite the technology transfer operations carried out for example by Eletrobras and Siderbras. As we have shown elsewhere,[7] in Mexico also, the position occupied by state-owned enterprises in the country's economy is considerable. The Mexican government uses Pemex as the spearhead of its strategy of support to small Central American countries, but also relies on Altos Hornos de Mexico for example, which owns steelworks in Honduras.

---

[6] See S. Lall, *The New Multinationals: The Spread of Third World Enterprises*, John Wiley & Sons, Chichester, 1983, and L. T. Wells, *Third World Multinationals, the Rise of Foreign Investment from Developing Countries*, MIT Press, Cambridge, 1983.

[7] J. P. Anastassopoulos and G. Blanc, 'Enterprises publiques et développement', *Revue Politiques et Management Public*, No. 1, Winter 1983.

In order to prepare the ground for multinationalization, the state-owned firms of developing countries deploy their managerial and technical skills in their operations abroad. On the other hand, in developed countries, the state-owned enterprises, even those which are invested with the crucial role of a public service, make a profitable use of their technological competence by exporting their engineering industry and hence going multinational. As previously mentioned, the French 'Sofre' enterprises were created with this aim in view, most of them with successful results. The British state-owned firms, though not encouraged by their government — even the Labour government which set them up — to go international, have also developed engineering activities overseas. Today, these industries are coordinated and promoted by an organization which is common to the entire public sector, the Nationalized Industries Overseas Group (NIOG), formed by the representatives of the 20 British state-owned groups (British Airports, British Railways, British Steel, London Transport, etc.). The members of NIOG earn 200 million pounds in consulting fees and nine billion pounds in exports. The essential role of this group is to allow each member enterprise to be informed of the foreign projects of the other participating firms, in order to enable them to profit mutually from the fallout of such operations. However, unlike the French 'Sofre' companies, the subsidiaries of British state-owned enterprises which export their engineering capacities have an extremely limited permanent staff and operate with the personnel of their parent company. For example, Placon Ltd, a subsidiary of the Port of London Authority, only has three permanent executives, despite the fact that it has started projects in at least twelve different countries.

More generally, it is noticeable that all developed countries and all countries considered to be in the process of industrialization export the technological skills developed by their public utilities (electricity, gas, transport, etc.). On the international market of engineering industries, the competitors are the governments concealed behind either their state or privately owned enterprises; their principal objective is to sell national skills abroad in order to promote exports (notably capital goods) to foreign countries.

THE NATIONALIZATION OF FRENCH MULTINATIONALS

In 1982, following the victory of the Left in France, a certain number of French multinationals were nationalized. This resulted in a unique situation: for the first time, enterprises which were already multinational were nationalized. It is interesting to examine how far nationalization entailed changes in the multinational strategy of the enterprises, notably for the five big industrial firms concerned: Rhône-Poulenc, Péchiney, Thomson, CGE and Saint-Gobain. For several of these firms however state ownership may only have been a provisional situation since Saint-Gobain was privatized in 1986 and CGE in 1987, following the return to power of a right-wing coalition which intends to privatize all the firms nationalized in 1982 — as well as other state-owned companies.

Both the government and the management of the enterprises asserted that nationalization would not lead to disinvestment abroad. Some company heads even made trips abroad — as for example M. Gandois, then head of Rhône-Poulenc, who went to Brazil in 1982 — in order to reassure foreign subsidiaries as well as the economic authorities of host countries. Upon assuming charge of the Ministry of Industry in 1984, Edith Cresson (who was also Minister of Foreign Trade) declared that nationalized firms should continue to set up abroad: she was in fact conforming to the policy adopted by the Socialist government. It must be recalled that one of the most important investments ever financed by a state-owned enterprise abroad was the 14 billion francs acquisition of Texas Gulf by Elf-Aquitaine in the United States following the victory of François Mitterrand in the 1981 elections, whereas a similar purchase, that of US Kerr McGee, had been opposed by President Giscard d'Estaing when he was in power. By the end of 1984, it was clear in French economic circles that Saint-Gobain and CGE wished to acquire sizeable industrial facilities abroad, preferably in the United States, without this project meeting objections from the shareholder-state.

Since 1982, the newly nationalized enterprises have undertaken a number of important strategic operations. Saint-Gobain, for example, has abandoned its activities in electronics, CGE and Thomson have concluded an agreement in the telephone sector, Péchiney has reorganized its industrial activities. However, these operations — which journalists have called the 'Great Monopoly' — have not affected the extent of multinationalization of the enterprises concerned. On the contrary, it can be argued that the restructuring, which was accompanied by very generous government financial aid — on an average, 12 or 13 billion francs per year for all the newly nationalized industries, that is to say far more than the capital obtained from private shareholders in former times — enabled a certain number of the new nationalized companies to consolidate and extend their activities abroad.

For example, the agreement between Thomson and CGE would have been almost impossible prior to nationalization. This agreement was concluded, with the blessing of the Minister of Industry, between the heads of the two companies, who acted with total freedom. The CIT-Alcatel branch of the CGE group took over Thomson's entire telephone activities. CIT now has a complete range of equipment without any duplications, owing to the suppression of one of Thomson's low-grade products and one of CGE's high-grade equipments. Following its nationalization, geographically CGE spread out more widely than in the past and went on to take over the entire telecommunications activities of ITT in 1986, thus becoming the second largest telecommunications firm in the world after AT & T. In 1985, Thomson bought the US firm Mostek in a major move to develop its semiconductor division, and in 1987 merged this division with SGS, the Italian semiconductor multi-national, thus creating the second largest group in Europe in this field, after Philips.

On the whole, a careful examination of post-1982 developments indicates that the managements of the newly nationalized firms have been able to exploit the situation to their advantage, benefiting from state aid while successfully avoiding excessive constraints. Thus, after it was nationalized, Péchiney compelled EDF to lower its electricity rates. In the same way, Rhône-Poulenc was able to abandon the low-grade products of its textile range, which largely contributed to its deficit, as well as its fertilizer activities. Moreover, Rhône-Poulenc is now better placed for achieving the coordination of its own activities with that of its subsidiary May and Baker, which operates essentially in the United Kingdom and in Commonwealth countries, notably India and Canada. However, the situation varies from one enterprise to another. Thus, Thomson obtained from the government a large grant in compensation for setting up a plant in Maxeville (France) where jobs were desperately needed.

No such compensation was given, on the other hand, to Saint-Gobain when it was compelled to withdraw from the sector of electronics against the wishes of its management, who seemed to enjoy less freedom of action than that of Thomson. The autonomy of nationalized industries seems to depend on the way the management of each enterprise conducts its relations with members of the government and high-ranking civil servants. The arguments developed in the first three sections of this chapter are also applicable to the management of enterprises in this category. In other words, their success depends on their ability to:

— exploit situations where the government's policy and the multination-alization plans of the enterprise converge — as for example in the context of aid to developing countries or of pro-European policies;

— prove that, in the long run, certain investments abroad will have a positive impact on the French economy, and that what is good for the enterprises is also good for France. For example, if Matra, Thomson or CIT-Alcatel wish to retain their place in the techno-logical race, it is essential that they invest in the United States;
— appear as national champions, who bring foreign exchange to France — as borne out by Table 5.1, which was drawn up by the Banque de France.

Table 5.1   *French balance of payments (billion francs).*

	Exports	Imports	Balance
1982			
Nationalized sector	140	111	29
French economy	621	711	−90
1983			
Nationalized sector	152	115	37
French economy	682	756	−74

Table 5.1 confirms the November 1984 report of the Haut Conseil du Sector Public (Public Sector Council), which showed that, between 1982 and 1983, the French nationalized sector was responsible for 45% of the reduction in the country's trade deficit. The management there-fore need only prove that investments abroad eventually result in a positive trade balance.

THE STRATEGIC AUTONOMY OF THE STATE-OWNED ENTERPRISE

The decision-making abilities of the management of state-owned enter-prises are of crucial importance in all multinationalization issues. We have seen that despite political, economic and even technological factors which encourage multinationalization, the situation varies considerably from one enterprise to another, depending on the manage-ment's ability to exploit the paradoxical situation of an enterprise which is also state-owned.

Some gifted writers have elaborated rational theories to explain the existence of enterprises which are simultaneously multinational and state-owned — a situation which at first glance often seems to be incongruous. For some, the explanation is to be found in the political leanings of the country of origin; a country subscribing to a free market ideology allows its state-owned enterprises, regarded as mere accidents of history, to operate like private companies, whereas on the other hand, an interventionist government considers such enterprises simply as instruments for implementing its national policy. However, the policy of the enterprise does not change overnight with a change of government, and ideology is often at odds with strategic operations already launched by the enterprises. For other theoreticians the explanation is economic and technological; certain activities must be carried out on a worldwide scale whereas for others internationalization is not necessary. Unfortunately, our study of individual cases showed that there are as many examples as counter examples. Admittedly, ideology and economic considerations are of great importance, but they alone, even when taken together, cannot be decisive. The state-owned enterprise is always allowed a certain leeway, which enables it to make its strategic choices. A large number (but certainly not all) of them have been able to implement a strategy of multinationalization, some by going along with the predominating tendencies of the government, others by placing themselves in opposition to the prevailing ideology. We contend that the explanation for successful multinationalization is probably to be found within the enterprise, in its corporate identity, rather than in the ideology of the government or in certain natural laws governing the sector of activity. The following chapter will deal with the influence of a firm's corporate identity on its ability to go multinational.

Chapter Six

From State-Owned to Multinational: The Ways of Corporate Identity

INTRODUCTION

In the preceding chapters we have analysed all the factors which apparently condition the multinationalization process of state-owned enterprises. This led us to examine what kind of strategic decisions were likely to enable such enterprises to overcome some of the major obstacles they meet in the course of their foreign expansion. The question we shall try to answer here can be phrased as follows: apart from the objective determinants in their economic environment — notably the policy of the controlling authorities and the characteristics of the sector of activity — which hinder, or, on the contrary, favour their line of action, why do certain enterprises seem to succeed better than others in really going multinational? Indeed, in the examples of state-owned enterprises we have examined, it appears that in situations which *a priori* are comparable, some enterprises resolutely embark on the way of multinationalization and manage to surmount the obstacles discussed above; others, in contrast, do not even envisage an international development, or abandon the idea as soon as they meet the first difficulty. Why is Sofretu, the subsidiary of the RATP, much more successful than Sofrerail, its counterpart with respect to the SNCF. Why has Renault become a true multinational, while British Leyland has remained insular? Why does Keppel Shipyard develop its set-ups abroad, whereas Howaldwerke confines its activities to Germany, its country of origin? Explanations based on strategic factors, notably the sector of activity and the policy of the owner-state, are not entirely satisfactory.

At this point, the question arises whether in the specific culture of each enterprise, in its own history, in the collective image shared by the staff, there are certain elements which either favour the multinationalization process, by some kind of internal pressure, or, on the contrary, prevent the enterprise from expanding abroad. The answer to this question can only be found within the enterprises themselves, in their 'corporate identity', which appears to be an additional explanatory factor for their propensity to multinationalize.

CORPORATE IDENTITY

The impact of the corporate identity of a state-owned enterprise on its multinationalization process is only one aspect of a much broader issue, namely the impact of the corporate identity of a firm (whether state or privately owned) on any strategy it chooses to implement. Managers, as well as business management academics, are well aware that even the best strategies do not necessarily lead to success, and that on the other hand certain firms seem to be successful without even clearly formulating a sound strategy. In fact, the corporate identity of a firm determines the way it operates as well as the forms of its development. The analysis of corporate identity will therefore provide further explanations for the success or failure of a firm's specific strategic manoeuvres.

Definition

The corporate identity of an enterprise — or of any organization — is the foundation of both its specificity and its cohesion. Corporate identity is what makes any enterprise different from others, and unique; at the same time all the individuals working in the enterprise adhere to such identity and unite in the pursuit of a common goal.

Corporate identity, which some authors, notably in the United States, call 'corporate culture' or 'organizational culture', can be defined as a collective image which comprises three main aspects:

— an image of the enterprise shared by all those working in it;
— the perception of the required qualities for succeeding within the enterprise;
— the perception of the distribution of power, which includes the internal power structure as well as the external sources of power to which the enterprise is subjected.

These concepts, which may seem extremely abstract at first sight, permit a better description and analysis of certain phenomena which are usually perceived in a purely intuitive way. The image that any employee has of his enterprise distinguishes it fundamentally from any other organization. For a particular enterprise, all these individual images are similar enough to allow the existence of a collective image. Such images make all employees perceive their enterprise as either 'powerful' or 'vulnerable', 'benevolent' and 'protective' or, on the contrary, as 'menacing', etc. A well-known example is that of IBM, in which all employees perceive the firm as powerful, as the 'best' in its field, as capable of succeeding in all ventures, as immune to any threat of competition. The perceived power of the firm is legitimized by the image of excellence shared by all its employees: 'We are the leaders because we are the best'.

The employees of a firm also share a common perception of the ideal qualities required to succeed within the enterprise. It is quite common to hear top managers assert: 'Our company needs people with this or that particular quality', or 'Only such and such kind of people can reach the top in our enterprise'. One firm will only hire 'ambitious and enterprising' executives, while another will reject 'unscrupulous adventurers' and prefer 'poised and organized' people who would be considered as 'bureaucrats' in the former. At Nestlé, a perfect executive must be fluent in at least five or six languages and be willing to travel throughout the world if the interests of the company are at stake. At Peugeot and Michelin, executives must above all be trustworthy, observe the law of silence to which these enterprises are deeply attached and furthermore must be irreproachable in their social behaviour.

Lastly, in all enterprises a shared perception of the distribution of power prevails, which has been described elsewhere[1] as the 'power chart' (*carte de pouvoir*). In firms like Procter and Gamble or General Foods, the marketing department holds most of the power; moreover, most of the top executives are the product of this department. At General Motors the financial department is in the dominant position, whereas at Dassault such a position is occupied by the technical division. The 'power chart' also includes the perception of the external sources of power to which the enterprise is subjected; the real power can be perceived as lying in the hands of an influential group of shareholders, or of a dominant supplier or customer, or even of the State. At Dassault, according to the employees, the real power was held by Marcel Dassault, the retired founder of the firm, who no longer had any official position.

All the components of corporate identity, which we deliberately cari-

---

[1] See J. P. Anastassopoulos, G. Blanc, J. P. Nioche and B. Ramanantsoa, *Pour une Nouvelle Politique d'Entreprise*, PUF, 1985.

catured in the above examples, exert considerable influence on the functioning and development of the enterprises. Though not easily apprehended, the corporate identity of a firm may be revealed by what some authors have called the 'symbolic creations' emerging from the organization; these symbolic creations reveal the main characteristics of the corporate identity. They result from the similarity in the behaviour and the lines of thought that prevail inside the enterprise and can be divided into myths, rituals and taboos.[2]

The myths are related to the history of the enterprise, to its days of glory, and depict these in an idealized way. The myth of Apple Computers' creation by the two Steves — Steve Jobs and Steve Wozniak — is particularly famous; they are said to have developed the prototype of their personal computer in their home basement near San Francisco and, although competing with the giant IBM, to have made their enterprise one of the major industrial successes of recent years (over one billion dollar turnover in 1983 and a 25% share of the world market in personal computers). In all enterprises there is a similar rewriting of history which is revealing of the way in which the enterprise is perceived by the people working in it.

Rituals constitute a convergent series of codes which determine the behaviour of individuals inside the enterprise. The way of dressing, working habits and other shared customs are elements of such rituals; employees express their sense of belonging to the enterprise by observing the prevailing rituals. For example, in some enterprises strict dark suits are the implicit rule, in others, executives are expected to give up part of their holiday, in one in particular — to be specific, IBM — all executives are required to praise the merits of their company in their social life.

Lastly, taboos concern painful subjects or events which are never referred to as they are not in accordance with the shared image of the enterprise. Strategic errors and failures often become taboos which are never alluded to within the enterprise.

The focalization of corporate identity

After having defined the concept of corporate identity more precisely and specified what its main components are and how it can be analysed, we must now explain what determines its particular nature and how it is structured.

---

[2] See footnote 1.

J. P. Larçon and R. Reitter[3] have shown that the corporate identity of a firm is partly determined by a number of political factors:

— the characteristics of the controlling authorities (shareholders, parent company, banks, etc.) and the objectives these assign to the firm, as well as the demands they make;
— the personality of company heads and top executives;
— the aims pursued by the firm and the strategy it chooses to implement.

A firm's corporate identity is also determined by structural factors such as the distribution of power, the internal organizational structure, rules, procedures and management systems.

Moreover, several empirical studies[4] have proved that a firm's corporate identity focalizes on a central element, which may be either:

— a product or an industry on which the 'business' of the firm, as well as the trade or skill of those working in it, is based; or
— a behaviour pattern which is an essential reference for the firm and to which the employees conform; or
— a 'charismatic leader' or a managing team who mobilizes the enterprise.

The nature of the object on which the corporate identity of a firm focalizes is an essential variable of its development. It has a considerable influence on the strategies the firm will or will not be able to implement successfully. Thus, for example, if the corporate identity focalizes on the product the firm manufactures and sells, all diversification strategies must be conducted cautiously as, in order to be successful, they require a change in the existing corporate identity. In the case of such a change not being achieved, a diversification move would be considered as betraying what constitutes the essence of the firm and would therefore, consciously or unconsciously, be rejected or even sabotaged by the personnel.

In a firm whose corporate identity focalizes on a bureaucratic behaviour pattern, that is to say whose functioning is based on an elaborate code of precise and strict rules and procedures, all modifications of strategy requiring creativity and initiative on the part of the employees

---

[3] J. P. Larçon and R. Reitter, *Structures de Pouvoir et Identité de l'Entreprise*, Nathan, 1979.
[4] See B. Ramanantsoa and C. Hoffstetter, 'La maîtrise de l'identité par la gestion du processus de focalisation, *Direction et Gestion*, no. 4, 1981.

would inevitably fail unless the organizational culture changed simultaneously.

An enterprise whose corporate identity focalizes on a 'charismatic leader' is *a priori* able to undergo varied and rapid strategic changes insofar as they are initiated and conducted by the leader. Such an enterprise may, on the other hand, meet serious problems when changes of leadership take place, if these are not planned carefully and long in advance.

In the case of state-owned enterprises, their 'state-owned' character — though having a variable impact and taking on diverse forms — is evidently one of the essential elements of their corporate identity; the precise nature of this 'public' corporate identity, and especially the object on which it focalizes, may be more or less compatible with a multinationalization strategy and can therefore help to explain why enterprises placed in similar situations (sector of activity, state intervention, etc.) seem to make totally different strategic choices with regard to multinationalization. State-owned firms which do not manage to go multinational seem to be hampered by their bureaucratic corporate identity, while those that succeed best on international markets seem to have an organizational culture quite similar to that of privately owned multinationals.

Our hypothesis is that foreign expansion can only take place if the firm's corporate identity is compatible with a multinationalization strategy; multinationalization therefore requires that a firm's bureaucratic culture give way to a more managerial culture, which can only be achieved by a change in the focalization of the firm's corporate identity.

THE TRADITIONAL STATE-OWNED CORPORATE IDENTITY: AN OBSTACLE IN THE WAY OF MULTINATIONALIZATION

Enterprises whose corporate identity is markedly affected by their state-owned status seem to have great difficulty in going multinational. The state-owned corporate identity may be analysed as one that is:

— either focalized on a bureaucratic behaviour pattern;
— or focalized on a product or a service regarded, within the enterprise, as being exclusively national.

A bureaucratic behaviour

A bureaucratic behaviour is based on an elaborate code of rules and procedures which determine the entire functioning of the enterprise. The fact that the corporate identity of a firm focalizes on a bureaucratic behaviour — which should not be understood here as necessarily having a pejorative connotation — may actually be an asset in certain situations and result in greater efficiency. A bureaucratic behaviour is particularly appropriate in the case of specialized, complex, large-scale, routine activities which furthermore require a very accurate coordination. Military organizations tend to function in a bureaucratic manner.

In the same way, most of the railway companies in the world (British Rail, Société Nationale des Chemins de Fer Français, Indian Railways, National Canadian Railways, to mention just a few examples) have a corporate identity focalized, at least partly, on a bureaucratic behaviour pattern. Respecting the codes, rules and procedures is essential to the proper functioning of the enterprise: it would indeed be disastrous to let a train driver or a shunting operator make decisions in an autonomous way. In the case of the SNCF, its bureaucratic corporate identity is revealed by the fact that even executives, who do not have to refer to the codes and rules concerning the traffic of trains, have to learn them by heart.

The form of control which the State exerts on state-owned enterprises determines the focalization of their corporate identity either on a bureaucratic or on a managerial behaviour pattern. A permanent monitoring at all levels of the enterprise, aiming at ensuring respect for preestablished rules and regulations, favours the emergence of a bureaucratic culture. In contrast, when the control of the State operates *a posteriori* and only concerns the realization of objectives defined in advance, the firm's corporate identity diverges from the bureaucratic model. The permanent interventions of the French government in the management of the Direction Générale des Postes (postal services) to fix tariffs, impose job creations or determine employment policies can only reinforce the extremely bureaucratic culture prevailing in the enterprise. On the other hand, the form of control exerted by the Singapore government on the Keppel Shipyard group, evaluating its management only on a profit basis, reinforces the managerial corporate identity of the firm.

When the corporate identity focalizes on a bureaucratic behaviour pattern, the multinationalization of the enterprise is far more difficult; in such a context, the internal resistance is extremely strong. As we have seen, the activity of the firm is organized according to rules and procedures to which the individuals must conform in their day-to-day work. Therefore, enterprises with a bureaucratic culture operate in a routine fashion. Any exceptional operation, for which there is no provision in the rules and regulations, cannot easily be carried out by such firms. Furthermore, the realization of an exceptional operation requires that one person, or a group of employees, take the risk of diverging from the system of rules and regulations, that is to say breaking the internal law of the enterprise. Clearly, such a conduct is neither encouraged nor rewarded, inasmuch as the entire functioning of the enterprise is based on the respect of the rules and regulations by all employees.

A product regarded as exclusively national

Multinationalization can be extremely difficult for state-owned enterprises whose corporate identity focalizes on a product or on a service which is regarded as being exclusively national — indeed regional or local — in scope. All international operations may be perceived as diverting the enterprise from its mission, its national objectives, for which it has been created and which are its *raison d'être*. The mission and the activity it implies, as conceived inside the enterprise, may not naturally lead to multinationalization.

Most public services offered by the State through large state enterprises are likely to be perceived as intended exclusively for the national community. Thus, in all countries, the telecommunications department is responsible for offering telephone services to the citizens; why should they try to sell their knowhow and their technical and management systems abroad? This would mean leaving the public service in order to 'go into business', in other words changing trades. In the eyes of the employees of telecommunications companies, implementing a multinationalization strategy would be as absurd as wanting to run the railway system or to manage gas and electricity distribution

In this connection, it might seem that what we have described as the traditional state-owned corporate identity is linked to a non-competitive market and a monopoly situation. The state-owned enterprises whose corporate identity focalizes either on a bureaucratic behaviour pattern or on an activity regarded as exclusively national would then all be monopoly public services. The lack of competition and the protection of a monopoly situation reinforce the bureaucratic tendencies of an enterprise which thus is not compelled to take into account the potential worldwide dimension of its market and of its environment in general.

However, the mere fact of being state-owned can produce similar effects to those of a non-competitive monopoly situation. State protection, and the security and durability it provides, usually results in the emergence of a traditional state-owned corporate identity.

In France, SEITA, the Société d'Exploitation Industrielle du Tabac et des Allumettes (state tobacco and matches company), had the monopoly for the distribution of tobacco and matches in the country for many years and is still responsible for collecting the taxes imposed on these products. In terms of production, SEITA has always faced the competition of American multinationals of the sector even on the French market, but this did not prevent it from developing a bureaucratic corporate identity and behaving more like a government administration than like an enterprise operating in a competitive environment. Moreover, the current difficulties of SEITA are due more to its inability to adapt to the change in demand on the French market — a preference for mild tobacco — than to the recent loss of its distribution monopoly — in fact most of the well-known brands are still distributed by SEITA.

In the same way, the state-owned group British Leyland, though operating in a very competitive sector, has had until recent years — because it was made up of previously independent companies — a fractionated corporate identity which, however, focalized on its product, as is often the case with car manufacturers. This product, however, was above all considered as being national or insular. Today in the automobile sector the competition operates on a worldwide scale, and all the rivals of British Leyland which have not only understood this and taken it into account in the formulation of their strategy but have also integrated it in their corporate culture have long been true multinationals. British Leyland, on the contrary, only acknowledged the multinational dimension of its business more recently and thus went into a joint venture with Honda in the early eighties.

Other enterprises like Indian Railways, the RATP and DSM — whose case we will examine in more detail later in this chapter — although state-owned and in a monopoly position, seem to have a corporate identity that has enabled them to go multinational.

Thus, what we have termed a traditional state-owned corporate identity cannot be systematically associated with monopolistic situations and the lack of competition. The mere fact of being owned and controlled by the State increases the probability for state-owned enterprises to have such a traditional state-owned corporate identity.

We have shown that such an identity is unfavourable to foreign expansion. Therefore, state-owned multinationals are enterprises which have succeeded in changing their corporate culture or in bypassing the obstacle it constitutes on their way towards multinationalization.

STATE-OWNED ENTERPRISES WITH A MULTINATIONAL CORPORATE IDENTITY

As we have seen in the course of this book, some state-owned firms are true multinationals. Their successful development as multinationals is precisely due to their particular corporate identity, which is quite different from the type we have just examined.

Referring to the same categories defined earlier, we shall now see that when the corporate identity of state-owned multinationals focalizes on a behaviour pattern, the latter is managerial and not bureaucratic; when it focalizes on a product or on a service, these are regarded as having a worldwide market by the staff. Lastly, the corporate identity of such enterprises sometimes focalizes on a charismatic leader who has an international strategic perspective for the firm.

Managerial behaviour

The managerial behaviour patterns on which the corporate identity of a firm may focalize are varied: certain firms consider themselves as being 'efficient', others as 'innovative' or 'brilliant', others as 'perfectionist' or 'individualistic'. For example, the corporate identity of IBM appears to be focalized on a 'planned' behaviour pattern. At IBM, all operations must be planned in advance, intermediate objectives must be fixed and all the discrepancies must be analysed and justified. The stock joke of the firm's commercial executives is: 'the planned loss of a customer is better than the unexpected winning of a new one'. Moreover, the worldwide organizational structure of IBM is based on a product and geographical area matrix which requires an elaborate planning system in order to function efficiently, hence reinforcing the firm's corporate identity.

In contrast, Matra's corporate identity focalizes on a behaviour pattern which could be termed 'ingenious' or 'cunning'; a 'good' executive at Matra is one who can seize opportunities. The success of the enterprise, as it is told by its own employees, is the result of exceptional operations such as the winning of special contracts and the takeover of enterprises, all conducted 'ingeniously'.

A managerial behaviour is typical of enterprises which, on the one hand, emphasize the importance of the market and try to adapt to it, and, on the other, pursue efficiency objectives and economic performance. Therefore it is somewhat surprising to find state-owned firms whose corporate identity focalizes on a managerial behaviour pattern. Indeed, there are more state-owned enterprises with a managerial culture among the firms nationalized recently than among public services in a monopoly situation.

To take an example the Keppel Shipyard group of Singapore has a corporate identity focalized on a managerial behaviour pattern. The principal objective of the firm, shared by the entire staff, is one of profitability and growth. All strategies regarded as favouring such an objective are massively supported by the employees. Thus, the multinationalization of Keppel Shipyard may be carried out in the most favourable internal climate, inasmuch as it is in line with these major objectives. The Norwegian group Norsk-Hydro provides another example of a state-owned enterprise whose corporate identity seems to focalize on a managerial behaviour pattern.

A worldwide product

A corporate identity focalizing on a product or on a service may facilitate the firm's multinational expansion insofar as this product is considered to be international in scope, that is to say adapted to a worldwide demand and market. In this context, multinationalization may occur without meeting internal opposition since it is convergent with the corporate identity. The managers as well as all employees of the enterprise support the multinationalization process as it is essential for the success of the product.

For example, at Assi — the Swedish paper group whose capital is held totally by the State — the multinationalization process is reinforced by slogans such as 'Europe is our natural market' which prevail in the enterprise.

In the case of Renault, its corporate identity appears to focalize on the automobile as a product which is easily identifiable, clearly differentiated and has a strong social and symbolic meaning. The multinationalization of the firm met relatively little resistance within the enterprise, most of the criticism originating from outside: the political parties, the unions and even the government. Indeed, all the employees of Renault realized that the success of their product required the multi-natioalization of the firm. On the other hand, the staff at American Motors easily accepted the takeover by Renault, a foreign state-owned group, owing to the fact that it was an enterprise in the same industry, manufacturing a similar product and working in the same trade. Even though the car models manufactured by American Motors had changed, employees were still in the same trade; in fact, Renault[5] and American Motors worked for the same cause.

Thus, it would seem that in the case of enterprises whose corporate identity focalizes on a product which can be manufactured by state as well as privately owned enterprises, the internal resistance to multinationalization is no stronger in the former than in the latter. In such a situation, and in the absence of external constraints imposed by the controlling authorities, state-owned enterprises tend to go multinational following a similar pattern to that of the private firms in the same industry.

However, in the case of Renault, it must be noted that the multinationalization of the firm was made possible by its charismatic leader, Pierre Dreyfus, who managed to keep the controlling authorities at arm's length while at the same time convincing the personnel that Renault products could and had to be sold throughout the world. This complementary focalization on a charismatic leader associated with the main focalization on a worldwide product made the firm's corporate identity extremely favourable to multinationalization. This explains in part why Renault managed to expand abroad faster and to a greater extent than Peugeot, its French private rival.

A charismatic leader

In general, the multinationalization process of a state-owned enterprise is facilitated by the presence at its head of a charismatic leader. If, on the one hand, multinationalization is one of the leader's main objectives, he will be able to motivate all the employees, internal resistance will disappear and the firm will develop a propensity to expand abroad. On the other hand, by obtaining greater autonomy from the controlling authorities, such a leader can free the enterprise from the external obstacles in the way of multinationalization imposed by the State which we described in Chapter Three. A charismatic leader, in most cases a

---

[5] Owing to its financial woes, Renault was obliged to sell its stake in American Motors to Chrysler Corporation in 1987.

real manager rather than a politician, has a clearer view of the firm's
interests at stake as far as multinationalization is concerned, and will
carry it out when the economic environment and competition require
that the firm engage in such a policy.

Enterprises with a charismatic leader usually have a corporate
identity which focalizes neither on a product nor on a specific behaviour
pattern; the specificity and the unity of such enterprises result from the
fact that all employees follow the leader – or the managing team – whose
position at the head of the enterprise is considered to be legitimate and
unquestionable.

A leader on whom the corporate identity of the enterprise may
focalize must have a strong or even authoritarian personality, be a man
of decision rather than compromise who tries to impose his own views
instead of seeking a consensus. In general, such a leader formulates
ambitious projects for the enterprise and manages to communicate his
enthusiasm to all the personnel. Most enterprises are run by a charismatic leader at some point in the course of their development. This
period is usually marked by important projects, the starting of new
activities and, more generally, by dramatic changes in the firm's
strategy.

For example, Mr Apfalter, the head of the Austrian Voest-Alpine
group, transformed his enterprise into a true multinational, similar to
all its private rivals (for instance Mannesman). In the same way, Alain
Gomez, another charismatic figure, was appointed chairman and
managing director of the Thomson group when it was nationalized in
1982; he took important restructuring decisions which, though
unpopular, were nevertheless necessary and which the previous
management had not succeeded in imposing on the firm. Pasquale
Pistorio, a former director of the American multinational group Motorola, was assigned the management of SGS by the IRI — the state
Italian holding company which controls it — in order to put the ailing
firm on its feet again. Within just a few years, Pasquale Pistorio
managed to make profits, to change working methods and to cut absen-
teeism, which was extremely high even according to Italian standards;
thus, he is transforming SGS into one of the most dynamic enterprises
in the field of semiconductors on a worldwide level. Colonel Ozires
Silva, the head of Embraer since the creation of the firm,[6] who is
convinced that only enterprises with a global market can succeed in the
field of aeronautics, managed to rally all the employees of the enterprise
to this objective and led Embraer to become one of the most multi-

[6] Colonel Ozires Silva was appointed head of Petrobras in 1986.

nationalized state-owned enterprises originating from a developing country. Thus, there are countless examples which prove that the personality of top managers is a crucial factor for the success of enterprises.

FROM NATIONALIZATION TO MULTINATIONALIZATION

The preceding analysis enables us to identify two categories of state-owned enterprise:

— Some that have a pronounced 'state-owned' corporate identity which focalizes on a bureaucratic behaviour pattern, a strictly national product or a public service activity.

— Others that have a managerial corporate identity which focalizes on a charismatic leader or a worldwide activity.

All these enterprises are above all state-owned and the ones that have a managerial corporate identity today — which therefore are the most multinationalized — previously had a traditional state-owned corporate identity; moreover, the latter may eventually develop a managerial corporate identity enabling them to go multinational. This suggests that there may exist a 'way' — or even several 'ways' — leading from our first category of state-owned enterprises to the second.

We shall now try to explore these 'ways' and show the essential part that corporate identity plays in the transformation which accompanies the multinationalization of an enterprise. As we have already stressed, the sector of activity of a firm is not the only factor which determines its propensity to go multinational. The corporate identity is another critical factor which explains why enterprises placed in similar situations can adopt radically different strategies, some becoming true multinationals while others remain confined to their domestic market.

Most state-owned enterprises — except the newly nationalized firms — originally have a corporate identity that is strongly influenced by their attachment to the public sector and which hinders their multinationalization strategies. Thus, the firms that have actually multinationalized are those which have managed to surmount the obstacle created by their corporate identity, or even transform the latter to a large extent.

'Breaking', 'broadening' or 'splitting up' corporate identity?

The most drastic, and also the most dramatic, transformation process may take place when the existing corporate identity not only hinders all development strategies but even jeopardizes the very survival of the enterprise. Certain state-owned enterprises whose corporate identity was extremely bureaucratic have managed to go multinational after having experienced a serious crisis which 'broke' the existing bureaucratic corporate identity and resulted in the emergence of a new identity focalized on a managerial behaviour pattern. Crises of this kind originate in the increasingly wide gap which exists between a rapidly changing environment and the routine functioning of the enterprise, as its bureaucratic corporate identity prevents all changes in strategies, hence all progressive adaptation to the imperatives of its environment. The crisis occurs when this gap is so wide that the actual existence of the enterprise is threatened. It leads to the emergence of a new corporate identity and entails important strategic moves: diversification, restructuring, multinationalization, etc., provided the enterprise has sufficient resources or receives them from the State.

The diversification, and later the multinationalization, of DSM occurred as a consequence of the crisis which shook the Dutch coal mines in the mid-sixties. This crisis obliged the enterprise to develop new activities in the fields of chemicals, plastics and fertilizers within a very short period of time, in order to compensate for its declining coal-mining activities. The new activities led DSM to go multinational as they had to be carried out on international markets. Moreover, this crisis gave way to a drastic transformation of the firm's corporate identity as well as of the forms of intervention of the Dutch State in its management. Before 1965, the enterprise was managed almost directly by the Ministry of Economic Affairs, functioned like a government administration and its corporate identity focalized on a bureaucratic behaviour pattern. The crisis led the State to transform DSM into a real enterprise, managed almost like a private firm and enjoying great autonomy; today, the control of the State is only exerted at the highest level in the enterprise and takes the form of an annual meeting of DSM's chairman with a representative of the Ministry of Economic Affairs who, in fact, ratifies the decisions made by the firm's management. Today, DSM's corporate identity is focalized on a managerial behaviour pattern, as shown by the fact that its management considers that the firm is comparable to the major private enterprises in the chemical industry; DSM even accuses Rhône-Poulenc of being an unfair competitor owing to the aid it received from the State after it was nationalized, while its own preferential access to low-cost Dutch natural gas is never mentioned and has become a real 'taboo'.

The transformations of the corporate identity of a firm, enabling the latter to go multinational, may sometimes take less dramatic forms. Without 'breaking' the existing corporate identity of the firm as in the case mentioned above, it may be possible to make it change by 'broadening' its focalization. Thus, an enterprise whose corporate identity focalizes on an activity initially considered as exclusively national in scope may successfully start to multinationalize if, at the same time, the internal perception of the enterprise's product or activity tends towards a perception which integrates the worldwide perspective of the product or the activity.

This is well exemplified by the multinationalization of Renault. In the cases of Aérospatiale and Embraer, their international development was paralleled by the personnel's progressive awareness that serving the domestic market would not justify the existence of the enterprise. The successes abroad of both enterprises reinforce the image of excellence that all their employees have of themselves and of the firm. In the particular case of Embraer, the pride in selling airplanes which are conceived and built by a Brazilian firm — in other words originating from a developing country — in the United States, the most powerful and technologically advanced country in the world, is one of the driving forces of the firm's multinationalization. This 'David and Goliath' corporate identity probably explains in part Embraer's success on the US market. In contrast, De Havilland, a state-owned Canadian competitor of Embraer which in principle enjoys a better technological situation, has had a very limited success in the United States.[7] Are not the corporate identities of the firms partly responsible for their respective success and failure?

In the case of enterprises whose corporate identity focalizes on a public service, the extent to which they may multinationalize and the internal resistance such a strategy will meet are strongly influenced by their stage of development; the last phase in the setting up of the public service itself is crucial as far as the evolution of the firm's corporate identity is concerned. Such enterprises have been created or nationalized with the aim of setting up and later managing a particular public utility, as, for example, the domestic telephone network, the railways, the postal services, urban transport, gas and electricity supply, etc. As long as they have not fulfilled their initial mission, that is to say as long as the country has not been provided with basic equipment and the service is not functioning properly, these enterprises cannot start to

---

[7] De Havilland was taken over by Boeing at the end of 1985.

expand abroad. They allocate all their resources and devote all their efforts to their mission and, at this stage, foreign operations would be considered as diverting from their principal objectives and betraying the national interest.

On the other hand, when most of the necessary equipment is virtually realized, and the service reaches a stable phase in its development after a period of rapid growth, the enterprise is able to liberate financial as well as human resources which it can use for important strategic moves, notably multinationalization or diversification. It is during this phase, when the essential mission of the enterprise can be considered as practically fulfilled, that the corporate identity of the enterprise is most likely to change easily and the initial focalization to 'broaden' in order to allow a development of the enterprise which is not strictly limited to its original mission.

If the enterprise is not given new objectives and new growth perspectives, in other words if its corporate identity does not focalize on a new object, it is most probable that the corporate identity of such a firm will evolve from a focalization on its original mission towards a focalization on a bureaucratic behaviour pattern, allowing a routine functioning of the public service but totally opposed to the multinationalization of the enterprise.

When the traditional state-owned corporate identity of the enterprise is evidently opposed to its foreign expansion, when the internal pressure is too strong and the 'broadening' of the identity seems difficult, the only way to develop international activities is the creation of a parallel organization separated from the main enterprise, which would thus have its own identity. In this case, the corporate identity of the enterprise is 'split up'.

In order to sell their knownow abroad, enterprises whose corporate identity was obviously focalized on their state ownership and their bureaucratic culture, such as the RATP or Indian Railways, had to set up subsidiaries, respectively Sofretu and RITES. In Great Britain, the NIOG, which comprises at least 20 small-sized engineering companies — subsidiaries of extremely bureaucratized, state-owned enterprises — was created with the same aim. These subsidiaries, which are not subjected to the rules and procedures concerning the functioning of the main organization, are more adapted to the international context, more flexible and thus more adaptable. The setting up of such parallel structures permits the emergence of a specific corporate identity which unifies the employees on foreign activities. Moreover, in this procedure, developing international activities quite different in nature from the main activity does not call into question the mode of functioning or the corporate identity of the enterprise, which are compatible with the main activity. Nevertheless, in the long run, the corporate identity will eventually evolve, notably owing to shifts of personnel between the two organizations. Failing this, a serious break-up could occur when the international activities have developed sufficiently to separate from the original enterprise. Thus, the creation of a parallel organization can be the starting point of a long process finally leading to a transformation of the corporate identity.

'Broadening' the focalization of the corporate identity is a long and perilous process which requires a transformation of the latter. In contrast, the creation of a parallel structure does not imply a short-term change in the corporate identity of the enterprise. Therefore it is not surprising to see that a great number of state-owned enterprises resorted to parallel structures in order to carry out their international activities. If we summarize the results of our analysis up to this point, we have identified three 'ways' which enable an enterprise whose traditional corporate identity represents an obstacle in the way of multi-nationalization to overcome the latter in order to implement an international strategy. The three 'ways' which imply a decreasingly radical transformation of the corporate identity are:

— 'Breaking' — generally at the moment of a serious crisis threatening the survival of the enterprise — the existing bureaucratic corporate identity and redefining, on the basis of renewed management systems and new objectives, a managerial corporate identity which is compatible with the multinationalization of the enterprise.
— 'Broadening' the corporate identity by including the initial object of focalization, in other words the public service as defined in the original mission of the enterprise, in a broader focalization encompassing international activities.
— Maintaining the traditional state-owned corporate identity in the main organization and creating parallel structures in order to develop international activities.

The 'non-conformist' leaders

State-owned enterprises may adopt various 'ways' in order to surmount the obstacles to multinationalization that their corporate identity represents, relying above all on individuals who become the driving force of foreign venture as well as the ferment of the evolution of the corporate identity.

As we have emphasized earlier in this chapter, the presence of a charismatic leader involved in international activities at the head of the enterprise facilitates the multinationalization process.

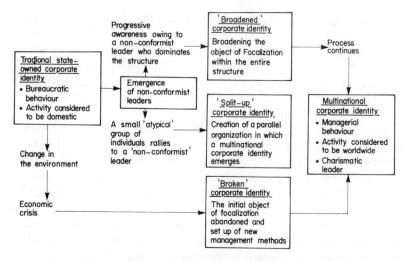

The ways of corporate identity

Indeed, we cited and analysed the decisive role such leaders played in the multinationalization of Renault, Voest-Alpine and SGS, to name only a few. More generally, the multinationalization of an enterprise with a strong state-owned and bureaucratic corporate identity can only be impelled by atypical, non-conformist individuals, outsiders who do not conform to the corporate identity of the enterprise and who are remote from the internal image of the ideal manager. Nonconformist leaders, who are not satisfied with acting in accordance with the traditional activity of the enterprise and its rules and regulations, try to stimulate new activities having high growth potential and at the same time allowing them greater freedom of action. Thus, this initiative can lead to the development of international activities and the multinationalization of the enterprise.

Very often the international expansion of a state-owned enterprise, notably the RATP (Parisian transport company) and DSM, can be traced to a non-conformist individual — or group of individuals — who does not strictly fit in with the corporate identity of the firm. When the corporate identity can evolve sufficiently to be able to include these non-conformist individuals and their international projects, the entire enterprise tends to go multinational. If, on the contrary, the gap between the non-conformist groups and the dominant corporate identity widens, parallel organizations with distinct identities will emerge. Through the exchange of personnel between the two organizations, the new structure can transform the corporate identity of the original body, making it focalize on increasingly multinational and managerial behaviour patterns. In this development there is often a transitional phase where the corporate identity of the entire group focalizes on a leader who encourages multinationalization, for example one of those who initiatied the parallel international organization.

The development of the activities of Sofretu and the shifts of personnel between Sofretu and the RATP seem to have already started the transformation of the corporate identity of the latter. The RATP, whose corporate identity was focalized on the Parisian underground and city bus transport systems, has evolved towards a corporate identity focalized on a larger notion of urban transport systems which facilitates its internationalization. The sale of its knowhow abroad is thus becoming an essential component of the object of focalization of the firm's corporate identity.

The different means of eliminating or bypassing the internal obstacles to multinationalization imply a transformation of the corporate identity; multinationalization obliges enterprises to change from a conventional state-owned corporate identity to one that is increasingly managerial. This may suggest that the more a state-owned enterprise is capable of going truly multinational, the more its corporate identity deviates from that of other state-owned enterprises which are barely multinational, and resembles that of private multinationals.

COMPARING THE CORPORATE IDENTITY OF STATE-OWNED AND PRIVATE MULTINATIONALS

Once a state-owned enterprise satisfies all the objective criteria of multinationalization as defined in Chapter Two, how can it be distinguished from a private multinational in terms of corporate identity?

Whether state-owned or private, an enterprise can be considered to be at the service of its shareholders, whose demands must be fulfilled. In the case of private shareholders, the aim of the enterprise is relatively simple and unequivocal, at least in theory: it must try to maximize the value of their investments on a long-term basis. When the capital of the enterprise is held by the State, these demands are more complex and often contradictory. Above all, they can clash with the interests of the enterprise itself, whereas for a private enterprise the interests of the shareholders and those of the enterprise are almost systematically convergent.

A private multinational manages its worldwide interests without concerning itself with the interests of its country of origin or those of the host countries. The psychological contract of individuals with the enterprise is relatively straightforward. The corporate identity does not require them to take into account, in their decisions and behaviour patterns, any element which is extraneous to the objectives and the interests of the enterprise itself.

In contrast, in a state-owned multinational the psychological contract is more complex because individuals are bound not only to the enterprise, but through it to the government and to the public interest. Thus, in their decisions, they are obliged to take into account the explicit or implicit objectives of the enterprise and to consider the public interest to a certain extent. Therefore, apart from the constraints imposed by the controlling authorities, the managements of most state-owned enterprises are seen to follow a kind of code of conduct which limits the possibilities open to the enterprise. For example, the management of DSM, though it claims that it runs the company like any private enterprise, admit that it could never consider investing in South Africa owing to the apartheid policy, precisely because of the state-owned nature of its company. The American employees of Voest-Alpine International enjoy advantages which are unusual in the country of free enterprise — social protection, longer paid holidays, etc. This is because the company follows the Austrian system. In France, when Renault is obliged to lay off personnel, it suggests a negotiable social plan to the unions, whereas its private rival Peugeot merely announces the cutbacks in staff that it proposes. Hydro-Quebec International loses important tender bids in certain developing countries because its management is unaware of the practice frequently resorted to by its private rivals of offering under-the-table commissions to certain well-placed middlemen — or possibly is reluctant to do this. To these broad principles must be added countless minor details which in daily usage differentiate the working methods of managers and which moreover vary from one state-owned enterprise to another, each manager interpreting his national responsibility in his own way and adopting his distinctive code of conduct. The management of Assi admits that the enterprise benefits from certain facilities (notably in terms of bureaucratic formalities, fiscal and legal regulations) in the host countries because it is state-owned. On the other hand, it compels itself to observe a strict code of conduct and thus be an irreproachable partner.

It may be inferred that in terms of corporate identity a state-owned enterprise, whatever the extent of its multinationalization, remains largely marked by its origin and its national attachments, whereas a private multinational frees itself progressively from these bonds and the constraints that they imply in the course of its multinationalization.

What can be said of the corporate identity of multinationals which were nationalized in 1982, such as Saint-Gobain, the Compagnie Générale d'Electricité, Péchiney, Rhône-Poulenc or Thomson in France? With respect to their multinationalization process, does the attachment of these enterprises to the public sector entail a 'regression' of their corporate identity towards a more 'traditional state-owned' model? According to our analysis, this regression may be effected through the progressive bureaucratization of behaviour patterns which were formally managerial and on which the corporate identity mainly focalized. For example, the bureaucratization may be caused by the repeated interventions of the State in the management of the enterprises in the form of multiple and contradictory directives which negate past agreements between the enterprise and the controlling authority. Eventually these interventions demoralize the management, which no longer dares to show any initiative or take risks. Even when the government policy regarding the enterprise is more or less coherent, certain changes of strategy urged by the government may clash with the objectives of the management if they happen to be too remote from the latter's assessment of what constitutes the interests of the enterprise in the context of international competition. In both cases, the management can manifest its opposition and its indignation, thus convincing its collaborators, and consequently a large number of executives, that in such conditions it is impossible to work as in the past. This would be the starting point of a de-responsibilization of the management which could trickle down to the lower levels.

Was this the case with the examples cited above? At first, we are inclined to answer in the negative. At any rate, seen from abroad where all factors relating to multinationalization are closely observed, nationalization has not brought about any immediate changes. However, the answer needs to be qualified: the experience is still too recent to allow any valid assessement to emerge. Enterprises can be compared to giant oil tankers: once launched, it takes time to change their course. The strategies developed in the eighties were formulated at the end of the seventies and it was not possible to change them abruptly. If any modifications have been actually made, they will be noticed only progressively. Moreover, the controlling authority is still not fully familiar with the newly nationalized enterprises and is easily intimidated when the latter protest vigorously and claim that the interventions disrupt the market forces. This might change in the future. For the moment, however, it is worth noting that a number of top executives left the enterprises either immediately aftr nationalization or six months or even one or two years later. This may not be of great significance, but it is nevertheless a 'negative' sign since these executives were convinced advocates of multinationalization and their successors, though defending multinationalization on principle, are sometimes incapable of understanding all its implications. Certain of the newly appointed executives visited all the foreign subsidiaries in order to assure them that nothing had changed. On the other hand, the chairman of one of the companies, when asked if he thought (like his predecessor) that in order to reach a top executive position it was essential to prove one's efficiency abroad, replied without much enthusiasm: 'Yes, it may help'. For advocates of internationalization, such a reply is hardly encouraging

As for the denationalized enterprises in Britain for example, once again it is too early to judge. However, the problem seems to be simpler since the enterprises, with the possible exception of Rolls Royce, were not, properly speaking, multinationals and thus did not have a multinational corporate identity. Their privatization places them in a situation comparable to that of their rivals. They will either be able to acquire a multinational corporate identity or fail to do so. In the first case the 'heritage' of their former nationalized status will not prove to be an obstacle, whereas in the second it will evidently be a burden. Only time will tell. So far an interesting fact can be noted: upon privatization, an enterprise like British Aerospace opened talks with large private industrial groups. If it joins up with such groups, its corporate identity will change rapidly. However, such a step is disapproved of by the Thatcher government, which on the contrary wants the newly privatized enterprises to float their shares among the general public instead of being immediately swallowed up by existing private groups. It is, however, interesting to see that these newly privatized firms tend to seek protection when they return to the private sector. It would seem that they wish to forget their former state-owned status as quickly as possible. We leave this question unresolved because these enterprises, being no longer state-owned, fall outside the scope of our study.

On the other hand, what can be said about the corporate identity of enterprises which remain in the public sector and which are true multinationals? They possibly have a hybrid corporate identity, the combination of two profoundly opposed natures. In our opinion, one of these natures will tend to dominate and relegate the other to a secondary position — in other words, in most cases, all conflicts will be resolved in favour of the dominant nature. This however is only a hypothesis. If the state-owned character predominates, it is unlikely that the enterprise acquires a true multinational corporate identity. It would rather be an instrument of its government's imperialistic desires, serving its state of origin in all the host countries. In the event of incompatibility between its service to the State — in the strongest sense of the term — and the local interests of the enterprise, the latter are totally sacrificed. On the other hand, if the multinational nature predominates, the enterprise will most likely soon cease to be a true state-owned company; its corporate identity will be almost identical to that of a private multinational and, in fact, it will undergo a virtual privatization. In this case, the State is reduced merely to the role of a shareholder, and in the event of clear victory of a political party opposed to state interventionism, the enterprise will be a ready candidate for a legal denationalization, provided such a step is acceptable to public opinion.

Thus, there are more and more state-owned enterprises which, judged by standard criteria, are true multinationals. However, we can ask ourselves whether state-owned enterprises with a true multinational corporate identity do or can exist.

Chapter Seven

A Tentative Typology of State-Owned Multinationals

INTRODUCTION

All through the preceding chapters we have progressively defined what state-owned multinational enterprises are. We have also shown that this term designates a great variety of firms, some of which are still in the process of multinationalization. Thus, it now seems necessary to introduce a certain order in the variety, in other words to draw up the typology of these 'state-owned multinationals'.

We started by showing that in a large number of countries and sectors of activity there exist state-owned enterprises which have foreign subsidiaries. However, at the same time we noted that many denied being multinational, whereas others rejected their state ownership. This was the beginning of a differentiation. Later, the analysis of the existing theories of the multinational firm as well as of the state-owned enterprise and particularly the comparison of these theories suggested as a preliminary hypothesis that state-owned multinationals experienced a real conflict. This led us to assert that some opted for their state-owned status and others for their multinational character. In this last chapter we shall try to define a typology of state-owned multinationals as accurately as possible, based on the theoretical opposition.

To do so, it might indeed be useful to go back to the theories and follow the same reasoning, in order to understand the situation of state-owned multinational enterprises. Thus, we have tried to acknowledge two generally accepted ideas: one which considers that the owner-state prevents its own enterprises from going multinational, the other which, in contrast, describes the State as the *'deus ex machina'* backing its firms, which become unfair competitors on the international scene. In fact, it appeared that the State put a spanner in the works of its state-owned enterprises. However, these could still invest abroad, though some found it easier to overcome the obstacles than others. Moreover, we showed that most of these firms do not deserve to be termed unfair competitors, since abroad they behave like private companies which also receive aid from their country of origin. Yet it is undeniable that some state-owned multinationals are 'fairer' than others.

It was thus necessary to examine more closely the state-owned multinationals themselves. We studied their strategies and their corporate identity and found the explanatory factors which, in our opinion, seem to determine the differing characteristics of these enterprises. As far as strategies are concerned, it is clear that, for each case, there are answers adapted to the particular circumstances in which an enterprise operates. Therefore the management wanting to multinationalize the enterprise always enjoys a considerable freedom of action. However, certain managers may make a better use of their autonomy because their enterprise itself possesses the characteristics favourable to multinationalization: this is what we have called the corporate identity.

At that point the circle was completed, since the corporate identity of an enterprise is related to its historical origin, which was our starting point. We now have a complete set of analytical data which should enable us to suggest categories of enterprise and to better understand how a particular enterprise can shift from one category to another in the course of its development.

THE CLASH OF TWO LOGICS: COMBINATION RATHER THAN OPPOSITION

Our purpose here is to try and go beyond the paradox which resulted in this book: multinational and state-owned. We wish to prove that enterprises with this status do exist, since we have shown that it was compatible with economic practices, whereas theory could only point out the contradiction of the situation. According to our observations, certain enterprises are more multinational than others. Therefore there is a variable, a factor which can be evaluated and which changes from one enterprise to another and from one period to another within the same enterprise. As far as the state-owned character is concerned, certain firms appear to be closely controlled by the State while others seem to behave according to their own wishes. Thus there is a second variable.

It would seem that an enterprise can be 'more or less state-owned' and 'more or less multinational'. Can these two variables be combined? For example, can there be enterprises that are 'very state-owned' and 'very multinational' at the same time, or 'very multinational' and 'barely state-owned', and vice versa? Indeed this is possible; however, before making an assertion, we must ensure that the combination of the two variables is valid, in other words that they are sufficiently independent from one another. Therefore, we must start by studying them separately, in order to find and consequently compare their respective determinants. The first variable, the state-owned character, proceeds from a precise logic, which is that of state intervention in the economy. The second one, the multinational character, results from the logic of the development of an enterprise within its market. Thus we can examine in turn what we shall call the state logic on the one hand and the entrepreneurial logic on the other, and combine them later.

State interventionism

How can the fact that a state-owned enterprise is utilized as a mere instrument in the hands of the State or, on the contrary, that it has great autonomy in relation to the latter be explained? We answered this question in Chapters Two and Three: there are historical circumstances leading to nationalization and above all there is the permanent interplay of ideology and economic imperatives, of principles and facts, which determines the behaviour of the owner-state. As we observed, two states inspired by greatly differing ideologies may have the same interventionist policy because objectively they are placed in the same economic situation. Conversely, the same economic situation may induce two successive ideologically opposed governments to develop contradictory policies within the same country. Thus there is a complex interaction of economic considerations and ideology.

All the same, our observations have led us to argue that two significant connections may be considered, as they are seen almost everywhere. First, the less a country is developed, the more the State, whatever its doctrine, intervenes in the economy. In this context we understand the development of a country not only in the sense of revenue per inhabitant, but also in relation to the wealth potential of the country or to a prior level of development. Thus, most of the European countries as they were in the immediate postwar period, or Canada and Australia today, should be included in the group of currently developing countries. The farther the country is from realizing its potential, the more the role of the State in filling the gap is important. This role would decrease with the reduction of the difference in wealth.

Secondly, the more the prevailing ideology is that of free enterprise and free market economy, the less the State intervenes directly in the economy. In this respect, the ideology of the government in power should not be confused with the prevailing ideology: even in the established democracies there can be a discrepancy between the two. Public opinion can change for example between two elections, but above all it can bring a government to power, basing itself on criteria which are more political than economic in nature. In countries where the enterprises traditionally resort to the State in difficult times, like France, Italy or Spain, even the free market governments are interventionist. In countries where individualism prevails over the State, which is suspected of waste and totalitarianism, as in the United States or in West Germany, even the governments most inclined to be interventionist remain moderate in this respect.

In all, the propensity of the State to intervene in the economy may be considered as the result of the comparison between the 'development gap' and the prevailing ideology, and it can be validly assumed that what is seen in the economy in general is true of the state-owned enterprise in particular. This does not provide a satisfactory explanation for the degree of government intervention *vis-à-vis* a specific state-owned enterprise; however, it gives the basis for general reflection. Therefore, we could draw up a double-entry matrix: one of its dimensions would be the development gap qualified as 'wide' and 'narrow' and the other the prevailing ideology qualified as 'free market' and 'interventionist'. The four resulting positions would each represent a certain propensity to state intervention:

— When the development imperative is high and 'etatism' or 'state interventionism' is the prevailing ideology, the propensity of the State to intervene tends to be maximal.
— In contrast, when the development imperative is low and the prevailing ideology is that of the free market, the propensity of the state to intervene tends to be minimal.
— In the other two cases, the result is less clear as either of the two explanatory factors may be decisive. At this stage, we can put forward as a hypothesis that a very high development imperative will be balanced by a dominant free market ideology resulting in an average propensity of the State to intervene, and that a prevailing ideology of 'state interventionism' will be balanced by a low development imperative (with the same result). Evidently, this is only an assessment, which is probably confirmed in an adequate number of examples but which can be invalidated in a particular example; indeed one of the two variables can have the

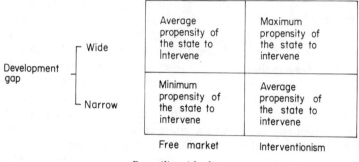

Prevailing ideology

upper hand. When the development imperative prevails we are in
the first position (maximum) and in the second one (minimum)
when the free market ideology dominates. Moreover, in practice
we observed such cases, which we will discuss later in the chapter.
The diagram gives a summary of these cases.

We shall now examine whether these tendencies appear at the level
of a particular enterprise. In order to do so, we must take into account
the specific characteristics of the enterprise. As there are no established
theories on the matter, we have to base our argument on our observations. The latter invalidate the most generally accepted ideas; for
example, the amount of competition the firm has to face is in no way
decisive, nor is the quality of its performance. In other words, a state-
owned enterprise may operate and be effective in a competitive sector
without freeing itself from the intervention of the government; for
instance, Saint-Gobain in France (which the State prevented from diversifying) or Assi in Sweden (which cannot lay off personnel). Competition, in particular international competition, is rather an argument
used by the enterprises in their negotiations with the controlling authorities in order to obtain greater autonomy. In the same way, deficit is
one of the arguments used by the controlling authorities to intervene
in the management of state-owned firms. In our view, the personality
of directors, on both sides, seems to be a factor as important as the
economic characteristics of the enterprise's sector of activity. The *esprit
de corps* of the enterprise, the management of its knowhow by
specialists — in a situation of power *vis-à-vis* the high-ranking civil
servants who do not know anything about the firm's technology — are
major determining factors in the achievement of autonomy. The attitude of the unions, which more or less tend to bypass the management
of the enterprise in their dealings with the government, is another
important element. Lastly, the nature of the problem posed is crucial.

Where a strategic decision of the enterprise directly conflicts with a priority national policy, any government will tend to intervene. If, on the other hand, the strategic decision of the firm has no political impact, the government will adopt a *laissez-faire* policy. If the option taken is vital for the enterprise, it will struggle to obtain its autonomy; otherwise it will accept state authority.

The entrepreneurial logic

How can the fact that an enterprise goes multinational, or, on the contrary, remains confined to the limits of its own country, be explained? Here again, the preceding chapters provided some answers which we will now examine in turn. The theories of multinational enterprises emphasize the existence or the absence of a 'competitive advantage' enabling a firm to set up abroad. The enterprise can do so in search of production factors that are more attractive than those it can use in its country of origin, or of customers to which it can sell its products, being able to outdo its local competitors thanks to technology, its *savoir-faire*, etc. The enterprise can also be obliged to set up production units by a government wanting to industrialize its country. All these reasons apply perfectly well to state-owned enterprises.

Thus, state-owned enterprises tend to consider an international venture to a lesser or a greater extent depending on the nature of their activities. We are cautious in saying 'tend to consider', for we are aware that, being state-owned, they do not necessarily act as they wish. However, if we only look at their intentions, the strategy they formulate themselves before their controlling authorities intervene to disturb its implementation, we can advance the hypothesis that they will try to set up abroad if it is to their advantage. This is also true of state-owned enterprises producing goods or services with a worldwide supply and having multinationals as rivals. In contrast, those whose activities have a particular character, specific to their country of origin and generally enjoying a domestic monopoly, prefer to limit themselves to their own protected market instead of facing local monopolies in foreign countries. This analysis, based on commonsense logic, is moreover confirmed by the relevant literature. Therefore, we may say that the prime factor in multinationalization relates to the sector of activity.

Nevertheless, our observations showed that reality was not quite in accordance with this assessment. We saw state-owned enterprises which, though in a sector involving an exclusively national public service, set up engineering subsidiaries which were true multinationals: for example Sofretu in France (a subsidiary of the Parisian underground transport system) or RITES in India (a subsidiary of the nationalized railways). Their development as multinationals was not hindered (sometimes, on the contrary, it was favoured) by the policies of their respective states, though the latter subscribe to an interventionist ideology and exert an extremely close control on their parent companies, which incur heavy losses. Nevertheless, there must be an additional explanatory factor for their success, since other comparable enterprises stagnate (Sofrerail, Hydro-Quebec International, etc.). Things would be simpler if the same factor — their own inability and not the controlling authority's opposition — was also responsible for the failure of some state-owned enterprises in their foreign expansion which their sector of activity should have favoured. Indeed, such cases do exist: for example British Leyland (in the automobile sector) in Great Britain and SEITA (in the tobacco sector) in France. In this regard, we presented a diagram in the preceding chapter centred on the specific qualities of the enterprise itself, not those of its sector of activity or its controlling authority. This diagram is based on the corporate identity of the enterprise.

We may say that a state-owned enterprise's tendency to become multinational depends both on its sector of activity and its corporate identity. There are, as we have seen, some corporate identities which are favourable to multinationalization and others that are unfavourable. Thus, the combination of these two explanatory factors would enable us to better determine the propensity of a state-owned firm to become multinational.

— When the sector of activity and the corporate identity are favourable, the propensity to multinationalization will evidently tend to be at a maximum.
— When the sector of activity as well as the corporate identity of the enterprise are unfavourable, the propensity to multinationalization will be at a minimum.
— When the sector of activity is favourable and the corporate identity of the enterprise is unfavourable, we can, once again, suppose that the two factors counterbalance one another and that in both cases the propensity to multinationalization is average.
— With the same reservation as above, since one of the two factors can sometimes eclipse the other, if the factor which clearly dominates is favourable to multinationalization the propensity is in the same position (maximum) as in the first case; if the dominant factor is unfavourable to multinationalization, the propensity is in

Influence of the sector of activity on multinationalization

	Favourable	Average propensity to go multinational	Maximum propensity to go multinational
	Unfavourable	Minimum propensity to go multinational	Average propensity to go multinational
		Unfavourable	Favourable

Influence of the corporate identity of the enterprise on multinationalization

the 'minimum' position. The diagram comprises all these hypotheses.

Thus, we have defined a way to determine the propensity of a state-owned enterprise to multinationalize. Since the explanatory diagram drawn up earlier, showing the degree of state intervention to which a particular state-owned enterprise is submitted in a given country, was too precise to apply to a specific enterprise, we shall now try to combine the State's logic and the entrepreneurial logic instead of opposing them.

THE NINE TYPES OF STATE-OWNED MULTINATIONALS

An analytical matrix

In order to make the above-mentioned combination valid, we must make sure that the two logics are sufficiently independent of one another; it is precisely for this reason that we tried to define the constituent elements. At this stage of our analysis the independence of the two logics is in no way evident; to establish it, we must reconsider the dividing up of the two logics into two explanatory factors for each of them, that is to say into four factors in all. These are what we have called the development gap on the one hand and the prevailing ideology on the other. Although we did not mention it earlier, the fact that the factors are independent within the same logic is noteworthy: mere observation shows that at a particular level of development the prevailing ideology can vary considerably (as seen in the opposed cases of Brazil and Mexico). In the same way, the attachment to a certain sector of activity can be related to widely different types of corporate identity, either favourable or unfavourable to multinationalization (as we have shown in opposing firms like Renault and British Leyland or Embraer and De Havilland). Therefore there are within each logic four clearly differentiated situations, although some are more frequent than others in reality. However, what is the result of the two/two combinations of the four factors?

Does the development gap determine, for example, the sector of activity? The state-owned enterprises of the less developed countries could thus mainly belong to sectors where multinationalization is not necessary, but this is not the case: in such countries, as in more developed ones, the state-owned firms belong to all kinds of sectors — monopolistic, competitive, industrial activities, services, etc. It appears that these two factors at least are not related. Secondly, does the development gap determine the corporate identity of the enterprise? This does not seem probable either. Indeed, some state-owned enterprises of less developed countries manage to go multinational while placed in particularly difficult circumstances, and certain state-owned firms in more developed countries do not become multinational though conditions are favourable. For instance, as we have mentioned above, RITES is typical of the first category while the National Coal Board belongs to the second type.

What is the role of the second factor, i.e. the prevailing ideology? The prevailing ideology could determine the sector of activity in the case, for example, of a non-interventionist ideology implying that state-owned enterprises should be limited to monopoly sectors. Is it so with the metallurgical sector in West Germany, with the oil and chemical industry in Norway and the chemical sector in the Netherlands? The answer is no. There are even countries with an interventionist ideology, like France, where a public service which is a monopoly, in this case water supply, is carried out by private enterprises. Therefore there is no close link between the above-mentioned factors. Finally, there is the question of whether there exists a causality relation between the prevailing ideology and the corporate identity of the enterprise. Although this would seem probable, it is not evident. There are countries with a prevailing interventionist ideology where public services succeed in going multinational (for example urban transport in France), thus proving to have a corporate identity particularly favourable to international venture. In contrast, there are other countries with a prevailing non-interventionist ideology in which state-owned enterprises in the competitive sector do not manage to go multinational (as in the case of German shipyards), probably because their corporate identity is an obstacle in the way of foreign expansion. Thus, the study of all possible combinations indicates that the state logic and the entrepreneurial logic can be considered as being sufficiently independent for the purpose of our analysis.

We should, however, mention one reservation imposed by a scientific analysis. The degree of state intervention with regard to a particular state-owned enterprise was described by us to depend on factors such as the *esprit de corps* of the enterprise or the personality of its managers. Evidently these factors are linked to the corporate identity of the enterprise, even if we do not know exactly how. In other words, a state-owned firm wanting to go multinational may obtain sufficient autonomy from the State owing solely to the fact that it is headed by a charismatic leader who is capable of uniting its subordinates as well as convincing its controlling authority. Thus our theories are distorted by a 'human' factor; however, we will incorporate this in our reasoning, for it does not confuse but on the contrary provides an explanation in cases where the stage logic and the entrepreneurial logic seem to be compatible.

In Chapter Six we discussed the importance of leaders who, though often 'non-conformist' at first, succeed in changing the corporate identity of the enterprise. When they manage to occupy the commanding seat they are capable of totally transforming the corporate identity from a bureaucratic and domestic model into a managerial and multinational one. Their influence can also extend to the relations between the enterprise and the State; indeed, when they act as a screen between the controlling authorities and the enterprise they allow the corporate identity of the latter to change more freely. In fact, they alone can prevent the state-owned enterprise from reaching what we shall present in the conclusion of this book as the inevitable 'breaking point', at which it is impossible for such an enterprise to go completely multinational without renouncing its allegiance to government policies and to the power of the controlling authority. Thus the leaders are a sort of human 'link' between the two logics in question; they allow the entrepreneurial logic to develop in the enterprise, which is its natural environment, and at the same time prevent the logic of the State from being disregarded.

This 'link' apart, the combination of the State's logic and the entrepreneurial logic makes possible the identification of a number of different types of state-owned enterprises. As we have seen, at least three degrees of 'etatism' can be defined, according to the minimal, average or maximal degree of intervention of the State in the state-owned enterprise. In the same way, three degrees of entrepreneurial logic may be determined, according to the minimal average or maximal propensity of the state-owned enterprise to go multinational. Therefore we can construct a six-entry crossed matrix with the latter and the three degrees of state intervention. This matrix comprises nine 'squares' representing

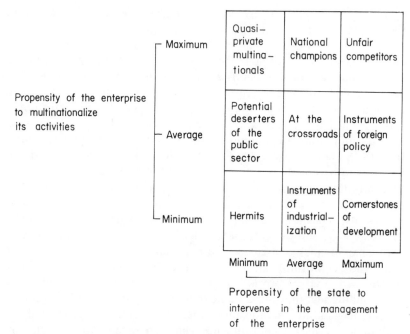

Propensity of the enterprise to multinationalize its activities

	Minimum	Average	Maximum
Maximum	Quasi–private multina–tionals	National champions	Unfair competitors
Average	Potential deserters of the public sector	At the crossroads	Instruments of foreign policy
Minimum	Hermits	Instruments of industrial–ization	Cornerstones of development

Propensity of the state to intervene in the management of the enterprise

A tentative typology of state-owned multinational firms. An analytical matrix

nine different types of state-owned enterprises. We have given them eloquent names which are not to be taken literally but rather as suggestions favouring further reflection. We shall now examine them in turn using the matrix presented here.

Type examples

1. The bottom left square of the diagram represents the 'hermits', that is to say enterprises which face hardly any state intervention in their management and which at the same time have little inclination to extend their activities abroad. According to our approach, state intervention is at a minimum when the prevailing ideology is that of a free market economy and the development gap is narrow. Therefore we can expect to find examples of enterprises of this type in the United States, West Germany, Norway, the Netherlands, etc. Moreover, the sector of activity of the enterprise does not lend itself to internationalization and the corporate identity is not compatible with such an aim. Enterprises of this type can be found in sectors with a 'domestic' nature — public

service monopolies, for example, particularly those with a bureaucratic functioning comparable to that of a government administration. We have not studied this type in detail, precisely because it does not succeed in multinationalizing. However, we can give some examples, if only to prove the validity of our analysis — the Tennessee Valley Authority or Amtrak in the United States. Both have a mission of collective service whose market is local by definition. They carry out their task following well-established procedures (their corporate identity focalizes on a bureaucratic mode of operation) and thus do not concern themselves with foreign markets. This immobility is reinforced by their non-interventionist government and the fact that they belong to one of the most developed countries in the world. It is interesting to note that they form an 'atypical type', since they should either be under private ownership (for example TVA is the only enterprise in its sector in the United States which was nationalized) or under greater government control.

2. The 'unfair competitors' represent the diametrically opposed type, and occupy the upper right-hand corner of the matrix. In this type, the propensity of the State to intervene and at the same time the propensity of the enterprise to go multinational are at a maximum. Since this multinationalization is carried out with the active aid of the State of the country of origin, these enterprises can be considered as unfair competitors because they benefit from greater advantages than their rival firms, who have to compete on unequal terms. If the State intervenes to a large extent, we can be sure that the enterprise belongs to a country with a wide development gap and a prevailing interventionist ideology. The example of developing countries immediately comes to mind, but it must be remembered that the 'development gap' defined by us should not be confused with the 'level of development'. We must therefore look for our examples in countries having an ambitious development programme because of their vast and unexploited economic potential. Owing to the sector of activity and the favourable corporate identity, the propensity of the enterprise to multinationalize is at a maximum. Enterprises with a managerial corporate identity are to be found in competitive industries with an international perspective. It is difficult to find enterprises which have all the requisites to fit into this model. It is therefore not surprising that we discovered practically no examples of true unfair competitors in Chapter Four. However, a number of firms have certain points of resemblance to this type and can be used to illustrate our analytical matrix. Thus Embraer, the Brazilian firm, belongs to an industry with an international perspective and has a corporate identity extremely favourable to internationalization. Moreover, Brazil is a country with considerable development needs. This example therefore tallies with our approach up to this

point, but the prevailing ideology tends, on the contrary, to be non-interventionist. In this case the development imperatives predominate over ideology, which explains the active interest taken by the government with regard to its favourite aeronautics firm. A second, but opposing, example is provided by the Airbus Industrie consortium, which can be likened to the 'unfair competitor' type, despite its denials. This enterprise has a well-established managerial identity, belongs to a sector of activity which is international by definition and is encouraged by a government, France, well known for its interventionist ideology — but not particularly 'underdeveloped'. In this case, ideology prevails over development factors. We had concluded too hastily that the propensity to state interventionism was maximum only when the two factors were extremely favourable to interventionism. Evidently, one of the two factors can sometimes predominate, resulting in a propensity to state interventionism which is either maximum or minimum but not average, as we had put forward in the form of a general hypothesis. In the cases cited above, this propensity is maximum and entails accusations of 'unfair competition' from other rivals, notably Americans.

3. The 'National champions' are similar to the preceding type because they are also subject to state intervention, though to a lesser degree. Moreover, since their propensity to multinationalization is very high, they occupy the middle square in the top row of our matrix. They are to be found in highly internationalized industries, and their corporate identity reinforces their foreign expansion. Their country of origin tends to be interventionist, either for ideological reasons or owing to development needs, thereby providing a wide range of possibilities. Countless examples can be found; it would possibly have been kinder to have placed Airbus in this category, but we will make amends by including its parent company, Aérospatiale. This French state-owned enterprise operates in civil and military aeronautics as well as space technology, which are all internationally competitive industries. Moreover, its internal identity favours multinationalization. The government observes its activities closely but refrains from imposing anti-economic burdens (like the Concorde programme in the past). Nor does it always meet its aid demands (in particular, as far as arms orders are concerned). Another enterprise which could fit into this category is ENI, which is in fact a holding company but whose oil division, Agip, could be cited as an example. The oil industry is one of the most worldwide sectors, and, since the days of Enrico Mattei, the corporate identity of Agip has favoured its international expansion. The Italian government does intervene, but more to appoint its chosen men (the *lottizzazione* system) than to define the firm's strategy. We have here a case of a developed country but with a prevailing interventionist

ideology, with the result that the two factors somewhat neutralize each other. Fewer examples can be found in developing countries. However, the Indian firm RITES is a notable exception, as we have seen in the course of our analyses.

4. The 'quasi-private multinational' type, which occupies the top left-hand corner of our matrix, includes a large number of enterprises. These enterprises have extensive multinational activities and are accorded considerable freedom of action by their government. They operate in internationally competitive industries and, in each case, the corporate identity is practically identical to that of their private counterparts. Since they belong to developed countries with a free market ideology, the government policy is non-interventionist. This is well exemplified by VIAG in Germany in the metallurgy sector or by Norsk-Hydro in Norway in the oil sector. When we interviewed the managements of this type of enterprise, we realized that state ownership is a relatively unimportant factor for them. This viewpoint is shared by their controlling authorities. In fact, one might wonder exactly why these enterprises are state-owned, and whether their privatization would bring any change in their situation. However, there must be a reason why they continue to be under state ownership, which can be discerned by examining the attitudes of the staff and the unions, as well as that of certain political parties. The fact that there are a great number of such enterprises throughout the world indicates that valid justifications for their situation do exist. Among the examples we have frequently cited in this book, we can include, though drawn from different contexts, Keppel Shipyard in Singapore, SGS (belonging to the IRI group) in Italy and DSM in the Netherlands. Certain French enterprises nationalized in 1982 — Rhône-Poulenc, Thompson (for household products), CGE (for cables), Saint-Gobain (for its traditional activities) — fall within this category, although they are somewhat different as the State intervenes to a certain extent in their management, albeit only with regard to specific issues. The above list suggests that our typology could cut across the business portfolio of diversified enterprises, in which some activities are managed almost in the manner of private industries whereas others are subject to state intervention. However, this shows the limits of all typologies, yet at the same time it encourages further analysis and a search for increasingly subtle differentiation criteria. In our analytical matrix we could have symbolised the enterprises by using circles or even clusters of points in order to emphasize the fact that they belong simultaneously to several types (with the circles cutting across the squares of the matrix). We have chosen not to do so, preferring to avoid further complicating our analysis.

5. The 'potential deserters' of the public sector are very close to those of the preceding category, though their propensity to go multinational is less marked (the middle square in the left-hand column of the matrix). In other words, the nature of their activities, or their corporate identity, is less favourable to their foreign expansion. This type includes, for example, high-technology enterprises which remain essentially exporters, as well as technology-minded firms which lack a commercial strategy. However, they must conform to only one of the two above criteria since otherwise they would be classified as 'hermits'. In this category state intervention is equally limited, probably because development imperatives do not call for an active role from the government, and the prevailing ideology tends to be that of the free market. However, once again exceptions can be found. The French company Matra, though specializing in high technology and more an exporting rather than a multinational firm, operates within a domestic environment which is predominantly interventionist. This autonomy is probably due to the charismatic personality of Jean-Luc Lagardère, its chairman, who, like the other company heads we mentioned earlier, can give an impetus to his enterprise while persuading the government to allow it total liberty of action. Possibly France is a country which we have classified too hastily as being interventionist. In any case, the enterprises belonging to this type tend to quit the public sector, following the example of 'quasi-private multinationals'. In order to do so, they need only further assert their multinationalization strategy (as in the case of Matra and its Datavision subsidiary in the United States). Another example is provided by the successful resistance of the Canadian Development Corporation to the pressure of the federal government, which sought to reduce it to a docile instrument of its Canadianization policy. Once again, this is due to its dynamic chairman, Anthony Hampson. This enterprise has become a deserter from the public sector, since it has been privatized. It appears that enterprises of this type possess exceptional qualities which enable them to break out of the shackles within which the others are confined. The holding company IPE, whose engineering subsidiary Profabril has already been cited, is in a similar situation. Enjoying a remarkable autonomy within the Portuguese public sector which is totally under the control of the State, it probably wishes to join the private sector. It has already started to sell a number of its subsidiaries (such as the store chain Expresso in 1984) to the private sector.

6. The situation of the 'instruments of industrialization' is quite different. Their propensity to go multinational is extremely low or even non-existent, whereas the intervention of the State in their management is far more pronounced. They occupy the middle square in the bottom

row of our matrix. They do not go multinational because they belong to a sector which is domestic in nature and because their corporate identity is closer to a bureaucratic rather than an entrepreneurial model. However, the State intervenes in their management, albeit moderately, because they are involved in the development process of the country or because of the prevailing interventionist ideology. These features are more common in developing countries than in industrialized nations, but they are also applicable to countries which have not yet realized their full development potential, like Spain or Canada. Thus, a group like INI in Spain essentially comprises enterprises of this type, which have not yet succeeded in going international (with the exception of ENASA) though they belong to industries as varied as the iron and steel industry, the chemical industry, the automobile and the arms industries. The official explanation is that they are too involved in the domestic market, where they benefit from government protection. The level of development of the country is possibly an explanatory factor but their corporate identity must also be taken into account (as illustrated by the foreign expansion of one such enterprise). Examples of this type may be found in less developed countries — Sidermex in Mexico, Siderbras in Brazil or BHEL in India. This seems to indicate that the reason for their lack of internationalization lies not in their corporate identity but rather in the economic conditions which determine their activities and in the attitude of their respective governments, which are little inclined to finance foreign operations in view of the firms' mediocre domestic performance. However, these enterprises retain a certain autonomy. Countless examples of this category may be found in industrializing countries.

7. The 'cornerstones of national development' closely resemble the preceding type. However, in this case state intervention in the management is more pronounced. They occupy the bottom right-hand corner of our matrix. The greater intervention of the State is probably due to the role they play in the economy, as well as the level of development of the country. Even when they are headed by a charismatic personality or have a corporate identity which favours foreign expansion, they are in fact the chosen instruments of their government. An enterprise like Pemex well exemplifies this type: it is responsible for more than half of Mexico's foreign currency and its growth rate determines the development rate of the country. Though it has the potential of a major oil multinational, it is restrained by its government because its strategic ambitions could disrupt the national economic equilibrium. This explains the poor results of its multinationalization strategy. Petroleos de Venezuela, Pertamina and Turkiye Petrolleri are in a similar situation, as they are involved to a large extent in the national development

policies of their respective countries, Venezuela, Indonesia and Turkey, whereas their foreign expansion is limited (Petroleos de Venezuela) or non-existent (Pertamina and Turkiye Petrolleri). In this case, the explanation is to be found in their control of natural resources which are essential to the country. A state-owned enterprise which exploits a raw material representing the national wealth of a country, especially a developing one, is most likely to fall into this category.

8. The 'instruments of foreign policy', like the preceding category, are equally subject to government control, but in this case the enterprises are far more multinationalized. They therefore occupy the middle right-hand square of our matrix. The reasons for state intervention are similar: these enterprises carry out activities which are essential to the national development. However, the reasons for the greater degree of multinationalization are more complex. They might lie in the nature of the competition (which can be international) or in other characteristics of the sector which have a bearing on multinationalization (for example the localization of production factors). But, in some cases the explanation can be found in the corporate identity of the enterprise, which may favour internationalization. All the above factors must be compatible with a strict state control, so that the strategy of the enterprise serves the government's foreign policy. Surprising as it may seem, certain enterprises do succeed in reconciling multinationalization with state interventionism. For example, an enterprise like Petrobras is international by force of circumstances (Brazil's oil resources being limited), multinational out of opportunism (its worldwide set-up facilitates its commercial activity) but, above all, serves the national objective. Not only does it ensure the fuel supplies of the country, but the foreign nations that it deals with are chosen according to the priorities of its government, which must be taken into account in the strategies of the enterprise. Other examples, though rare, can be found, as for instance the Office Chérifien des Phosphates, which, however, is in a somewhat different situation. This state-owned enterprise, which is the leading industrial group in Morocco, exploits one of the principal resources of the country, but, at the same time, it has managed to go beyond the national frontiers and assert itself as one of the major actors on the world phosphate market. Its success is probably due to the personality of its chairman, Karim Lamrani, who enjoys the full support of the King. In fact, he was twice appointed Prime Minister while continuing to carry out his managerial functions at the Office Chérifien des Phosphates. Certain Middle Eastern oil companies also fall into this category, as for example Iranian Oil (partnering BP in the Iranian British Steamship Company and in the exploitation of the 15/13 block of North Sea oil, in both cases having equal equity participation with the British

firm) and Kuwait Petroleum (which took over the European assets of Gulf in 1983).

9. The 'enterprises at the crossroads', which occupy the central square of our matrix, have some features in common with the preceding types without really falling into any specific category. By its very definition, this type is less clearly differentiated than the others. Its propensity to go multinational is 'average', as is the propensity of the State to intervene in its management. The indeterminate nature of these 'average' features precludes any clear-cut definition of a type. Thus we have a series of individual cases rather than a definite category. For example, ENASA, belonging to the Spanish INI group, which we classified as an 'instrument of industrialization', has marked itself out from the group by going multinational to a greater extent. The explanation is probably to be found in the corporate identity of the enterprise itself, rather than in its sector of activity (heavy vehicles), which is comparable with that of the other sectors in the same category. CIT-Alcatel, belonging to the French group CGE, provides a very different example. We have classified this enterprise (but only partially) as a 'quasi-private multinational'. However, within this type, it is less internationalized and more dependent on the State (for research and development and government contracts). Owing to this dependence, which is also a form of protection, it was less prepared for an international venture, though it is now increasingly expanding abroad, as shown by its projected purchase of ITT's telecommunication operations. GIOL of Argentina, ASV of Norway and Balmer-Lawrie of India are all enterprises at the crossroads, each for specific reasons. This category comprises enterprises which are only in transit. What is their final destination? This is the question to which we will now turn.

THE DYNAMICS OF STATE-OWNED MULTINATIONALS

All the enterprises mentioned above do not remain in one type for ever; on the contrary, in the course of their development they can shift from one category to another. In this respect the limits which we have set between the different types are less clearly established in reality than in our matrix; they serve to differentiate tendencies and situations in which a particular feature dominates. Therefore the shift of an enterprise from one category to another is not sudden but occurs progressively, and only time allows the definition of such changes and their successive phases.

There are only two possible ways through which an enterprise may become a state-owned multinational: either it is state-owned and becomes multinational progressively or it is multinational and is suddenly nationalized. Thus, there is a slow way — not to say a 'natural' way — and a rapid way — which may be 'artificial'; here the entrepreneurial logic is taken to be natural and the rapid emergence of policies, of the State's logic, which distort the former, to be artificial. Admittedly, this is a point of view. We could also mention the issues of the national interest being corrupted by the sirens of multinationalization. . . . However, we shall not discuss these two points since our main concern is the multinationalization process in itself and not the significance it is given according to an established set of values.

Considering our examples, it would seem that the two access ways to the state-owned multinational status are of unequal importance: in fact, only the French industrial groups nationalized in 1982 have followed the 'rapid way' mentioned above. It is too soon yet to analyse the consequences nationalization may have had on the multinational strategy of the groups concerned. A vast majority of state-owned multinationals are enterprises which originally were state-owned and later became multinational thereby following the 'slow way'. The shifts of the latter within our matrix can be described as falling into two models, the 'north model' and the 'south model', which we will now discuss further.

The 'north model' vs the 'south model'

The 'north model' is that of the more developed countries, which explains its name (referring to the North–South talks between industrialized countries and developing ones). Of the two opposing forces, the propensity to state interventionism and the propensity to multinationalization of activities, the latter is dominant. Thus, in this category, the states are more inclined to free market ideology and the enterprises are more involved in worldwide competition; the constraints of the owner-state are less burdensome and the managerial corporate identity of the enterprises rebels and struggles against them. At worst (for them) they will become 'national champions': they all more or less aspire to be 'quasi-private multinationals'.

The force which drives them, in other words the propensity to expand abroad, can intensify and in principle enable them to reach increasingly

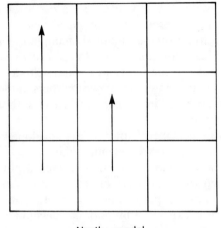

North model

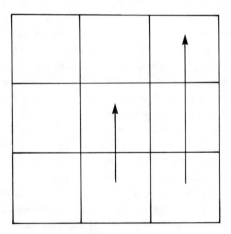

South model

high levels of multinationalization; however, freeing themselves from the control of the State is more difficult, which explains why, in this model, there are only vertical arrows. In fact, we are considering here enterprises which are already — and which remain — state-owned; their control by the State is therefore well established and does not change. For example, CIT-Alcatel, which we placed 'at the crossroads' in our matrix, is too dependent on the State to shift towards the left of the matrix (towards the 'potential deserters' or the 'quasi-private multinationals'): if it continues to expand abroad, as it seems to be doing, it will tend to become a 'national champion'. In the same way, VIAG, which we have considered as a 'quasi-private multinational', is very unlikely to move to the right in the matrix, that is to say towards a greater control by the state. As shown by the standard development of the enterprises observed in the past, these shifts, though not impossible, are most improbable.

The 'south model' is evidently that of less developed countries which are nevertheless in the process of industrialization — otherwise they would have no state-owned multinational, even a potential one. Our diagram shows that the propensity of the State to intervene is higher than the propensity of the enterprises to go multinational. The preeminence of the State is explained by national development problems as well as the lack of experience of the enterprises in such countries. This does not prevent them from going multinational; however, their foreign expansion is slower and more limited. One of the most important factors which determine it is the emergence within the enterprises of a type of manager who is inclined to venture abroad and, at the same time, is competent enough to carry out such an operation. Nevertheless, for all these enterprises, which are primarily state-owned and secondarily multinational, the control of the State will not lessen as they go more multinational. Countries of the 'south model' have a well-established interventionist tradition; in the event of a state-owned enterprise becoming international, the State will have an additional reason to keep a close eye on it. The State will first be wary of the emergence of a 'State within the State' that the international dimension represents and, secondly, it will regard the enterprise as the ideal instrument of its foreign policy. In our view this is the way to the 'unfair competitors' type: at the final stage of their multinationalization, certain enterprises in this category will not compete fairly for they will be supported by their State. However, as we noted earlier, examples of this type are rare. Firms like Petrobras or the Office Chérifien des Phosphates could tend towards this situation if their respective governments would let them further develop as multinationals, which they have opposed up to now. In the same context, the natural development, for example of Pemex or Petroleos de Venezuela, is to extend their activities abroad, thereby joining the above category; in the case of Siderbras or Sidermex, they would normally shift towards the middle square of the matrix (see p. 174), in other words towards the type we called 'at the crossroads', which we shall examine within the scope of the dynamics of state-owned multinationals.

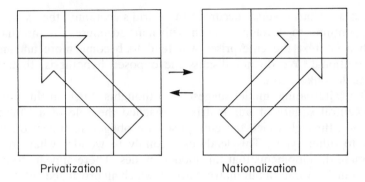

Privatization   Nationalization

The 'alternating model'

The 'alternating model', which we could also call the 'oscillating' model, is that of the enterprises whose development is disrupted by radical changes of government policy. We have already mentioned such a situation in the case of Great Britain (and of British Columbia in Canada) but other countries could be included in this model. France is one of them, since the 1982 nationalization wave was highly political in nature and perceived as such by public opinion and also because the return to power of a free market oriented majority will entail privatizations, following the example of Great Britain. The debate on privatization is quite common throughout the world and is revived by international organizations such as the World Bank or the International Monetary Fund. In West Germany and also in countries in the process of industrialization, which periodically realize that their public sector is a burden, the issue of privatization recurs sporadically. In Mexico and Brazil, the government regularly threatens certain state-owned enterprises with privatization because of their losses. Clearly, this reveals a paradoxical situation for it would be almost impossible for such enterprises to find private shareholders unless they adopted radically opposed management policies — notably in the social field. The 'alternating model' could be schematized as in the diagram.

In fact, it is an alternation of two opposed movements concerning the propensity of the State to intervene; this alternation is not linked to the strategies of the enterprises but rather to the political changes in their country of origin. As seen in our diagram, all nine cases share the common feature of an increasing internationalization. This is rather a bias on our part than an established law. Indeed, it seems to us that, unless a serious reversal occurs in the world's economy, the exchanges will continue to develop — even with marked pauses — and that in such a context the enterprises will tend to become more and more international. We do not dismiss the opposed hypothesis, though it seems less likely to us.

Our 'alternating' model suggests two thoughts. First, in this model, the central square of our matrix is assigned the role of a 'shunting station', through which the enterprises are obliged to transit on their way to other types. This leads us secondly to wonder what are the ultimate developments that this model implies. There appears to be at least one 'way out' of our matrix through which all privatized enterprises pass. As revealed by concrete examples, such a 'way out' does exist and has been followed, notably by British Aerospace, British Telecom and the Canadian Development Corporation. Nationalization implies a 'way into' the matrix, which has been followed by the French groups nationalized in 1982. Once inside the matrix, what are the main development patterns that a firm may experience? Our model suggests that if state intervention was maintained for a long enough period, all firms would tend to be 'unfair competitors'. However, such a development has not yet occurred in the countries which we studied. It may be too early to draw definite conclusions as the nationalizations referred to here are still too recent. Indeed, such a development may never take place, as the ideological evolution of the western world, even in countries where socialists are in power, is marked by an increasing rejection of state intervention.

Considering the cases of enterprises which enable us to draw more general conclusions, it seems that the high degree of multinationalization of a firm is incompatible in the long run with excessive state interventionism. The idea of the State intervening only to favour the multinationalization of the firm, though developed by critics of unfair competition, is unrealistic. Some actions of the State will indeed favour multinationalization but others will hinder it, for the State is not a unique actor but in fact a complex organization with various and often conflicting objectives, whose intervention may take extremely diverse forms. Furthermore, an enterprise which has become a true multinational has developed a specific corporate identity, strategic objectives and management methods which are diametrically opposed to those of the State. The State and the enterprise may have convergent views concerning multinationalization, albeit limited to particular foreign investment operations. Other foreign expansion decisions may be rejected or delayed and countless day-to-day problems may impair the relations between the State and the enterprise.

Thus, such a combination of a high degree of multinationalization with strong state interventionism suggests that the situation will eventually reach a breaking point. The upper left-hand corner of our matrix shows a 'way out', whereas the upper right-hand corner seems to be a dead end. The many vetos checking further foreign expansion operations opposed by the State will discourage the employees, lead to a loss of enthusiasm for international development, and hence to the decline of the enterprise; it must be remembered that on international markets competition is fierce. Though not impossible, international 'relational' strategies are difficult to sustain in the long run since they depend on short-lived bilateral agreements.

The breaking point is reached when the international development of state-owned multinationals is hindered rather than favoured by state intervention. What happens beyond this breaking point — the decline of the enterprise or an increased *laissez-faire* policy of the State — remains an open question which we will discuss as a conclusion to this research. However, before ending this chapter, we will try to apply our typology analysis to most of the state-owned enterprises we have mentioned in the course of our book.

POSITIONING STATE-OWNED MULTINATIONALS IN THE MATRIX

In order to illustrate our analysis on the 'north' and 'south' models, we will present our typology according to two different groups: one which comprises all enterprises from 'northern' countries, the other all enterprises from 'southern' countries (see diagram).

In the 'northern' group, most of the enterprises are positioned above the diagonal, the only exceptions being Spanish firms, that is to say firms belonging to a country which could also be considered as part of the 'southern' group.

In the 'southern' group, most enterprises are concentrated in exactly the opposite part of the matrix. The only exception is that of Keppel Shipyard. Once again, should Singapore still be considered as a developing country?

It is quite clear that there are far more state-owned multinationals in the 'northern' group than in the 'southern' group, which confirms the observations we have made throughout the preceding chapters.

Southern group

		ICCI
	RITES	Embraer
		Petrobras / Iranian Oil / YPF / OCP
Keppel Shipyard	GIOL / Balmer-Lawrie	PDVSA Pemex / CVRD
	Siderbras Sidermex / BHEL	Indian Oil / Turkiye Petrolleri

Northern group

NIOG / Airbus		
SGS Péchiney / Saint-Gobain / Elf-Aquitaine / Agip Sofretu		
VIAG / Rhône-Poulenc / Renault / HQI		
DSM Assi / Salzgitter		
Norsk Hydro / CGE / Voest-Alpine / Cogéma / Thomson Aérospatiale	ENASA	
Matra	CIT-Alcatel	
CDC	ASV	
IPE / British Aerospace	British Leyland	
BRIC	CASA	
TVA / Portucel / Amtrak	SEAT	

Lastly, many public services, from either developed or developing countries, have not been included in our tables as they are not multinational and not even in the process of becoming so. They would be positioned in the form of a cluster along the bottom line on the right-hand side of the matrix.

Nationalization and Multinationalization: The Breaking Point in Perspective

We have so far considered state-owned multinationals as a novel category of enterprise which, nevertheless, forms part of the contemporary scene. If we limit ourselves to our definition of Chapter Two, we find that a large number of enterprises can be classified as state-owned multinationals — a minimum of 10% of their turnover must be achieved in at least two different countries other than the country of origin, while the government of the latter must obviously hold more than 50% of their shares. However, this definition does not encompass the central question posed in this book, for it does not take into account the reasons underlying the nationalization and the multinationalization of an enterprise, which in our opinion can often prove to be contradictory. In the preceding chapters, we affirmed that this contradiction was 'manageable' or that at least it could be resolved concretely in different ways. This led us to propose a typology of state-owned multinationals. Finally, we must follow our reasoning to its logical conclusion and ask ourselves whether an enterprise which continues indefinitely its multinationalization as well as its nationalization (in other words, its service to the government of its country of origin) reaches a point where the contradiction between the two opposed logics becomes too pronounced, and can no longer be resolved. In order to identify the breaking point beyond which the conflict becomes irreconcilable, it is necessary to recall the logics involved.

The principle of nationalization is well known — a number of large enterprises must be made to serve the national interest by playing a key role in the economic development of the country. It must, however, be noted that there are a certain number of contradictions inherent in this principle, giving it a dialectical character. The state-owned enterprise must serve the political and industrial policy and contribute to the macroeconomic objectives (employment, foreign trade, prices, etc.), but, in order to be an effective instrument, it must be managed efficiently. The possible contradictions are theoretically best resolved by negotiated agreements, based on the strategic planning of the enterprise, in the context of an explicit national plan.

The logic of multinationalization has also been the subject of countless studies, most of them from an economic rather than a managerial perspective. In our opinion, a true multinationalization policy consists of a twofold convergent movement, starting simultaneously from the top and the base. At the top, corporate headquarters define the major strategic orientations and allocate the resources among the different fields of activity of the enterprise. At the base, the different units — set up by definition in a number of countries — frame development projects for their different activities, drawing on their first-hand knowledge of the territory. These two movements meet in an integrated planning process or any decision-making process which acts as a substitute. Thus, for us, a true multinational is not merely an enterprise with an international strategy, however deliberate, nor one which collects dividends from its foreign, and very likely well-placed, investments.

Our definitions of a state-owned enterprise on the one hand and of the multinational on the other need to be further elaborated. In fact, strategy by itself is not enough. It is formulated and implemented through specific organizational structures, in which the decision-making processes play an important part. In the long run, a corporate identity characteristic of each distinctive enterprise emerges through these structures. The standard state-owned enterprise is a more centralized company, owing to its submission to the controlling authority of the State and its mission of public service (or at least its commitment to the national interest) which unifies the employees at all levels. The standard multinational is very different, with an extremely decentralized structure and its corporate identity focalized above all on a 'managerial' behaviour pattern centred on adaptability and mobility, which are the factors for success. These two natures can coexist for a certain time, but we feel that sooner or later the contradictions will become irreconcilable and the enterprise will have to make a definite choice. It can either pursue its multinationalization, thereby abandoning its mission of public service, or it can give priority to the latter, in which case it will no longer be a true multinational.

Can a state-owned enterprise which sets up abroad go as far as forgetting its primary mission of public service? In our opinion, it is inevitable, and even essential, if the enterprise wishes to remain in the race, in the context of the major oligopolies which characterize the world economy. First, it is essential in terms of technology. Investing heavily in research and development is not enough; the enterprise must be able to offer products and services which can compete with those of other companies. Moreover, it is crucial (but still rare) that the engineers and researchers are allowed sufficient mobility, in order to provide them with varied experience. Next, the enterprise's abandoning of its national mission is vital for reasons of economic efficiency. Placed in a situation comparable to that of private companies, the state-owned enterprise must create an economic surplus; it must generate cash flows which enable it to compete on equal terms; its managers cannot function differently compared to those of private companies.

If, as we have suggested, a large number of development projects are proposed by the base, can they be rejected by the top echelon each time they are vetoed by the shareholder-state? Can the opposition of the government be long accepted by the management, against the wishes of its decentralized units? It is not possible to check all attempts at initiative and responsibility without provoking a reaction of indignation and rejection. The management tends to avoid such a predicament by acting as a screen between the enterprise and the controlling authority, mitigating the repressive measures of the latter in order to permit the enterprise to extend its activities abroad. The more the management plays such a role, the more difficult it is for the controlling authority to be aware of and understand developments beyond its frontiers. The government can thus be kept at a distance, being warned that an excessive interference can lead to the bankruptcy of the company, which will be unable to cope with international competition.

In this hypothesis, the interventionist State meets with failure. Its directives are followed only on rare occasions, when they are not incompatible with the strategy of the enterprise. A truly interventionist government cannot content itself with such a secondary role. It will exert greater pressure, and be tempted to resort to authoritarian measures such as arbitrarily imposed decisions, replacement of recalcitrant managers, etc. The press will take up the issue and revive the controversy concerning nationalization, the dismissed managers will voice their grievances in the media, providing arguments for political parties opposed to the existing government. At the same time, government objectives can be sabotaged from within the enterprise — not deliberately, but rather as the combined result of the reaction of a number of refractory individuals — tending to justify the assumption that nationalization can be dangerous. The commercial failures of the company compared to its rivals will be highlighted and all unsatisfactory financial results proclaimed with much publicity in order to make the taxpayer apprehensive. In such a situation, any change of government will lead to a privatization policy.

However, the government does not always behave in the manner evoked above. Instead of increasing its pressure on the enterprise which goes multinational it can lessen its control, seeking to avoid the difficult consequences described in the preceding paragraph. However, in this case it ceases to be interventionist and the reconciliation of nationalization and multinationalization is achieved through the predominance of the latter. We have thus a virtual privatization, whereby a political crisis can be averted. The breaking point can be avoided through the State renouncing its role, bringing us to the 'quasi-private multinational' category of our typology. In this case, as in the preceding one, the State must beat a retreat, either voluntarily or under the pressure of public opinion. Yet the State can react in other ways — what if it succeeds in imposing its views on the enterprise? In our opinion, this would lead to the relegation of the multinationalization principle to a secondary role. Let us assume that once the government has replaced a certain number of managers, the resulting resignations eliminate most of the internal opposition to government directives. The enterprise is now totally subservient to the State. The government can possess a certain degree of political acumen: the issue of nationalization need not necessarily be problematic. In such a situation the enterprise can be run entirely according to government objectives, which may very well include plans for setting up abroad. However, our observations have indicated that in such cases multinationalization is never extensive because all initiatives come from the top echelons, whereas the base merely executes orders. Abroad, the enterprise lacks a fighting spirit and tends increasingly to rely on its government for conquering or retaining its hold on the market. This attitude is due to the certainty that in the event of any conflict between the development possibilities of the enterprise and any government policy the former will invariably be obliged to renounce its claims. The international expansion of the company becomes of secondary importance, taking place only when it does not hamper the official policies (or if the general management, in the absence of any initiative from its units, makes some attempt at decisive action).

Let us go a step further and assume that the State has an entrepreneurial outlook, and that instead of imposing a check on the enterprise it wins it over. For example, it can offer generous financial aid, accord substantial grants for research and development, ensure lucrative public markets and help in export. However, in the context of an interventionist State, the enterprise remains an instrument to serve the national interest, notwithstanding the financial advantages generously granted by the State to compensate for its lack of autonomy. Can a state-owned enterprise go multinational in such circumstances? Though we earlier replied in the affirmative, it must be added that such an enterprise can never be a true multinational. It should be emphasized that a government which consistently uses its state-owned multinationals as a tool for furthering its policies inevitably creates fragile and inadequate multinationals, in other words enterprises of inferior calibre, totally dependent on state aid. More precisely, each time the government opposes a decision of the enterprise which conforms to a multinationalization logic, it also becomes bound to grant state aid to the company in question. If a large number of state-owned multinationals are subjected to repeated government checks and consequent promises of aid, their economic situation can soon become explosive and uncontrollable.

This risk seems greater for developing countries than for developed ones. Admittedly, the developing countries do not yet possess state-owned enterprises which are extensively multinational. However, it is only a question of time and, given the current crisis, the development of such enterprises may be more rapid than is generally foreseen. Yet developing countries lack experience or any long tradition in this field. Their managers have so far known the international scene only as exporters, and their high-ranking civil servants and politicians habitually reason from a purely nationalistic point of view. As they become increasingly aware of the immense possibilities offered by foreign markets, they are tempted to go all out to set up abroad, without really knowing the rules of the game. They attempt to achieve all at the same time: create powerful enterprises, capable of defending the country's interests on the international scene. In this perspective, considerations of economic profitability are relegated to a secondary position, at least during the initial expansionist phase.

However, the 'unfair competitors' which launch an attack on positions so far held by private multinationals in fact prove to be giants with feet of clay. Their governments cannot long sustain them in their onslaught against their private competitors for the national resources are not inexhaustible. This can lead to catastrophic results — either a hasty retreat or a foolhardy venture into increasingly daring operations. However, at the same time, this also signals the beginning of a greater autonomy for the state-owned enterprises of the developing countries concerned, hence a progression towards quasi-privatization, which we discussed above. Thus it appears that in the long run the state-owned enterprises of developing countries must choose between two alternatives. They can either remain national, engaging in export, with a limited number of set-ups abroad depending on specific situations, or they can sever their links with the State — taking advantage of a political upheaval for example — and become true multinationals.

The picture is very different in developed countries, or at least in those which have a free market ideology and are exposed to international competition. We may say that state-owned enterprises which go multinational will be increasingly privatized, whether formally or in practice. However, there is no alternative solution. Apart from 'purely' national public services — though it might be asked if they can remain so indefinitely — all state-owned enterprises are obliged to expand abroad for the sake of their survival. In fact, no other long-term possibilities are feasible. In this respect, the events in France and in Britain in the early eighties are revealing. At first glance, the two countries appear to be diametrically opposed, since one pursued a policy of nationalization and the other of privatization. It can be argued that in both cases the objective was the development — and therefore the multinationalization — of the enterprises concerned. However, in that case, why were the means utilized so radically different? In our opinion the difference can be explained as follows.

In France, the nationalization of the large industrial groups can be considered as a step in their multinationalization process. The State intervened at the right moment in order to reinforce their capital and their credit, to enable them to invest in research and development and to benefit from national protection. All these advantages were lacking under private ownership during the preceding free market governments. Nationalization gave a new lease of life to these enterprises and facilitated redeployment. On the other hand, state ownership could never lead to the paralysis of the enterprises (owing to the disruptive effect of repeated state interventions) since it would thereby become inacceptable to public opinion. Thus, either the government leaves the enterprises to benefit from its largesse and enjoy a large measure of autonomy or, after the next elections, the new party in power privatizes the nationalized companies. In the first case, we have a virtual privatization, in the second, a legal one. Hindsight will show that for these enterprises nationalization was largely profitable and gave an impetus to their multinationalization strategy.

Britain is already in the second phase since the initial phase of nationalization met with failure. The previous governments — whether Labour or Conservative — were unable to give the British state-owned enterprises the means or the autonomy necessary for their multinationalization. Thus we had an unacceptable situation, of the kind evoked above. Privatization was envisaged as the most effective method of encouraging the enterprises to go multinational. Thatcher and Mitterrand therefore apparently had a common goal! All factors, including ideology, are shaped by circumstances.

Today, it seems indisputable that enterprises must go multinational in order to ensure their survival in our competitive world. Compared to this compulsion, the state or private ownership of a company is a secondary issue. Generally, state ownership is not favourable to multinationalization, but, as we showed, in specific circumstances it can have a beneficial impact. Above all, the legal status of a company is of lesser importance than its relations with the government. Though very much in fashion at the moment, we do not anticipate a massive surge of privatizations throughout the world, even throughout Europe. Moreover, with the increasing internationalization of economies, there will be more and more 'state-owned multinationals'. However, of these two terms, the latter will inevitably eclipse the former. Whether state-owned or private, multinationals will be above all multinationals.

Annex:

Enterprises Studied

Enterprise	Country of origin	Sector of activity	State owner-ship %	Creation or national-ization year	1983 turnover[g]	Exported turnover (%)	Foreign turnover (%)	1983 net results	No. of industrial subsidiaries abroad	Main host countries
State-owned multinationals										
Aérospatiale	France	Aeronautics	100	1970	3 152	61	3	−47	5	USA, Singapore
Agip (ENI)	Italy	Oil products	100	1926	14 750[f]	NA	NA	220[f]	Multiple[a]	Africa, Europe
Assi	Sweden	Paper products	100	1942	634	80	9	0.097	8	Denmark, UK
CIT-Alcatel (CGE)	France	Telecom	100	1982[b]	1 717	23	NA	7.8	2	USA
Cogéma (CEAI)	France	Nuclear	100	1976	431[f]	36	NA	0.04	Multiple[a]	North America, Africa,
CGE	France	Diversified	100	1982[b]	8 195	24	39	52	Multiple[a]	USA, Germany
DSM	Netherlands	Chemicals	100	1902	6 926	62	NA	57	Multiple	USA, Europe, Mexico
Elf-Aquitaine	France	Oil products	67	1941	18 188	9	21	488	Multiple	Europe, USA, Africa
Embraer	Brazil	Aeronautics	55[d]	1969	276[f]	50	NA	25[c]	2	Europe, USA
ENASA	Spain	Automobile	100	1946	57.2[c]	36	NA	−2.13[f]	4	UK, Latin America
Keppel Shipyard	Singapore	Shipbuilding	70	1968	33.3	8	NA	0.04	2	Philippines
Norsk-Hydro	Norway	Oil products	51	1945	4 077	86	NA	67	Multiple	Qatar, Europe, UK
Péchiney	France	Aluminium	100	1982[b]	3 806	36	25	−61	Multiple [a]	Canada, Australia, Africa
Petrobras	Brazil	Oil products	100	1953	16 258	NA	NA	486	Multiple[a]	Africa, Middle East
Renault	France	Automobile	95	1945	14 467	34	48	−206	Multiple[a]	USA, Europe
Rhône-Poulenc	France	Chemicals	100	1982[b]	5 657	31	38	13	Multiple[a]	Brazil, USA, UK
Saint-Gobain	France	Diversified	100	1982[b]	7 595	16	49	53	Multiple[a]	USA, Germany, Brazil
Salzgitter	Germany	Iron and steel	100	1951	3 774	35[a]	27[c]	273	Multiple[a]	Europe, USA, Latin America
SGS	Italy	Electronics	100	1972[b]	230	NA	84	0.250	4	France, Malta, Singapore, Malaysia
Thomson	France	Electronics	100	1982[b]	6 492	35	21	−141	Multiple[a]	Spain, Singapore, Germany
VIAG	Germany	Métals	100	1945	2 309	23	8	31.6	Multiple[a]	USA, Canada, Europe
Voest-Alpine	Austria	Métals	100	1945	6 632	72	NA	−2	Multiple[a]	Europe, USA
YPF	Argentina	Oil products	100	1922	6 782	NA	NA	−4 643	3	Ecuador, Péru, Bolivia

Enterprise	Country of origin	Sector of activity	State owner-ship %	Creation or national-ization year	1983 turnover^e	Exported turnover (%)	Foreign turnover (%)	1983 net results	No. of industrial subsidiaries abroad	Main host countries
State-owned enterprises in the process of multinationalization										
Balmer-Lawrie (IBP)	India	Diversified	65	1972^b	40^c	32^c	1.9	−0.24^c	2	Dubai, Saudi Arabia
BHEL	Indonesia	Electricals	100	1963	943^c	15^c	0	0.49^c	—	—
CASA	Spain	Aeronautics	72	1943^b	30^f	69	NA	0.3^f	2	Indonesia, Brazil
CVRD	Brazil	Mining	100	1942^b	1 642^e	80	0	344	1	USA
Matra	France	Diversified	51	1982^b	1 340	72	NA	4.5	1	USA
OCP	Morocco	Phosphates	100	1956	1 200^f	70	NA	NA	1	Belgium
Pemex	Mexico	Oil products	100	1938	16 140	79^b	NA	−5	1	Spain
Petroleos de Venezuela	Venezuela	Oil products	100	1976	6 012	95^b	NA	712	1	Germany
Siderbras	Brazil	Iron and steel	100	1973	2 500^f	NA	NA	−100^f	2	Latin America
Engineering Companies										
Hydro-Quebec Int.	Canada	Engineering	100	1978	NA	—	100	NA	7	India, Bangladesh, Saudi Arabia
ICCI	Indonésia	Engineering	100	1979	NA	—	100	NA	1	Saudi Arabia
NIOG	UK	Engineering	100	1976	230^f	—	100	3.75^f	Multiple^a	Europe, Middle East
RITES (IR)	India	Engineering	100	1974	21.7^f	—	76	4.5^f	10	Africa, Ceylon
Sofretu (RATP)	France	Engineering	100	1961	17.9^f	—	84	0	Multiple^a	America, Africa

[a] Over 10.
[b] Nationalization year.
[c] 1982 figures.
[d] Voting rights.
[e] In million US dollars. *Source: Fortune 500*, except f.
[f] Estimate.

Selected Bibliography

Acocella, N., *L'Impresa Pubblica Italiana e la Dimensione Internazionale, Il Caso dell'IRI*, Einaudi, Torino, 1983.

Agmon, T. and Kindleberger, C. (eds), *Multinationals from Small Countries*, MIT Press, Cambridge, 1977.

Aharoni, Y., 'The state-owned enterprise as a competitor in international markets', *Columbia Journal of World Business*, Spring 1980.

Allen, M. and Ghertman, M., *An Introduction to the Multinationals*, MacMillan, London, 1982.

Anastassopoulos, J. P., 'The French experience: conflicts with the government, in Vernon, R. and Aharoni, *State-Owned Enterprise in the Western Economies*, Croom Helm, London, 1981.

Anastassopoulos, J. P., 'The strategic autonomy of government-controlled enterprises operating in a competitive economy', PhD diss., Columbia University, 1973.

Anastassopoulos, J. P., *La Stratégie des Entreprises Publiques*, Dalloz, Paris, 1980.

Baer, W., *The Brazilian Economy, Growth and Development*, Praeger, New York, 1984.

Balassa, B., *'Comments on A. M. Choksi's "State intervention in the industrialization of developing countries: selected issues"'*, World Bank Paper, 1979.

Baumann, H. G., 'Merger theory, property rights and the pattern of US direct investment in Canada', *Weltwirtschaftliches Archiv* **III**, 4, 1975.

Baumol, W. (ed.), *Public and Private Enterprise in a Mixed Economy*, St Martin's Press, New York, 1980.

Bergsman, J., *'Growth and equity in semi-industrialized countries'*, World Bank Staff Working Paper No. 351, 1979.

Bery, S., *'Public sector enterprises in India: a descriptive survey'*, Domestic Finance Studies No. 28, 1976, Public and Private Finance Division, Development Finance Department, The World Bank.

Bhagwati, J. and Desai, P., *India: Planning for Industrialization*, Oxford University Press, London, 1970.

Bhatt, V. V., 'Decision making in the public sector', *Economic and Political Weekly* **13**, No. 13, May 1978, pp. 30–48.

Bizaguet, A. *et al.*, *Les Entreprises Publiques dans la CEE*, Dunod, Paris, 1967.

Blitzer, C., Clark P. and Taylor, L., *Economy-Wide Models and Development Planning*, Oxford University Press, London, 1975.

Bloch-Lainé, F., *Profession: Fonctionnaire*, Seuil, Paris, 1976.

Boccara, P., *Etudes sur le Capitalisme Monopoliste d'Etat, Sa Crise et Son Issue*, Editions Sociales, Paris, 1973.

Boiteux, M., 'Planning investments in public enterprises: the experience of Electricité de France', Paper from Conference on Public and Private Enterprises in a Mixed Economy, Mexico, 1978.

Boublil, A., *Le Socialisme Industriel*, PUF, Paris, 1977.

Brachet, Ph., *L'Etat-Patron*, Syros, Paris, 1974.

Brachet, Ph., *Entreprises Nationalisées et Socialisme*, CERF, Paris, 1978.

Brown, W. E., 'Island of consensus power: MNCs in the theory of the firm', MSU, *Business Topics*, Summer 1976.

Buckley, P. J. and Dunning, J. H., 'The industrial structure of US direct investment in the UK', *Journal of International Business Studies*, Summer 1976.

Buckley, P. J. and Pearce, R. D., 'Overseas production and exporting by the world's largest enterprises', *Journal of International Business Studies*, Spring/ Summer 1979.

Carey-Jones, N. S., Patankar, S. M. and Poodhoo, M. J., *Politics, Public Enterprise and the International Development Agency*, Croom Helm, London, 1974.

Carillo Castro, A., *Las Empresas Publicas en Mexico*, INAP, Mexico, 1976.

Caves, R. E., 'International corporations: the industrial economics of foreign investment', *Economica*, February 1971.

Caves, R. E., 'The causes of direct investment: foreign firm's shares in Canadian and UK manufacturing industries', *Review of Economics and Statistics*, August 1974.

Centre Européen des Entreprises Publiques, *Les Entreprises Publiques dans la CEE*, 1981.

Chenery, H. B., 'Interaction between industrialization and exports', *American Economic Association*, 1980.

Chevallier, J., '*Les entreprises publiques en France*', Documentation Française, N.E.D. No. 4507–08, 1979.

Choksi, A. M., '*State intervention in the industrialization of developing countries, selected issues*,' World Bank Staff Working Paper No. 341, 1979.

Club Socialiste du Livre, *L'agression: l'Etat Giscard Contre le Secteur Public*, Paris, 1980.

Collective, 'La politique monopoliste contre le secteur public et nationalisé, Special issue, *Economie et Politique*, November 1974.

Comité Nora, *Rapport sur les Entreprises Publiques*, 1967.

Commission de Verification des Comptes des Entreprises Publiques, *Rapports d'Ensemble* (I à XIV).

Conte, A., *Hommes Libres*, Plon, Paris, 1973.

Cornell, R., 'Trade of multinational firms and nation's comparative advantage',

Paper presented to a conference of Multinational Corporations and Governments, UCLA, November 1973.

Cotta, A. and Ghertman, M. (eds), *Les Multinationales en Mutation*, PUF, Paris, 1983.

Dangeard, F., *Nationalisations et Dénationalisations en Grande-Bretagne*, La Documentation Française, Paris, 1983.

Donges, J. B., 'A comparative survey of industrialization policies in fifteen semi-industrialized countries', *Weltwirtschaftliches Archiv*, No. 112, 1976.

Donges, J. B. and Riedel, J., '*The expansion of manufactured exports in developing countries: an empirical assessment of supply and demand issues*', Institut für Weltwirtschaft, Kiel Working Papers, No. 49, 1976.

Doz, Y., 'Multinational strategy and structure in government-controlled business', *Columbia Journal of World Business*, Fall 1980.

Dreyfus, P., *La Liberté de Réussir*, J. C. Simoens, Paris, 1977.

Drouot, G. and Bonnaud, J., *Deux Entreprises Publiques Face à Leur Avenir: Air France et la SNCF*, PUF, Paris, 1979.

Dunning, J. H., 'The determinants of international production', *Oxford Economic Papers*, November 1973.

Dunning, J. H., 'Trade location of economic activity and the multinational enterprise. A search for an eclectic approach', in Ohlin, B., Hesselborn, P. O. and Wiskman, P. J. (eds) *The International Allocation of Economic Activity*, London, MacMillan, 1979.

Dunning, J. H., 'Explaining changing patterns of international production: in defense of the eclectic theory', *Oxford Bulletin of Economics and Statistics*, November 1979.

Dunning, J. H., 'Toward an eclectic theory of international production', *Journal of International Business Studies*, Spring–Summer 1980.

Dunning, J. H. and Buckley, P. J., 'International production and alternative models of trade', *Manchester School of Economic and Social Studies* **45**, December 1977.

Dupuis, M., *Nationaliser, Quels groupes? Pourquoi? Comment?* Editions Sociales, Paris, 1974.

Economist, 'The state industry Merry-Go-Round', *Economist*, December 1978.

EROPA, 'Eastern Regional Organization for Public Administration, (The role of public enterprise in development)', Manila Conference, June 1978.

Evans, P., *Dependent Development, the Alliance of Multinational, State and Local Capital in Brazil*, Princeton University Press, New York, 1979.

Franck, J. R. , 'Public and private enterprises in Africa', in Ranis, G. *Government and Economic Development*, Yale University Press, New Haven, 1971.

François-Marsal, F., *Le Dépérissement des Entreprises Publiques*, Calmann Lévy, Paris, 1973.

Gallais-Hamono, G., *Les Nationalisations. A quel Prix? Pour Quoi Faire?* PUF, Paris, 1977.

Gantt, A. and Lutto, G., '*Financial performance of government-owned corporations in less developed countries*', Staff Papers of the IMF, No. 25, 1968, pp. 102–142.

Garner, M., 'Governments and public enterprises, their relationships abroad', *The Banker*, March 1980.

Gaudy, R., *Et la Lumière fut Nationalisée*, Editions Sociales, Paris, 1978.

Ghertman, M., *Les Multinationales*, Que Sais-je? PUF, Paris, 1982.

Girgis, M., *Industrialization and Trade Patterns in Egypt*, Kieler Studien, Tübingen, 1976.

Gordon, D., *Development Finance Companies, State and Privately Owned*, The World Bank, Washington, 1983.

Grassini, F. and Scognamiglio, C. (eds), *Stato e Industria in Europa: l'Italia*, Il Mulino, Bologna, 1979.

Grieve Smith, J. (ed.), *Strategic Planning in Nationalized Industries*, MacMillan, London, 1984.

Guisinger, S., 'Direct controls in the private sector,' in Hugues, H. and Wall, D., *'Industrial development policy'*, World Bank and UNIDO Paper, 1980.

Haas, J., 'Les caractéristiques de l'industrialisation des principaux pays en voie de développement', Annex II in Berthelot, Y. and Tardy, G. *Le Défi Economique du Tiers Monde*, Documentation Française, Paris, 1978.

Hafsi, T., *Entreprise Publique et Politique Industrielle*, McGraw Hill, Paris, 1984.

Hamilton, C., *Public Subsidies to Industry: The Case of Sweden and its Ship-building Industry*, The World Bank, Washington, 1983.

Hanson, A. H., *Public Enterprise and Economic Development*, Routledge and Kegan Paul, London, 1965.

Hanson, A. H., 'Organization and administration of public enterprises' Paper from United Nations Seminar on the Organization of State-Owned Enterprises, Asia and Far East Economic Commission, Bangkok, 1966.

Hirsch, S., 'Capital or technology? Confronting the neo-factor proportions and neo-technology account of international trade', *Weltwirtschaftliches Archiv* **114**, 1974.

Hirsch, S., 'An international trade and investment theory of the firm', *Oxford Economic Papers*, July 1976.

Holland, S., *The State as Entrepreneur*, Weidenfield and Nicolson, London, 1972.

Horst, T., 'Firm and industry determinants of the decision to invest abroad: an empirical study', *Review of Economics and Statistics*, August 1972.

Horst, T., 'The industrial composition of US exports and subsidiary states to the Canadian market', *American Economic Review*, March 1972.

Horst, T., 'American exports and foreign direct investments', *Harvard Institute of Economic Research Discussion* 362, May 1974.

Hsing, M., *Taïwan: Industrialization and Trade Policies*, Oxford University Press, London, 1970.

Hufbauer, G. C., 'The impact of national characteristics and technology on the commodity composition of trade in manufactured goods', in Vernon, R. (ed.) *The Technology Factor in International Trade*, Columbia University Press, New York, 1970.

IIAP, 'Les entreprises publiques', *Revue Française d'Administration Publique*, October–December 1977.

International Development Research Center, Kuala Lumpur conference on 'The Needs for Research in the Field of Management of state-Owned Enterprises in Asia', Country studies: India, South Korea, Singapore, 1976.

IPEA, *A Empresa Publica no Brasil: Uma Abondagem Multidisciplinar*, SEMOR, Brasilia, 1980.

Jha, P. S., *The Public Sector in India: Pioneering Role of the State in Industry*, Oxford University Press, London, 1980.

Johnson, H., 'The efficiency and welfare implications of the international corporation,' in Kindleberger, C. P. (ed.) *The International Corporation*, MIT Press, Cambridge, 1970.

Jones, L. P., *Public Enterprises and Economic Development: The Korean Case*, Korean Development Institute, Seoul, 1975.

Killick, J., *Development Economics in Action*, St Martin's Press, New York, 1978.

Knickerbocker, F. T., *Oligopolistic Reaction and the Multinational Enterprise*, Cambridge, Harvard University Press, 1973.

Kojima, K., 'A macro-economic approach to foreign direct investment', *Hitotsubashi Journal of Economics*, June 1973.

Krueger, A. O., *Foreign Trade Regimes and Economic Development: Liberalization Attempts and Consequences*, Praeger, New York, 1978.

Kubo, Y. and Robinson, S., '*Sources of industrial growth and structural change: a comparative analysis of eight countries*', World Bank Paper, 1979.

Kumar, K., 'Multinationalization of third-world public sector enterprises,' in Kumar, K. and McLeod, M. G. *Multinationals from Third World Countries*, Lexington Books, 1981.

Kumar, K. and McLeod, M. G., *Multinationals from Third World Countries*, Lexington Books, 1981.

Lal, D., 'Public enterprises', in Hugues, H., and Wall, D., '*Industrial development policy*,' World Bank and UNIDO Paper, 1980.

Lall, S., *Developing Countries in the International Economy*, MacMillan, London, 1981.

Lall, S. and Streeten, P., *Foreign Investment, Transnationals and Developing Countries*, MacMillan, London, 1982.

Lamont, D. F., *Foreign State Enterprises, a Threat to American Business*, Basic Books, New York, 1979.

Lamont, D. F. and Smith, H., 'Economic policy and international corporate strategy in a world of state-enterprise capitalism', Paper from Academy of International Business Annual Meeting, November 12–14, 1976.

Land, J. W., 'The role of public enterprises in Turkish economic development', in Ranis, G. *Government and Economic Development*, Yale University Press, New Haven, 1971.

Laufer, R. and Burlaud, A., *Le Management Public: Gestion et Légitimité*, Dalloz, Paris, 1980.

Le Pors, A., *Les Béquilles du Capital*, Seuil, Paris, 1977.

Lietaer, B., *Europe + Latin America + The Multinationals*, Gower Publishing Company, Farnborough, 1979.

Little, I. M. D., Scitovski, T. and Scott, M. F. G., *Industry and Trade in Developing Countries: A Comparative Study*, Oxford University Press, London, 1970.

Macauley, S. H. O. T., 'Management of Public enterprises: the Sierra Leone experience,' in Rweyemamu and Hyden, *A Decade of Public Administration in Africa*, East African Literature Bureau, 1979.

Marois, B., 'Le comportement multinational des entreprises françaises nationalisées', *Revue Française de Gestion*, March–April 1977.

Maxcy, G., *Les Multinationales de l'Automobile*, PUF, Paris, 1982.

Mazzolini, R., *Government-Controlled Enterprises: International Strategic and Policy Decision*, John Wiley, New York, 1979.

Mazzolini, R., 'European government-controlled enterprises: explaining international strategic decisions', *Journal of International Business Studies*, Winter 1979.

Mazzolini, R., 'Are state owned enterprises unfair competition?' *California Management Review*, Winter 1980.

Menzies, H. D., 'US companies in unequal combat', *Fortune*, April 1979.

Merril, W. C. and Schneider, N., 'Public firms in oligopoly industry', *Quarterly Journal of Economics*, **80**, 1966, pp. 400–412.

Mitra, J. D., '*The capital goods sector in LDCs: a case for state intervention?*' World Bank Staff Working Paper No. 343, 1979.

Monsen, J. and Walters, K., *Nationalized Companies, a Threat to American Business*, McGraw Hill, New York, 1983.

Morin, F., *La Banque et les Groupes Industriels à l'Heure des Nationalisations*, Calmann-Lévy, Paris, 1977.

OECD, 'Industrialization in the Third World', *OECD Observer*, March 1980, pp. 41–48.

Olisa, M. S., 'Factors affecting the performance of public enterprise in Nigeria', in Rweyemamu and Hyden, *A Decade of Public Administration in Africa*, East African Literature Bureau, 1979.

Owen, R. F., '*Interindustry determinants of foreign direct investments: a perspective emphasizing the Canadian experience*', Working Paper in International Economics (G. 79.03), Princeton University, 1979.

Parry, T. C., '*Trade and no trade performance of US manufacturing industry: "Revealed" comparative advantage*', Manchester School of Economics and Social Studies, June 1973.

Parry, T. C., '*Methods of servicing overseas markets: the UK owned pharmaceutical study*', University of Reading, Discussion Paper (series 2) 27, 1976.

Political and Economic Planning, *Atlantic Tariffs and Trade*, a report by PEP, Allen and Unwin, Winchester, MA, 1967.

Premchand, A., 'Government and public enterprises: the budget link', *Finance and Development*, January 1978.

Pryke, R., *The Nationalized Industries, Policies and Performances since 1968*, Martin Robertson, Oxford, 1981.

Ramanadham, V. U., *The Nature of Public Enterprise*, Croom Helm, London, 1984.

Ramanantsoa, B. and Hoffstetter, Ch., 'La maîtrise de l'identité par la gestion du processus de focalisation: une nouvelle donnée stratégique?' *Direction et Gestion*, June–July 1981.

Redwood, J., *Public Enterprise in Crisis, The Future of Nationalized Industries*, Basil Blackwell, Oxford, 1980.

Revue Française de Gestion, *L'entreprise Publique en Question*, Nos 20 and 21, Special issues, 1979.

Robson, W. A., *The Nationalized Industries*, Martin Robertson, London, 1981.

Roy, S. K., *Corporate Image in India: A Study of Elite Attitudes Towards Private and Public Industry*, New Delhi, 1974.

Rugman, A., *International Diversification and the Multinational Enterprise*, Lexington Books, Lexington, 1979.

Saint Geours, J., *Pouvoir et Finance*, Fayard, Paris, 1979.

Saunders, R. J., Warford, J. J. and Mann, P. D., '*Alternative concepts of marginal cost for public utility pricing: problems of application in the water supply sector*', World Bank Staff Working Paper No 259, 1977.

Saussois, J. M., *Les Aides Fédérales à l'Industrie Américaine*, FNEGE-ESCP, Paris, 1984.

Schacter, G. and Cohen, B. C., 'State economic enterprise and economic development', Research report No. 32, North-eastern University, Department of Economics, 1971.

Schneider, N., 'Mixed oligopoly: a study in the control of industry in a developing economy', Unpublished PhD dissertation, University of California, Berkeley, 1966.

Shirley, M., '*Managing state-owned enterprises*'. World Bank Staff Working Paper, No. 577, 1983.

Siddhartan, N. S. and Lall, S., 'The monopolistic advantages of multinationals; lessons from foreign investment in the US', *The Economic Journal*, September 1982.

Sigmund, P., *Multinationals in Latin America, the Politics of Nationalization*, University of Wisconsin Press, 1980.

Simai, M., 'The public sector and the international economic positions of developing countries', *Acta Economica* **22**, 1979, pp. 127–142.

Sinha, R. K., *Economics of Public Enterprises*, South Asian Publishers, New Delhi, 1983.

Smith, H. F., *Public Enterprises and Economic Development*, University of South California Press, 1964.

Sobhan, R., 'The nature of the state and its implications for the development of public enterprises in Asia', *Journal of Contemporary Asia*, May 1980, pp. 410–433.

Stanbury, W. and Thompson, F. (eds), *Managing Public Enterprises*, Praeger, New York, 1982.

Stevens, C. V., 'Determinants of investment', in *Economic Analysis and the Multinational Enterprise* (ed. J. H. Dunning), Allen and Unwin, Winchester, MA, 1974.

Stoffae, Ch. and Victori, J., *Nationalisations*, Flammarion, Paris, 1977.

Stopford, J., Dunning, J. and Haberich, K., *Directory of the Largest Multinational Corporations*, Sijthoffand Noordhoff International Publishing Co.

Swedenborg, B., *The Multinational Operations of Swedish Firms: An Analysis of Determinants and Effects*, Almquist & Wiksell International, Stockholm, 1979.

Taylor, L., *Macro Planning Models for Developing Countries*, McGraw Hill, New York, 1984.

Teritra, O., 'Development strategy investment decisions and expenditure patterns of a public development institution: the case of the Western Nigeria Development Corporation, 1949–1962', *Nigeria Journal of Economic and Social Studies* **8**, 1966, pp. 235–258.

Tomlinson, J., *The Unequal Struggle? British Socialism and the Capitalist Enterprise*, Methuen, London and New York, 1982.

Trebat, T. J., 'An evaluation of the economics of public enterprises in Brazil', unpublished PhD Dissertation, Vanderbilt University, 1978.

Tupper, A. and Doern, B. (eds), *Public Corporations and Public Policy in Canada*, Institute for Research on Public Policy, Montreal, 1981.

Tyler, W., 'Brazilian industrialization and industrial policies: a survey', *World Development* **4**, 1976, pp. 863–882.

Tyler, W., 'Manufactured export expansion and industrialization in Brazil', *Kieler Studien* **134**, Tübingen, 1976.

Umo, J. U., 'Public sector earning functions and implications for investment in human capital: the Nigeria case, *The Developing Economies*, May 1980, pp. 309–328.

United Nations, 'Regional session on technical and managerial problems of African public enterprise', Economic Commission For Africa, Yaounde, 7–14 August 1978, documents E/ECA/PAMM/PA/1–9.

United Nations, *Strengthening Public Administration and Finance for Development in the 1980s*, ESA/ST/SER.E/13, 1978.

United Nations, 'Role of the public sector in promoting the economic development of LDCs', Economic and Social Council, Second ordinary session, 1979, Point 3 on the agenda, The Secretary-General's Report, E/1979/66.

United Nations, *Manual For Improving Management in Public Administration*, United Nations, New York, 1980.

UNCNRET, *State Petroleum Enterprises in Developing Countries*, Pergamon Policy Studies, 1979.

UNIDO, 'The role of the public sector in the industrialization of the developing countries', Expert Group Meeting, Vienna, 14–18 May 1978, ID/WG.298/1–12.

Vernon, R., 'International investment and international trade in the product cycle', *Quarterly Journal of Economics*, May 1966.

Vernon, R., 'The location of economic activity', in Dunning, J. H. (ed.) *Economic Analysis and the Multinational Enterprise*, Allen and Unwin, Winchester, MA, 1974.

Vernon, R. and Aharoni, Y. (eds), *State-Owned Enterprise in the Western Economies*, Croom Helm, London, 1981.

Walstedt, B., *'State manufacturing enterprise in a mixed economy, the Turkish case*, World Bank Publications, The John Hopkins University Press, Baltimore, 1980.

Walters, K. D. and Monsen, R. J., 'State-owned business abroad: new competitive threat', *Harvard Business Review*, March–April 1979.

Wellisz, S., 'Lessons of twenty years of planning in developing countries', *Economica* **38**, 1972, pp. 121–135.

Wells, L. T. Jr, *Third World Multinationals, the Rise of Foreign Investment from Developing Countries*, MIT Press, Cambridge, 1983.

Werneck, L. R. F., 'Rapid growth, equity and the size of the public sector', *Brazilian Economic Studies*, IPEA, No. 5, 1979, Rio de Janeiro.

White, E., Campos, J. and Ondarte, G., *Las Empresas Conjuntas Latino-Americanas*, Instituto para la Integración de America Latina, Buenos Aires, 1977.

Wolf, B., 'Industrial diversification and internationalization: some empirical evidence', *Journal of Industrial Economics*, December 1977.

World Bank, *World Development Report*, 1979, Chapter V: Government support for industrialization.

Index of enterprises cited

General Index